Elements of Literature

First Course

Holt Multicultural Reader

- Respond to and Analyze Texts
- Apply Reading Skills
- Develop Vocabulary and Practice Fluency

HOLT, RINEHART AND WINSTON

A Harcourt Education Company

Orlando • Austin • New York • San Diego • London

Cover

Photo Credit: *Landschaft Mit Gelben Vögeln* (1923/32) by Paul Klèe (1879–1940). Watercolor on blackened ground on drawing paper mounted on cardboard. (35.5 x 44 cm). Private Collection. ©2005 Artists Rights Society (ARS), New York/VG Bild-Kunst, Bonn. Snark/Art Resource, NY.

Printed in the United States of America

ISBN 0-03-078592-8

5 6 7 8 9 1689 14 13 12 11 10

4500246278

Contents

To the Student xi

A Walk Through the Book xiii

• PART ONE •

READING LITERATURE 1

COLLECTION 1 Facing Danger 2

Academic Vocabulary for Collection 1 3

Before You Read: The Dive 4

Literary Focus: Conflict 4

Reading Skills: Retelling 4

Vocabulary Development 5

René Saldaña, Jr. — **The Dive** — SHORT STORY 6

Skills Practice: Plot/Conflict Chart 16

Skills Review: Vocabulary and Comprehension 17

Before You Read: Lifesaving Service 18

Literary Focus: Suspense and Foreshadowing 18

Reading Skills: Making Predictions 18

Vocabulary Development 19

Eleanora E. Tate — **Lifesaving Service** — SHORT STORY 20

Skills Practice: Suspense Boxes 32

Skills Review: Vocabulary and Comprehension 33

COLLECTION 2 Living Many Lives 34

Academic Vocabulary for Collection 2 35

Before You Read: Seventh Grade 36

Literary Focus: Character Traits 36

Reading Skills: Making Inferences 36

Vocabulary Development 37

Gary Soto — **Seventh Grade** — SHORT STORY 38

Skills Practice: Character Traits Chart 48

Skills Review: Vocabulary and Comprehension 49

Before You Read: The War of the Wall **50**
Literary Focus: The Narrator 50
Reading Skills: Making Inferences 50
Vocabulary Development 51
Toni Cade Bambara — **The War of the Wall** . . . . SHORT STORY . . . **52**
Skills Practice: Narrator Detector 64
Skills Review: Vocabulary and Comprehension 65

Before You Read: Virtue Goes to Town **66**
Literary Focus: Character Traits 66
Reading Skills: Making Predictions 66
Vocabulary Development 67
Laurence Yep — **Virtue Goes to Town** . . . . FOLK TALE . . . **68**
Skills Practice: Character Traits Chart 76
Skills Review: Vocabulary and Comprehension 77

COLLECTION 3 Living in the Heart **78**
Academic Vocabulary for Collection 3 79
Before You Read: Hum **80**
Literary Focus: Theme 80
Reading Skills: Identify Cause and Effect 80
Vocabulary Development 81
Naomi Shihab Nye — **Hum** . . . . SHORT STORY . . . **82**
Skills Practice: Theme Chart 104
Skills Review: Vocabulary and Comprehension 105

Before You Read: in the inner city **106**
Literary Focus: Universal Themes 106
Reading Skills: Reading Poetry 106
Lucille Clifton — **in the inner city** . . . . POEM . . **107**
Skills Practice: Theme Chart 109
Skills Review: Reading Comprehension 110

Before You Read: My Father's Song **111**
Literary Focus: Discovering Theme 111
Reading Skills: Making Inferences About Theme 111
Simon J. Ortiz — **My Father's Song** . . . . POEM . . **112**
Skills Practice: Thematic Graph 114
Skills Review: Reading Comprehension 115

COLLECTION 4 Point of View: Can You See It My Way? 116
Academic Vocabulary for Collection 4 117
Before You Read: That October 118
Literary Focus: Point of View 118
Reading Skills: Making Predictions 118
Vocabulary Development 119
D. H. Figueredo **That October** . . . . SHORT STORY . . 120
Skills Practice: Narrator Chart 130
Skills Review: Vocabulary and Comprehension 131

Before You Read: Identity 132
Before You Read: why some people be mad at me sometimes 132
Literary Focus: Speaker and First-Person Point of View 132
Reading Skills: Finding Units of Meaning—Stanzas 132
Julio Noboa Polanco **Identity** . . . . POEM . . 133
Lucille Clifton **why some people be mad at me sometimes** . . . . . . POEM . . 135
Skills Practice: Stanza Chart 136
Skills Review: Reading Comprehension 137

Before You Read: Madam C. J. Walker 138
Literary Focus: Biography and Third-Person Point of View . . . 138
Reading Skills: Finding the Main Idea 138
Vocabulary Development 139
Jim Haskins **Madam C. J. Walker** . . . . BIOGRAPHY . . 140
Skills Practice: Main Idea Chart 150
Skills Review: Vocabulary and Comprehension 151

COLLECTION 5 Worlds of Words: Prose and Poetry 152
Academic Vocabulary for Collection 5 153
Before You Read: *from* How the Alvarez Girl Found Her Magic 154
Literary Focus: Forms of Prose—Essay 154
Reading Skills: Discovering the Main Idea 154
Vocabulary Development 155
Julia Alvarez ***from* How the Alvarez Girl Found Her Magic** . . . . . . ESSAY . . 156
Skills Practice: Main Idea Chart 162
Skills Review: Vocabulary and Comprehension 163

Before You Read: The Smartest Human I Ever Met: My Brother's Dog Shep **164**
Literary Focus: Forms of Prose—Essay 164
Reading Skills: Comparison and Contrast 164
Vocabulary Development 165
Victor Villaseñor — The Smartest Human I Ever Met: My Brother's Dog Shep . . . . . ESSAY . . 166
Skills Practice: Comparison-and-Contrast Chart 171
Skills Review: Vocabulary and Comprehension 172

Before You Read: Dreams / Dream Variations **173**
Literary Focus: Figures of Speech 173
Reading Skills: Punctuation Clues 173
Langston Hughes — Dreams . . . . . POEM . . 174
Langston Hughes — Dream Variations . . . . . POEM . . 175
Skills Practice: Figures of Speech 177
Skills Review: Reading Comprehension 178

Before You Read: A Poem for Langston Hughes **179**
Literary Focus: Poetry—Rhythm and Rhyme 179
Reading Skills: Reading Aloud 179
Nikki Giovanni — A Poem for Langston Hughes . . . . . POEM . . 180
Skills Practice: Rhyme List 182
Skills Review: Reading Comprehension 183

Before You Read: María in School **184**
Literary Focus: Forms of Prose—Novel 184
Reading Skills: Making Inferences 184
Vocabulary Development 185
Judith Ortiz Cofer — María in School . . . . . NOVEL EXCERPTS 186
Skills Practice: Inference Chart 192
Skills Review: Vocabulary and Comprehension 193

COLLECTION 6 Our Literary Heritage: World Folk Tales 194

Academic Vocabulary for Collection 6 195

Before You Read: The Clever Magistrate **196**
Literary Focus: Folk Tales 196
Reading Skills: Predicting 196
Vocabulary Development 197

Linda Fang — The Clever Magistrate ..... FOLK TALE 198
Skills Practice: Folk Tale Chart 204
Skills Review: Vocabulary and Comprehension 205

Before You Read: How the Animals Kept the Lions Away **206**
Literary Focus: Motifs in Folk Tales 206
Reading Skills: Retelling 206
Vocabulary Development 207

Inea Bushnaq — How the Animals Kept the Lions Away ..... FOLK TALE 208
Skills Practice: Retelling Chart 214
Skills Review: Vocabulary and Comprehension 215

Before You Read: The Old Woman Who Lived with the Wolves **216**
Literary Focus: Folk Tales 216
Reading Skills: Cause and Effect 216
Vocabulary Development 217

Chief Luther Standing Bear — The Old Woman Who Lived with the Wolves ..... FOLK TALE 218
Skills Practice: Cause-and-Effect Chart 224
Skills Review: Vocabulary and Comprehension 225

COLLECTION 7 Literary Criticism: Where I Stand 226

Academic Vocabulary for Collection 7 227

Before You Read: Dear Benjamin Banneker **228**
Literary Focus: Biography 228
Reading Skills: Evaluating the Biography 228
Vocabulary Development 229

Andrea Davis Pinkney — Dear Benjamin Banneker ..... BIOGRAPHY 230
Skills Practice: Fact/Imagination and Opinion Chart 240
Skills Review: Vocabulary and Comprehension 241

Before You Read: The Whistle . . . 242
Literary Focus: Biographical Approach . . . 242
Reading Skills: Summarizing . . . 242
Vocabulary Development . . . 243
Anne Estevis — **The Whistle** . . . SHORT STORY . . 244
Skills Practice: Biographical Approach Chart . . . 250
Skills Review: Vocabulary and Comprehension . . . 251

COLLECTION 8 **Reading for Life** . . . **252**
Academic Vocabulary for Collection 8 . . . 253

Before You Read: Museum Announcement / Press Release / Metro Map . . . **254**
Reading Skills: Analyzing Public Documents . . . 254
Museum Announcement . . . ANNOUNCEMENT . . 255
Press Release . . . PRESS RELEASE . . 256
Metro Map . . . MAP . . 257
Skills Practice: Information-Locator Wheel . . . 258
Skills Review: Reading Comprehension . . . 259

Before You Read: VividPlayer Download Instructions . . . **260**
Literary Focus: Analyzing Technical Directions . . . 260
VividPlayer Download Instructions . . . TECHNICAL DIRECTIONS . . 261
Skills Practice: Technical Directions Organizer . . . 262
Skills Review: Reading Comprehension . . . 263

• PART TWO •
READING INFORMATIONAL TEXTS 264

Academic Vocabulary for Part 2 265

Before You Read: Hard at Work **266**
Reading Skills: Understanding Text Structures 266
Vocabulary Development 266
Ritu Upadhyay Hard at Work .... MAGAZINE ARTICLE .. 267
Skills Practice: Text Structures Chart 271
Skills Review: Vocabulary and Comprehension 272

Before You Read: I Am a Native of North America **273**
Reading Skills: Analyzing Comparison and Contrast 273
Vocabulary Development 273
Chief Dan George I Am a Native of North America .... ESSAY .. 274
Skills Practice: Comparison-and-Contrast Chart 279
Skills Review: Vocabulary and Comprehension 280

Before You Read: Feng Shui Your Room **281**
Reading Skills: Analyzing Cause and Effect 281
Vocabulary Development 281
E. Renee Heiss Feng Shui Your Room .... ARTICLE .. 282
Skills Practice: Cause-and-Effect Chart 285
Skills Review: Vocabulary and Comprehension 286

Before You Read: All Together Now **287**
Reading Skills: Tracing an Author's Argument 287
Vocabulary Development 287
Barbara Jordan All Together Now .... SPEECH .. 288
Skills Practice: Argument Chart 291
Skills Review: Vocabulary and Comprehension 292

Before You Read: Bernie Williams: Yankee Doodle Dandy **293**
Reading Skills: Identifying the Main Idea 293
Vocabulary Development 293
Joel Poiley Bernie Williams: Yankee Doodle Dandy .... ARTICLE .. 294
Skills Practice: Main Idea Chart 299
Skills Review: Vocabulary and Comprehension 300

Before You Read: Coming to Amreeka: The First Wave of Arab Immigrants (1880–1924) **301**
Reading Skills: Summarizing 301
Vocabulary Development 301
Aida Hasan Damuni — **Coming to Amreeka: The First Wave of Arab Immigrants (1880–1924)** . . . . ARTICLE . . **302**
Skills Practice: Summary Chart 305
Skills Review: Vocabulary and Comprehension 306

Before You Read: The First Mexican Americans **307**
Reading Skills: Evaluating Evidence 307
Vocabulary Development 307
Stephen Currie — **The First Mexican Americans** . . . . MAGAZINE ARTICLE . . **308**
Skills Practice: Evidence Chart 311
Skills Review: Vocabulary and Comprehension 312

Before You Read: So You Want to Start a Club **313**
Reading Skills: Analyzing Information in Public Documents 313
So You Want to Start a Club . . . . PUBLIC DOCUMENT . . **314**
Skills Practice: Key Information Chart 316
Skills Review: Reading Comprehension 317

Index of Authors and Titles **318**

Vocabulary Development **319**

To the Student

A Book for You

A book is like a garden carried in the pocket.
—Chinese Proverb

The more you put into reading, the more you get out of it. This book is designed to do just that—help you interact with the selections you read by marking them up, asking your own questions, taking notes, recording your own ideas, and responding to the questions of others.

A Book Designed for Your Success

The *Holt Multicultural Reader* goes hand in hand with *Elements of Literature.* It is designed to help you interact with the selections and master language arts skills.

The book has two parts, each of which follows a simple format:

Part 1 Reading Literature

To help you master how to respond to, analyze, evaluate, and interpret literature, The *Holt Multicultural Reader* provides—

For each collection:

- The academic vocabulary you need to know to master the literary skills for the collection, defined for ready reference and use.
- Selections printed in an interactive format to support and guide your reading. As you read and respond to these selections, you will apply and extend your skills and build toward independence.

For each selection:

- A Before You Read page that preteaches the literary focus and provides a reading skill to help you understand the selection.
- A Vocabulary Development page that preteaches selection vocabulary and provides a vocabulary skill to use while reading the prose selections.
- Literature printed in an interactive format to guide your reading and help you respond to the text.
- A Skills Practice graphic organizer that helps you understand the literary focus of the selection.
- A Skills Review page that helps you practice vocabulary and assess your understanding of the selection you've just read.

Part 2 Reading Informational Texts

To help you master how to read informational texts, this book contains—

- The academic vocabulary you need to know to understand informational reading skills, defined for ready reference and use.
- A Before You Read page that preteaches a reading skill to help you comprehend the selection. Selection vocabulary is also pretaught on this page.
- Informational selections in an interactive format to guide your reading and help you respond to the text.
- A Skills Practice graphic organizer that helps you understand the reading focus of the selection.
- A Skills Review page that helps you practice vocabulary and assess your understanding of the selection you've just read.

A Book for Your Own Thoughts and Feelings

Reading is about *you.* It is about connecting your thoughts and feelings to the thoughts and feelings of the writer. Make this book your own. The more you give of yourself to your reading, the more you will get out of it. We encourage you to write in it. Jot down how you feel about the selection. Question the text. Note details you think need to be cleared up or topics you would like to learn more about.

A Walk Through the Book

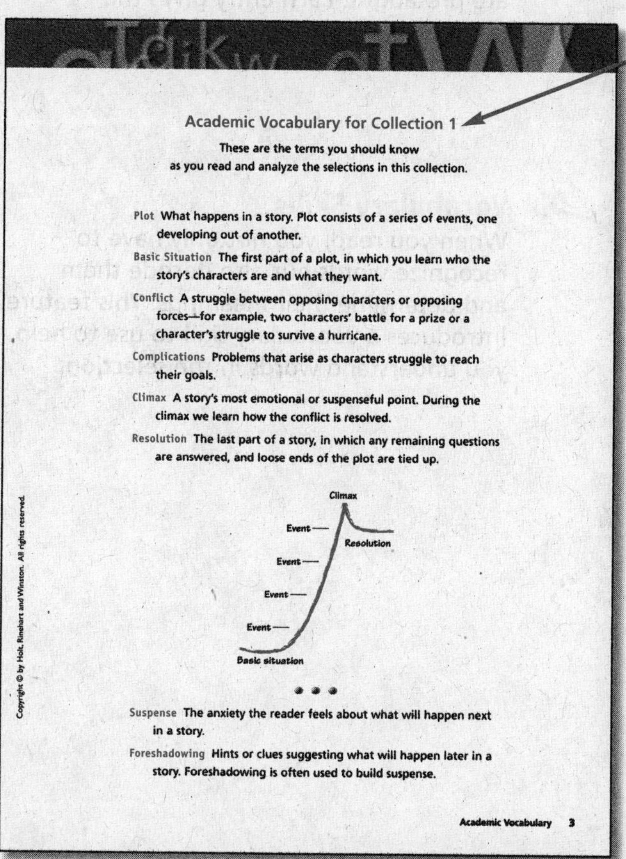

Academic Vocabulary for Collection 1

These are the terms you should know as you read and analyze the selections in this collection.

Plot What happens in a story. Plot consists of a series of events, one developing out of another.

Basic Situation The first part of a plot, in which you learn who the story's characters are and what they want.

Conflict A struggle between opposing characters or opposing forces—for example, two characters' battle for a prize or a character's struggle to survive a hurricane.

Complications Problems that arise as characters struggle to reach their goals.

Climax A story's most emotional or suspenseful point. During the climax we learn how the conflict is resolved.

Resolution The last part of a story, in which any remaining questions are answered, and loose ends of the plot are tied up.

• • •

Suspense The anxiety the reader feels about what will happen next in a story.

Foreshadowing Hints or clues suggesting what will happen later in a story. Foreshadowing is often used to build suspense.

Academic Vocabulary 3

Academic Vocabulary

Academic vocabulary is the language of books, tests, and formal writing. Each collection begins with the terms, or academic language, you need to know to master the skills for that collection.

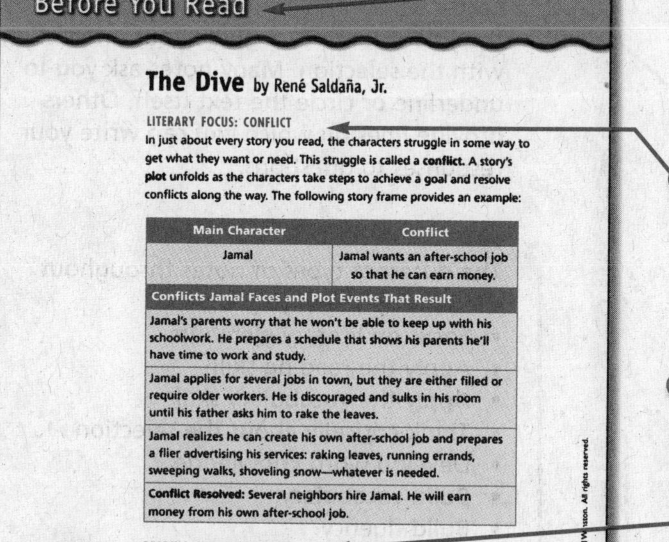

Before You Read

The Dive by René Saldaña, Jr.

LITERARY FOCUS: CONFLICT

In just about every story you read, the characters struggle in some way to get what they want or need. This struggle is called a **conflict**. A story's **plot** unfolds as the characters take steps to achieve a goal and resolve conflicts along the way. The following story frame provides an example:

Main Character	Conflict
Jamal	Jamal wants an after-school job so that he can earn money.
Conflicts Jamal Faces and Plot Events That Result	
Jamal's parents worry that he won't be able to keep up with his schoolwork. He prepares a schedule that shows his parents he'll have time to work and study.	
Jamal applies for several jobs in town, but they are either filled or require older workers. He is discouraged and sulks in his room until his father asks him to rake the leaves.	
Jamal realizes he can create his own after-school job and prepares a flier advertising his services: raking leaves, running errands, sweeping walks, shoveling snow—whatever is needed.	
Conflict Resolved: Several neighbors hire Jamal. He will earn money from his own after-school job.	

READING SKILLS: RETELLING

You probably retell stories often in real life—recounting for a friend the events in an exciting movie or filling in your neighbor on a story you just read, for instance. When you retell a story, you use your own words to bring its most important events to life.

As you read "The Dive," pause every so often to retell what has happened. Look for the Retell notes in the margins of the story, and jot down the important events.

SKILLS FOCUS

Literary Skills Understand conflict.
Reading Skills Retell story events.
Vocabulary Skills Clarify word meanings using restatement.

4 Part 1 Collection 1: Facing Danger

Before You Read

Previewing what you will learn builds success. This page tells you what the selection is about and prepares you to read it.

Literary Focus

This feature introduces the literary focus for the selection.

Reading Skills

This feature provides a reading skill for you to apply to the selection. It ties into and supports the literary focus.

Language Arts Skills

The skills covered with the selection are listed here.

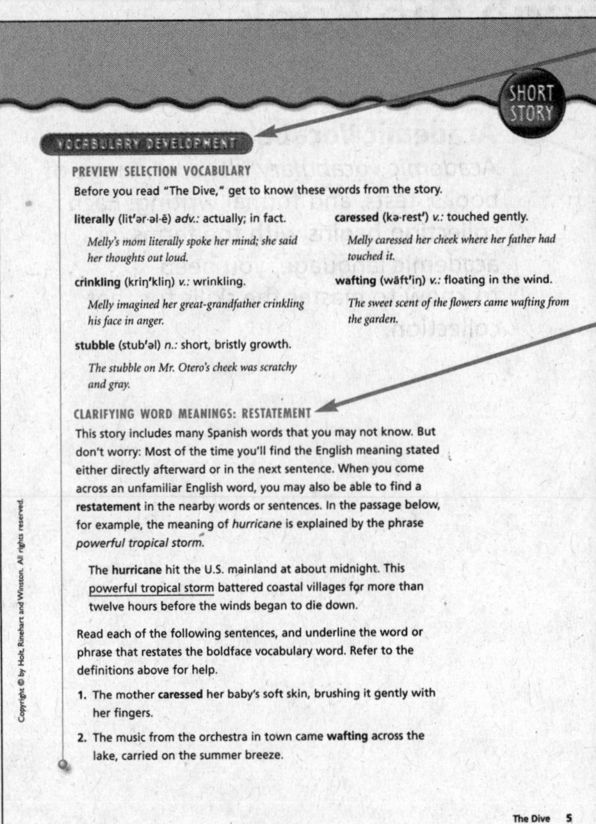

SHORT STORY

VOCABULARY DEVELOPMENT

PREVIEW SELECTION VOCABULARY

Before you read "The Dive," get to know these words from the story.

literally (lit'ər·əl·ē) *adv.:* actually; in fact.

Melly's mom literally spoke her mind; she said her thoughts out loud.

crinkling (kriŋ'kliŋ) *v.:* wrinkling.

Melly imagined her great-grandfather crinkling his face in anger.

stubble (stub'əl) *n.:* short, bristly growth.

The stubble on Mr. Otero's cheek was scratchy and gray.

caressed (kə·rest') *v.:* touched gently.

Melly caressed her cheek where her father had touched it.

wafting (wäft'iŋ) *v.:* floating in the wind.

The sweet scent of the flowers came wafting from the garden.

CLARIFYING WORD MEANINGS: RESTATEMENT

This story includes many Spanish words that you may not know. But don't worry: Most of the time you'll find the English meaning stated either directly afterward or in the next sentence. When you come across an unfamiliar English word, you may also be able to find a **restatement** in the nearby words or sentences. In the passage below, for example, the meaning of *hurricane* is explained by the phrase *powerful tropical storm.*

The **hurricane** hit the U.S. mainland at about midnight. This powerful tropical storm battered coastal villages for more than twelve hours before the winds began to die down.

Read each of the following sentences, and underline the word or phrase that restates the boldface vocabulary word. Refer to the definitions above for help.

1. The mother **caressed** her baby's soft skin, brushing it gently with her fingers.
2. The music from the orchestra in town came **wafting** across the lake, carried on the summer breeze.

The Dive 5

Vocabulary Development

Vocabulary words for the selection are pretaught. Each entry gives the pronunciation and definition of the word as well as a context sentence.

Vocabulary Skills

When you read, you not only have to recognize words but also decode them and determine their meanings. This feature introduces a vocabulary skill to use to help you understand words in the selection.

The Dive

René Saldaña, Jr.

BACKGROUND: Literature and Social Studies

In addition to including many Spanish words, this story contains several details about Mexican American culture. Like many Mexican American families, the different generations of the Oteros stay deeply and lovingly connected. Female elders like Mamá Tochi, the main character's grandmother, are respected and looked to for advice. Mamá Tochi shares the wisdom of her long life by telling *cuentos,* or stories, that serve as "life lessons." One of her *cuentos* involves a game of Mexican bingo, or Loteria—a type of bingo in which the tokens are cards bearing such colorful images as La Chalupa (the canoe) and El Gallo (the rooster).

IDENTIFY

Who is Mr. Otero?

WORD STUDY

Underline the restatement that tells you the meaning of the Spanish phrase *Tan locos* in line 3. (*Mi'ja* means "my child.")

"Look at them, Papi," said Melly to her father.

Mr. Otero cast his line into the water again and looked up and to his right. "Tan locos, mi'ja. It's a crazy thing to do."

From upriver, Melly and her father could see five or six boys fixing to jump from Jensen's Bridge. They pounded their chests, inched their way to the edge, then dove in all at once, some headfirst, others feet first, and one balled up. The boys disappeared underwater, leaving behind them different-sized splashes, then Melly heard the echoes of their jumping screams a full second or two after they'd gone under. By then, they were shooting up out of the water, their

"The Dive" from *Stories: Finding Our Way* by René Saldaña, Jr. Copyright © 2003 by René Saldaña, Jr. Reproduced by permission of Random House Children's Books, a division of Random House, Inc.

6 Part 1 Collection 1: Facing Danger

Side-Column Notes

Each selection is accompanied by notes in the side column that guide your interaction with the selection. Many notes ask you to underline or circle the text itself. Others provide lines on which you can write your responses to questions.

Types of Notes

The different types of notes throughout the selection help you—

- Focus on literary elements
- Apply the reading skill
- Apply the vocabulary skill
- Think critically about the selection
- Develop word knowledge
- Build vocabulary
- Build fluency

Vocabulary

The vocabulary words that were pretaught are defined in the side column and set in boldface in the selection, allowing you to see them in context.

Fluency

Successful readers are able to read fluently—clearly, easily, quickly, and without word identification problems. In most selections you'll be given an opportunity to practice and improve your fluency.

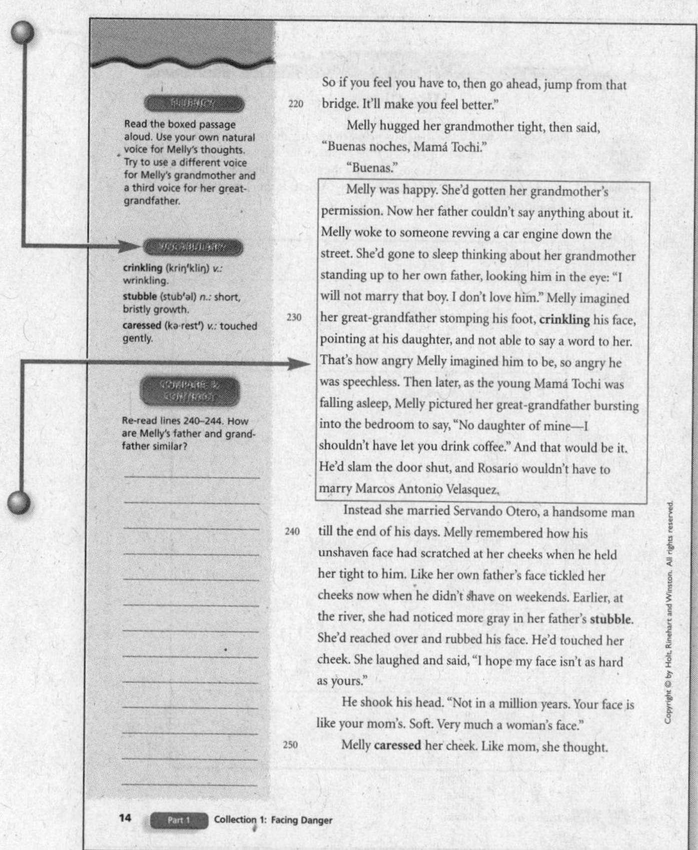

FLUENCY

Read the boxed passage aloud. Use your own natural voice for Melly's thoughts. Try to use a different voice for Melly's grandmother and a third voice for her great-grandfather.

VOCABULARY

crinkling (kriŋ′kliŋ) *v.:* wrinkling.

stubble (stub′əl) *n.:* short, bristly growth.

caressed (kə·rest′) *v.:* touched gently.

COMPARE & CONTRAST

Re-read lines 240–244. How are Melly's father and grandfather similar?

So if you feel you have to, then go ahead, jump from that bridge. It'll make you feel better."

Melly hugged her grandmother tight, then said, "Buenas noches, Mamá Tochi."

"Buenas."

Melly was happy. She'd gotten her grandmother's permission. Now her father couldn't say anything about it. Melly woke to someone revving a car engine down the street. She'd gone to sleep thinking about her grandmother standing up to her own father, looking him in the eye: "I will not marry that boy. I don't love him." Melly imagined her great-grandfather stomping his foot, **crinkling** his face, pointing at his daughter, and not able to say a word to her. That's how angry Melly imagined him to be, so angry he was speechless. Then later, as the young Mamá Tochi was falling asleep, Melly pictured her great-grandfather bursting into the bedroom to say, "No daughter of mine—I shouldn't have let you drink coffee." And that would be it. He'd slam the door shut, and Rosario wouldn't have to marry Marcos Antonio Velasquez.

Instead she married Servando Otero, a handsome man till the end of his days. Melly remembered how his unshaven face had scratched at her cheeks when he held her tight to him. Like her own father's face tickled her cheeks now when he didn't shave on weekends. Earlier, at the river, she had noticed more gray in her father's **stubble**. She'd reached over and rubbed his face. He'd touched her cheek. She laughed and said, "I hope my face isn't as hard as yours."

He shook his head. "Not in a million years. Your face is like your mom's. Soft. Very much a woman's face."

Melly **caressed** her cheek. Like mom, she thought.

14 Part 1 Collection 1: Facing Danger

Meet the Writer

A short biography of the writer appears after each literature selection.

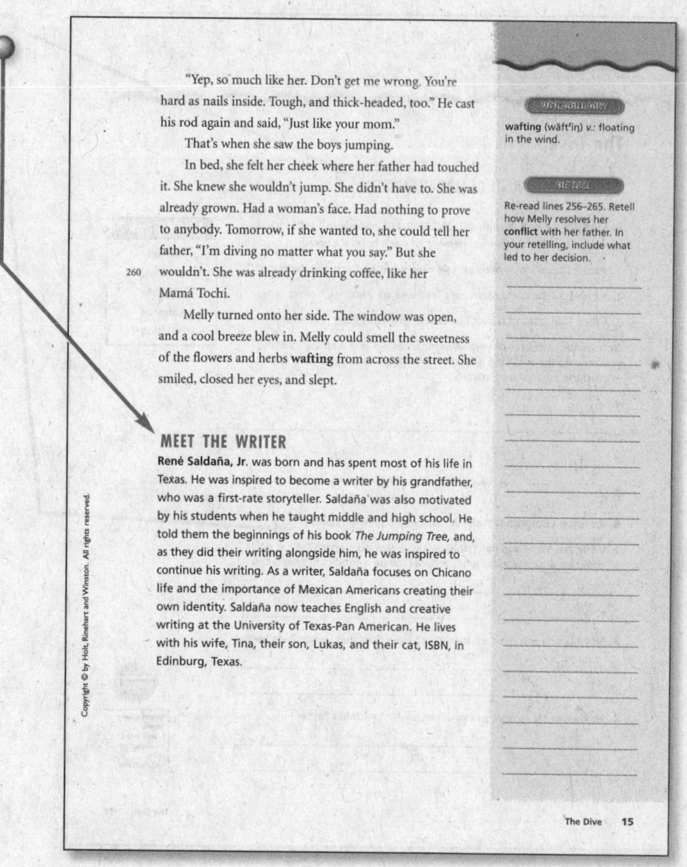

"Yep, so much like her. Don't get me wrong. You're hard as nails inside. Tough, and thick-headed, too." He cast his rod again and said, "Just like your mom."

That's when she saw the boys jumping.

In bed, she felt her cheek where her father had touched it. She knew she wouldn't jump. She didn't have to. She was already grown. Had a woman's face. Had nothing to prove to anybody. Tomorrow, if she wanted to, she could tell her father, "I'm diving no matter what you say." But she wouldn't. She was already drinking coffee, like her Mamá Tochi.

Melly turned onto her side. The window was open, and a cool breeze blew in. Melly could smell the sweetness of the flowers and herbs **wafting** from across the street. She smiled, closed her eyes, and slept.

VOCABULARY

wafting (wäft′iŋ) *v.:* floating in the wind.

RETELL

Re-read lines 256–265. Retell how Melly resolves her **conflict** with her father. In your retelling, include what led to her decision.

MEET THE WRITER

René Saldaña, Jr. was born and has spent most of his life in Texas. He was inspired to become a writer by his grandfather, who was a first-rate storyteller. Saldaña was also motivated by his students when he taught middle and high school. He told them the beginnings of his book *The Jumping Tree,* and, as they did their writing alongside him, he was inspired to continue his writing. As a writer, Saldaña focuses on Chicano life and the importance of Mexican Americans creating their own identity. Saldaña now teaches English and creative writing at the University of Texas-Pan American. He lives with his wife, Tina, their son, Lukas, and their cat, ISBN, in Edinburg, Texas.

The Dive 15

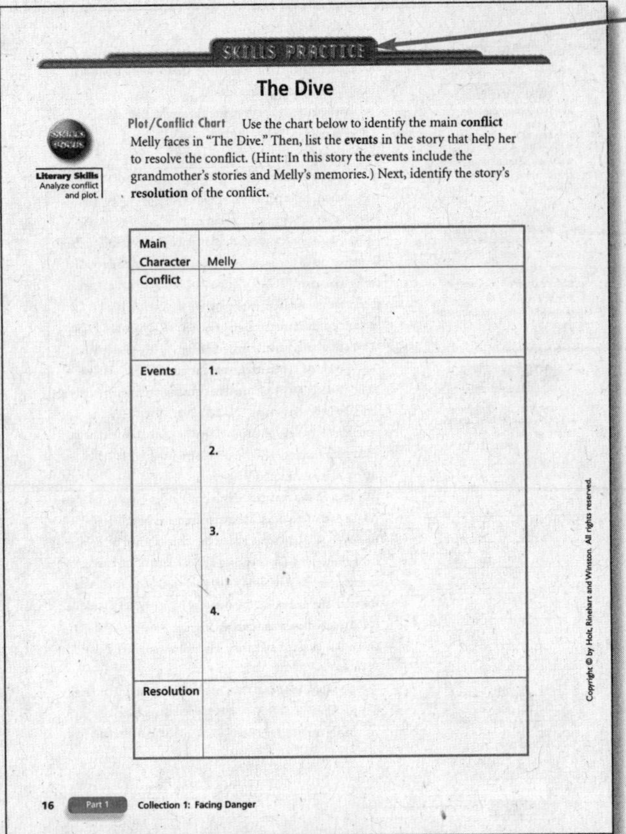

SKILLS PRACTICE

The Dive

SKILLS FOCUS

Literary Skills Analyze conflict and plot.

Plot/Conflict Chart Use the chart below to identify the main **conflict** Melly faces in "The Dive." Then, list the **events** in the story that help her to resolve the conflict. (Hint: In this story the events include the grandmother's stories and Melly's memories.) Next, identify the story's **resolution** of the conflict.

Main Character	Melly
Conflict	
Events	**1.** **2.** **3.** **4.**
Resolution	

Skills Practice

Graphic organizers help reinforce your understanding of the literary focus in a highly visual and creative way.

Skills Review

The Dive

VOCABULARY AND COMPREHENSION

A. Clarifying Word Meanings: Restatement Read each sentence below and underline the restatement of each boldface word.

1. Patty's **literally** true account told only what had actually happened.
2. At his surprise party, Grandpa's face was **crinkling** with smile lines.
3. When Dad doesn't shave, his **stubble** grows in short and scratchy.

Next, write sentences of your own for **caressed** and **wafting** in which you provide the meaning in a restatement. [For help, you may want to re-read the examples on page 5.]

4. __________

5. __________

Word Bank

literally
crinkling
stubble
caressed
wafting

B. Reading Comprehension Answer each question below.

1. What are Melly and her father doing as the story opens? What do they see, and how does what they see cause a conflict between them?
2. To whom does Melly turn for advice? How does that person help Melly?
3. How does Melly finally resolve her conflict with her father?

SKILLS FOCUS

Vocabulary Skills Clarify word meanings by using restatement.

Skills Review: Vocabulary

Test your knowledge of the selection vocabulary and the vocabulary skill by completing this short activity.

Reading Comprehension

This feature allows you to see how well you've understood the selection you have just read.

Part One

Reading Literature

Collection 1	Facing Danger
Collection 2	Living Many Lives
Collection 3	Living in the Heart
Collection 4	Point of View: Can You See It My Way?
Collection 5	Worlds of Words: Prose and Poetry
Collection 6	Our Literary Heritage: World Folk Tales
Collection 7	Literary Criticism: Where I Stand
Collection 8	Reading for Life

Collection 1

Facing Danger

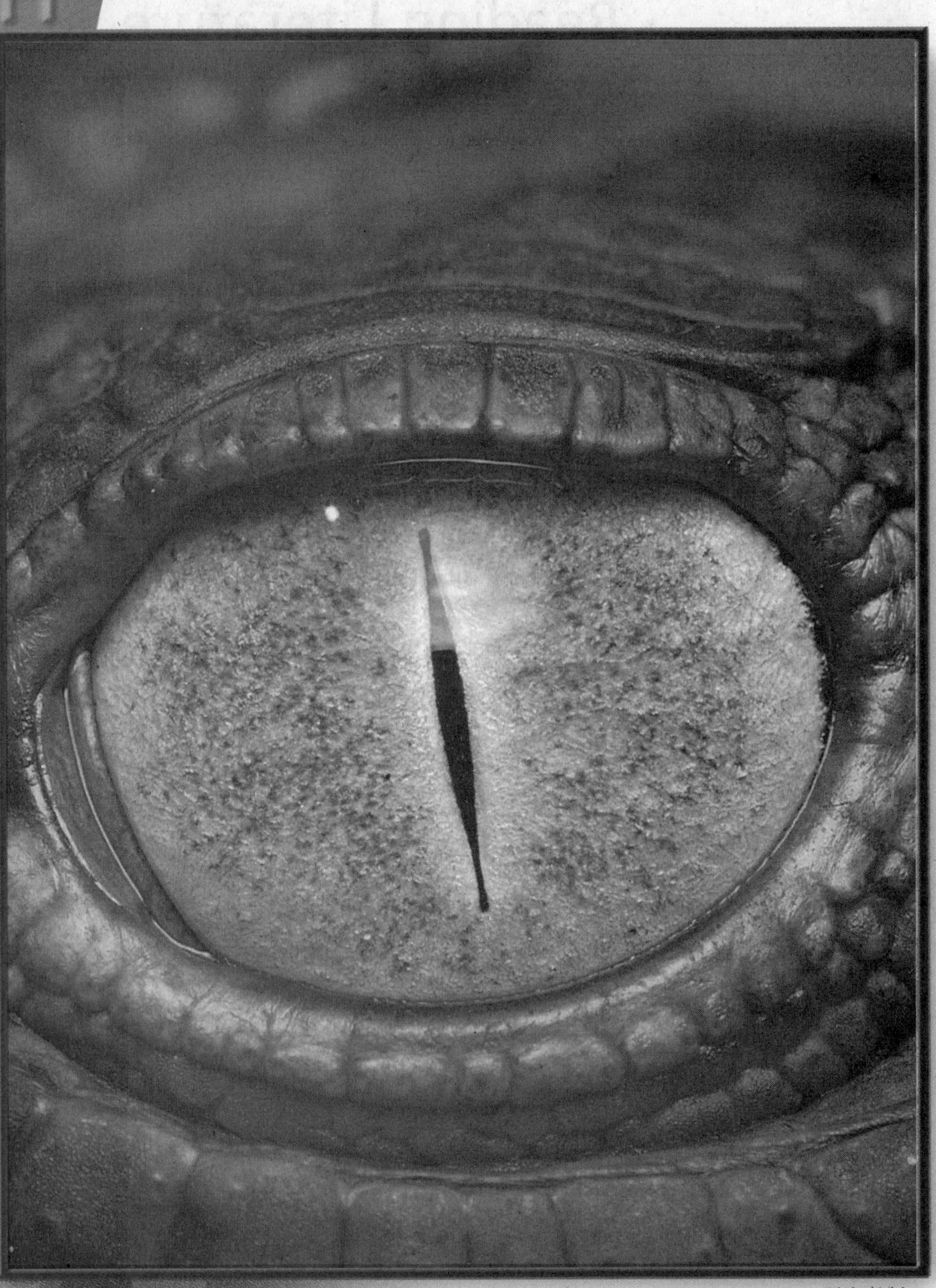

Digital Vision.

Academic Vocabulary for Collection 1

These are the terms you should know as you read and analyze the selections in this collection.

Plot What happens in a story. Plot consists of a series of events, one developing out of another.

Basic Situation The first part of a plot, in which you learn who the story's characters are and what they want.

Conflict A struggle between opposing characters or opposing forces—for example, two characters' battle for a prize or a character's struggle to survive a hurricane.

Complications Problems that arise as characters struggle to reach their goals.

Climax A story's most emotional or suspenseful point. During the climax we learn how the conflict is resolved.

Resolution The last part of a story, in which any remaining questions are answered, and loose ends of the plot are tied up.

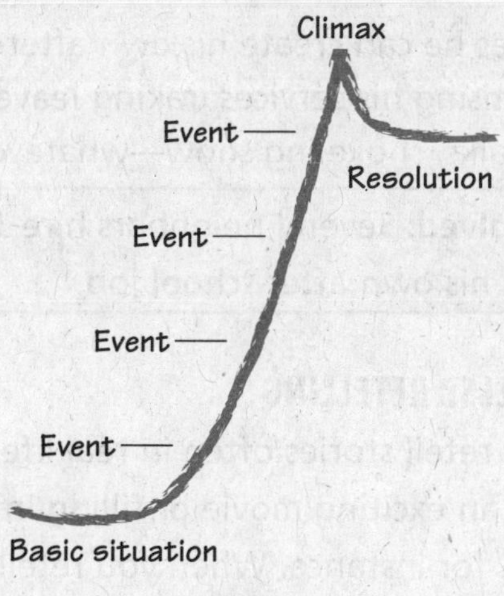

• • •

Suspense The anxiety the reader feels about what will happen next in a story.

Foreshadowing Hints or clues suggesting what will happen later in a story. Foreshadowing is often used to build suspense.

Before You Read

The Dive by René Saldaña, Jr.

LITERARY FOCUS: CONFLICT

In just about every story you read, the characters struggle in some way to get what they want or need. This struggle is called a **conflict.** A story's **plot** unfolds as the characters take steps to achieve a goal and resolve conflicts along the way. The following story frame provides an example:

Main Character	Conflict
Jamal	Jamal wants an after-school job so that he can earn money.
Conflicts Jamal Faces and Plot Events That Result	
Jamal's parents worry that he won't be able to keep up with his schoolwork. He prepares a schedule that shows his parents he'll have time to work and study.	
Jamal applies for several jobs in town, but they are either filled or require older workers. He is discouraged and sulks in his room until his father asks him to rake the leaves.	
Jamal realizes he can create his own after-school job and prepares a flier advertising his services: raking leaves, running errands, sweeping walks, shoveling snow—whatever is needed.	
Conflict Resolved: Several neighbors hire Jamal. He will earn money from his own after-school job.	

Literary Skills Understand conflict.

Reading Skills Retell story events.

Vocabulary Skills Clarify word meanings using restatement.

READING SKILLS: RETELLING

You probably retell stories often in real life—recounting for a friend the events in an exciting movie or filling in your neighbor on a story you just read, for instance. When you retell a story, you use your own words to bring its most important events to life.

As you read "The Dive," pause every so often to retell what has happened. Look for the Retell notes in the margins of the story, and jot down the important events.

VOCABULARY DEVELOPMENT

PREVIEW SELECTION VOCABULARY

Before you read "The Dive," get to know these words from the story.

literally (lit′ər·əl·ē) *adv.:* actually; in fact.

Melly's mom literally spoke her mind; she said her thoughts out loud.

crinkling (kriŋ′kliŋ) *v.* used as *adj.:* wrinkling.

Melly imagined her great-grandfather crinkling his face in anger.

stubble (stub′əl) *n.:* short, bristly growth.

The stubble on Mr. Otero's cheek was scratchy and gray.

caressed (kə·rest′) *v.:* touched gently.

Melly caressed her cheek where her father had touched it.

wafting (wäft′iŋ) *v.* used as *adj.:* floating in the wind.

We smelled the sweet scent of the flowers, wafting from the garden.

CLARIFYING WORD MEANINGS: RESTATEMENT

This story includes many Spanish words that you may not know. But don't worry: Most of the time you'll find the English meaning stated either directly afterward or in the next sentence. When you come across an unfamiliar English word, you may also be able to find a **restatement** in the nearby words or sentences. In the passage below, for example, the meaning of *hurricane* is explained by the phrase *powerful tropical storm.*

> The **hurricane** hit the U.S. mainland at about midnight. This powerful tropical storm battered coastal villages for more than twelve hours before the winds began to die down.

Read each of the following sentences, and underline the word or phrase that restates the boldface vocabulary word. Refer to the definitions above for help.

1. The mother **caressed** her baby's soft skin, brushing it gently with her fingers.
2. The music from the orchestra in town came **wafting** across the lake, carried on the summer breeze.

The Dive

René Saldaña, Jr.

BACKGROUND: Literature and Social Studies

In addition to including many Spanish words, this story contains several details about Mexican American culture. Like many Mexican American families, the different generations of the Oteros stay deeply and lovingly connected. Female elders like Mamá Tochi, the main character's grandmother, are respected and looked to for advice. Mamá Tochi shares the wisdom of her long life by telling *cuentos,* or stories, that serve as "life lessons." One of her *cuentos* involves a game of Mexican bingo, or Loteria—a type of bingo in which the tokens are cards bearing such colorful images as La Chalupa (the canoe) and El Gallo (the rooster).

IDENTIFY

Who is Mr. Otero?

WORD STUDY

Underline the restatement that tells you the meaning of the Spanish phrase *Tan locos* in line 3. (*Mi'ja* means "my child.")

"Look at them, Papi," said Melly to her father.

Mr. Otero cast his line into the water again and looked up and to his right. "Tan locos, mi'ja. It's a crazy thing to do."

From upriver, Melly and her father could see five or six boys fixing to jump from Jensen's Bridge. They pounded their chests, inched their way to the edge, then dove in all at once, some headfirst, others feet first, and one balled up. The boys disappeared underwater, leaving behind them different-sized splashes, then Melly heard the echoes of their jumping screams a full second or two after they'd gone under. By then, they were shooting up out of the water, their

© LWA-Dann Tardif/CORBIS

arms raised in the air. They'd done it. Most of the boys in Three Oaks had to dive from the bridge at one time or other to prove themselves real men. Today was their day.

Melly saw the boys crawl from the river and turn over on their backs, stretched out like lizards sunning themselves on the bank. Reeling in her line, she thought, So what if they can dive off the bridge! I could do it too if I wanted. Who said it was just for the guys to do?

"You'll do nothing of the kind," said Mr. Otero.

"Huh?"

"You said you could dive too if you wanted?"

"I didn't say anything. You must be hearing things."

He smiled. "Just like your mother. Talking your thoughts aloud." He reached over and touched his rough hand to her cheek.

RETELL

Pause at line 15. Explain what the boys on the bridge are doing, and why.

INFER

Re-read lines 2 and 18. Where are Melly and her father? What are they doing?

VOCABULARY

literally (lit′ər·əl·ē) *adv.:* actually; in fact.

INTERPRET

Pause at line 40. What disagreement does Melly have with her father? Do you think that a **conflict,** or struggle, will develop between them? Why or why not?

PREDICT

Pause at line 47. What do you think Melly will eventually do in this story? Why?

Melly blushed. She stood and set her rod on a rock, then stretched. She held her face and wondered if it was red from the sun. Red from her father's touch?

All along she'd actually been talking. She'd heard the same thing from her tías, from Mamá Tochi, and from her sister, Becky. "Your mom **literally** spoke her mind," the aunts all told her.

"You're so much like your mother," Mr. Otero told her, casting again.

"She probably would've jumped," she said.

"Probably so, but I said you won't do it. ¿M'entiendes?"

"Yes, sir. I understand. No jumping from the bridge." She looked downriver, then set her sight on the bridge. Her face was warm, and she imagined her mother jumping from the bridge, her long black hair in a ponytail, or all loose and curly; her mother slicing into the water, then exploding out, all smiles and laughter. Beautiful.

"What?"

"What what?"

"Never mind. Just like your mother."

That evening, Melly went to visit her grandmother, Mamá Tochi, down the street from where Melly lived with her father and her sister, who'd only recently left for college.

Mamá Tochi had lived on her own ever since Melly's grandfather died five years ago. When Mamá Tochi's children all moved and married, each begged her to come live with them, but she refused. She said, "For decades I took care of both your father and myself when you left the house for work and school, and before that I took care of the six of you, from dirty diapers to broken hearts, so what makes you think I need to be looked after?"

Mr. Otero, Melly's dad, was the only one to pull up stakes and move to be closer to Mamá Tochi when Papá 'Tero died. Moving was easy for him. His own wife had died a year before his father's passing, and he once confessed to Mamá Tochi, "With Aurelia gone, I don't know that I can do right by our two girls."

Melly knocked at her grandmother's and walked in. It was early evening, so she knew that Mamá Tochi would be out in her backyard garden with her babies: the herbs that ran up along the house; then the rosales, four bushes of them, red, yellow, white, and pink, big as trees almost; countless wildflower patches; and Melly's favorite, the esperanza bushes, the yellow bells soft on her cheeks. The backyard smelled like honey tasted.

She went out the screen door and said, "Mamá Tochi. Where are you?" Melly could hear the water splashing, but couldn't quite make out her grandmother.

"Aqui, mi'jita. I'm over here." Mamá Tochi was hidden behind the esperanza bush, watering it with her pail. She'd set the hose at the base of one of the rosales. "You don't even have to tell me why you're here. You want to jump from that crazy bridge."

Sometimes Melly thought her grandmother could read minds, see into the future, even talk to the dead. Melly couldn't figure out why she came over for advice. She never got anything but cuentos from Mamá Tochi, stories that somehow served as life lessons. That time Melly had had the chance to cheat on her end-of-term exam her ninth-grade year, Mamá Tochi said, "I remember a time I was calling bingo. Playing that night was my worst enemy, Perla. I kept an eye all night on her four cards, praying a secret prayer that she'd lose every time. On one of her cards I could see all she needed was El Gallo. Without knowing

WORD STUDY

Re-read the paragraph beginning with line 59. Underline the **restatement** clue that helps you understand the meaning of the **idiom** "to pull up stakes."

VISUALIZE

Underline the details that help you picture and smell Melly's grandmother's backyard (lines 67–72).

INTERPRET

Pause at line 85. What kind of relationship do Melly and her grandmother have? Underline details that support your response.

IDENTIFY

Reread lines 85–97. Circle the words that tell you this is a **flashback**—an account of something that happened earlier.

why, I pulled a card from the middle of the deck instead of the top. I pulled La Chalupa, and Manuela won. I was afraid to even look at the top card. I collected all the others and shuffled them real fast. What if it had been El Gallo? I wasn't able to look in Perla's eyes for two weeks and a half, that's how guilty I felt."

Lessons to be learned that time? You do it, you'll get caught. You'll feel worse if you don't get caught.

"It won't be cheating, really, Mamá Tochi. The teacher's already said chances of me passing are slim. There's stuff on the test we've never studied even."

Mamá Tochi sat on the porch swing and said, "You're a big girl. You'll know what to do."

That night, Melly considered what her grandmother had said. She saw herself three years later, marching for graduation, everyone taking photos, everyone smiling, everyone happy, except she wouldn't be because she'd remember having cheated that time back in the ninth grade. She didn't sleep at all that night. The next day, even before the exam was handed out, two boys and one girl were called out of class. Earlier in the week, they had asked Melly if she wanted a look at the test. They'd found it in one of the teacher's desks and ran off a copy. The morning of the test, she told them, "No thanks. I'll just try my best. I'll fail on my own terms, you know." Then they got busted, and Melly passed the test by two points. "A pass is a pass," said Mamá Tochi. That's just what Melly's mom used to say.

Tonight, Melly said, "What d'you mean? I'm here to visit with my favorite Mamá Tochi."

"Don't give me that. Your papi's already called. He's worried you're gonna jump and get tangled up in the weeds at the bottom of the river and drown."

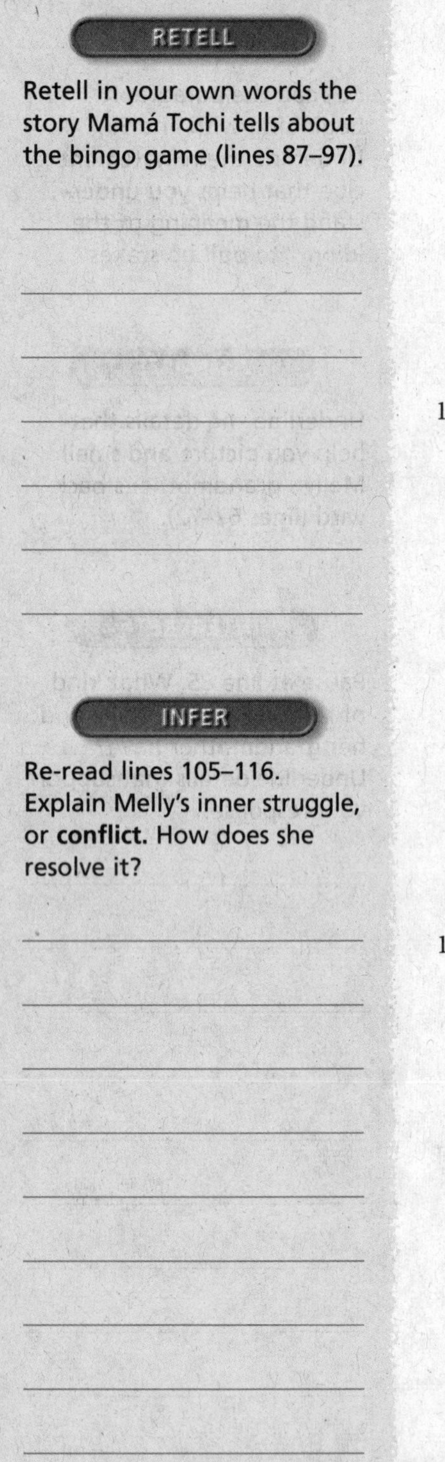

RETELL

Retell in your own words the story Mamá Tochi tells about the bingo game (lines 87–97).

INFER

Re-read lines 105–116. Explain Melly's inner struggle, or **conflict**. How does she resolve it?

IDENTIFY

Circle the word in line 120 that tells you the story has shifted back to the present time.

Melly said, "Ah, Papi knows there's no weeds down there. And besides, no one's ever drowned at the bridge before."

Mamá Tochi put down the pail, turned off the hose, then said, "Sit down. I'll bring coffee."

Melly sat under the orange tree. Papá 'Tero had built the table and chairs years ago. He also had carved each of his children's and grandchildren's names and dates of birth into the tabletop in a great big circle. At the center were his name and Mamá Tochi's: Servando Otero and Rosario Garcia de Otero, their dates of birth, and the date of their wedding. Melly traced Mamá Tochi's name.

"I put two spoons of sugar and a little milk in yours, just like you drink it," said Mamá Tochi.

"Gracias," said Melly. "It's not that high of a jump—ten, fifteen feet at most."

"That's not high. About two of my rosebushes, right." Mamá Tochi looked up where the top of the invisible bush would be.

"I mean, if the guys can do it— Aren't you the one always saying, 'You can do anything and everything you set your heart to'?"

"You're right, mi'jita. Anything is possible. How's your coffee?"

"Good, thank you, Mamá Tochi."

"Mi'jita, have I ever told you that my mother never let me drink coffee? It was a grown-up thing to do. I didn't take my first drink of it until I was twenty-one."

Melly knew there was a reason Mamá Tochi was telling her this. She just had to figure it out. She had to pay attention, then sleep on it, and if she hadn't figured it out by after school tomorrow, she'd have to come visit a second

INFER

What do the details in lines 130–136 tell you about Melly's family?

INFER

Re-read lines 139–148. What inner struggle, or **conflict**, is Melly trying to resolve? How is her grandmother helping her?

time, get another story, then try to figure out two lessons instead of one.

"I'd gotten my first job as a seamstress," Mamá Tochi continued. "My first paycheck, I told my mother, 'First thing I'll buy is a cup of coffee at Martin's Café.' My mother said, 'Then you'll buy for us all.' And so I did, a cup of coffee and a piece of sweet bread for everyone, all thirteen of us. I spent every peso I'd made, and I didn't sleep all night. But I loved the taste so much I haven't stopped, even when Dr. Neely told me I should. What does he know?"

She sat across the table from Melly and sipped her coffee.

Melly thought she'd figured out the lesson: that she should dive, and then she wouldn't be able to stop. She'd be as old as Mamá Tochi and diving would still be in her blood, and one day she'd jump from a bridge too high for such a frail woman and break every bone in her body and drown. But she'd be doing what she loved.

"This is some good coffee," Mamá Tochi said.

"Sure is. Good bread, too."

"Twenty-one, can you believe it? Today you kids have all these fancy cafés in your fancy bookstores where you go and study with all your friends. What was that drink you bought me once? Iced café mocha? Why ruin a good cup of coffee with chocolate syrup? Why ruin it by pouring it into a paper cup? Not like in the old days. A little crema, a pinch of sugar, and steaming hot in a clay jar."

It only seemed like Mamá Tochi had finished telling her story. Melly knew better, so she leaned back, ready for more. She knew she hadn't figured out her grandmother's riddle yet.

EVALUATE

Re-read lines 159–174. Melly thinks she has figured out the meaning of her grandmother's story. Do you think Melly has come to the right conclusion? Why or why not?

COMPARE & CONTRAST

Re-read lines 177–183. Underline the things Mamá Tochi identifies as aspects of life "nowadays." Circle the details that describe life in Mamá Tochi's day. How are the present and the past different?

"Nowadays, you babies grow up too fast. You're women before you're girls. You never get to be girls, some of you. It's not a bad thing, the way the world is today. You have to know more sooner, and be able to survive it. In my day, all I had to worry about was drinking my first cup of coffee, my first job, and hoping my family would choose the right man for me. They did that back then, you know, chose your husband. My father tried to find the man for me, and—well, let's just say, I was ahead of my time when I told my father I would not marry Marcos Antonio Velasquez. Papá told me, '¿Y tu, quien te crées?[1] I was twenty-three then, and getting too old to be playing this game, my father said. But I—I had to take a stand sometime. After all," she said, and laughed. Melly imagined Mamá Tochi's young face laughing, her wrinkles somehow gone. "After all, I was a woman now. I was drinking coffee at Martin's every Friday afternoon on my way home. But I didn't smoke like some of the others. I tried that once, but once was all I needed. I didn't like the taste. Coffee, now there's taste. Tobacco? Take it or leave it. Better leave it." She sipped some more, then said, "Mi'jita, it's getting late. You better go home before your papi calls looking for you."

Melly stood and helped her with the cups and plate of bread. She hooked the screen door shut. She didn't close the inside door. Mamá Tochi always said she wanted to smell her flowers. "And what's there in this house to steal? I wish someone would come and take that television. It's just something else I have to dust." Melly knew Mamá Tochi was teasing. She liked to watch her Mexican soaps.

"Dive if you want, mi'jita. I know you can make it. You won't drown. You're strong like all those boys, and smarter.

1. **¿Y tu, quien te crées?:** Spanish for "And you, who do you think you are?"

IDENTIFY

Re-read lines 194–200. How did Mamá Tochi "take a stand" when she was twenty-three?

EVALUATE

What advice does her grandmother give Melly in lines 217–220? Are you surprised by what she says? Do you think it is good advice? Why or why not?

So if you feel you have to, then go ahead, jump from that bridge. It'll make you feel better."

Melly hugged her grandmother tight, then said, "Buenas noches, Mamá Tochi."

"Buenas."

Melly was happy. She'd gotten her grandmother's permission. Now her father couldn't say anything about it. Melly woke to someone revving a car engine down the street. She'd gone to sleep thinking about her grandmother standing up to her own father, looking him in the eye: "I will not marry that boy. I don't love him." Melly imagined her great-grandfather stomping his foot, **crinkling** his face, pointing at his daughter, and not able to say a word to her. That's how angry Melly imagined him to be, so angry he was speechless. Then later, as the young Mamá Tochi was falling asleep, Melly pictured her great-grandfather bursting into the bedroom to say, "No daughter of mine—I shouldn't have let you drink coffee." And that would be it. He'd slam the door shut, and Rosario wouldn't have to marry Marcos Antonio Velasquez.

Instead she married Servando Otero, a handsome man till the end of his days. Melly remembered how his unshaven face had scratched at her cheeks when he held her tight to him. Like her own father's face tickled her cheeks now when he didn't shave on weekends. Earlier, at the river, she had noticed more gray in her father's **stubble**. She'd reached over and rubbed his face. He'd touched her cheek. She laughed and said, "I hope my face isn't as hard as yours."

He shook his head. "Not in a million years. Your face is like your mom's. Soft. Very much a woman's face."

Melly **caressed** her cheek. Like mom, she thought.

FLUENCY

Read the boxed passage aloud. Use your own natural voice for Melly's thoughts. Try to use a different voice for Melly's grandmother and a third voice for her great-grandfather.

VOCABULARY

crinkling (kriŋʹkliŋ) *v.* used as *adj.:* wrinkling.

stubble (stubʹəl) *n.:* short, bristly growth.

caressed (kə·restʹ) *v.:* touched gently.

COMPARE & CONTRAST

Re-read lines 240–244. How are Melly's father and grandfather similar?

"Yep, so much like her. Don't get me wrong. You're hard as nails inside. Tough, and thick-headed, too." He cast his rod again and said, "Just like your mom."

That's when she saw the boys jumping.

In bed, she felt her cheek where her father had touched it. She knew she wouldn't jump. She didn't have to. She was already grown. Had a woman's face. Had nothing to prove to anybody. Tomorrow, if she wanted to, she could tell her father, "I'm diving no matter what you say." But she wouldn't. She was already drinking coffee, like her Mamá Tochi.

Melly turned onto her side. The window was open, and a cool breeze blew in. Melly could smell the sweetness of the flowers and herbs **wafting** from across the street. She smiled, closed her eyes, and slept.

MEET THE WRITER

René Saldaña, Jr. was born and has spent most of his life in Texas. He was inspired to become a writer by his grandfather, who was a first-rate storyteller. Saldaña was also motivated by his students when he taught middle and high school. He told them the beginnings of his book *The Jumping Tree,* and, as they did their writing alongside him, he was inspired to continue his writing. As a writer, Saldaña focuses on Chicano life and the importance of Mexican Americans creating their own identity. Saldaña now teaches English and creative writing at the University of Texas-Pan American. He lives with his wife, Tina, their son, Lukas, and their cat, ISBN, in Edinburg, Texas.

VOCABULARY

wafting (wäft′iŋ) *v.* used as *adj.:* floating in the wind.

RETELL

Re-read lines 256–265. Retell how Melly resolves her **conflict** with her father. In your retelling, include what led to her decision.

SKILLS PRACTICE

The Dive

Literary Skills Analyze conflict and plot.

Plot/Conflict Chart Use the chart below to identify the main **conflict** Melly faces in "The Dive." Then, list the **events** in the story that help her to resolve the conflict. (Hint: In this story the events include the grandmother's stories and Melly's memories.) Next, identify the story's **resolution** of the conflict.

Main Character	Melly
Conflict	
Events	**1.** **2.** **3.** **4.**
Resolution	

Skills Review

The Dive

VOCABULARY AND COMPREHENSION

A. Clarifying Word Meanings: Restatement Read each sentence below and underline the restatement of each boldface word.

Word Bank
literally
crinkling
stubble
caressed
wafting

1. Patty's **literally** true account told only what had actually happened.
2. At his surprise party, Grandpa's face was **crinkling** with smile lines.
3. When Dad doesn't shave, his **stubble** grows in short and scratchy.

Next, write sentences of your own for **caressed** and **wafting** in which you provide the meaning in a restatement. [For help, you may want to re-read the examples on page 5.]

4. ______________________________

____

5. ______________________________

____

B. Reading Comprehension Answer each question below.

1. What are Melly and her father doing as the story opens? What do they see, and how does what they see cause a conflict between them?

____

____

2. To whom does Melly turn for advice? How does that person help Melly?

____

____

3. How does Melly finally resolve her conflict with her father? ____________

____

____

Vocabulary Skills
Clarify word meanings by using restatement.

Before You Read

Lifesaving Service by Eleanora E. Tate

LITERARY FOCUS: SUSPENSE AND FORESHADOWING

A "page turner" is an exciting story; you're so eager to find out what happens that you read page after page, not wanting to stop. One key ingredient in page turners is **suspense**—the feeling of uncertainty that propels you to keep reading. To build suspense, writers may create an eerie setting or withhold certain information in order to keep you guessing.

To build suspense, writers sometimes plant clues in their stories. These clues hint at what might happen later. The use of such clues or hints is called **foreshadowing.** As you read "Lifesaving Service," look for examples of foreshadowing.

READING SKILLS: MAKING PREDICTIONS

Which of the following types of predictions have you made recently: the outcome of a baseball game? which of your classmates will become class president? what inventions will come about over the next few years? Making predictions is part of participating in life. Likewise, you participate more fully in a story when you make predictions about it. To make predictions when you read,

- pay attention to what the narrator tells you about the story's characters and their situations
- from clues in the text, make smart guesses about what might happen next
- read on to find out if your predictions were on target. It's okay to change and adjust your predictions as you read

Literary Skills Understand suspense and foreshadowing.

Reading Skills Make predictions.

Vocabulary Skills Clarify word meanings by using examples.

VOCABULARY DEVELOPMENT

PREVIEW SELECTION VOCABULARY

The following words appear in "Lifesaving Service." Take the time to preview these words before you begin the story.

commercial (kə·mʉr′shəl) *adj.:* involving the buying and selling of goods.

Richard had been a commercial fisherman, selling the fish he caught in order to make a living.

enlist (en·list′) *v.:* join an organization or cause.

When he heard Richard's stories, Tucker wanted to enlist in the lifesaving service.

qualifications (kwôl′ə·fi·kā′shənz) *n.:* qualities or skills needed to do a job.

Tucker had many of the qualifications needed for lifesaving.

heaves (hēvz) *n.:* shoves or lifts performed with great effort.

It took two mighty heaves to get the heavy man back onto his raft.

recognition (rek′əg·nish′ən) *n.:* acknowledgment; something done as an expression of appreciation.

The lifesaving service finally received recognition many years after its members had all died.

CLARIFYING WORD MEANINGS: EXAMPLES

Sometimes you can figure out the meaning of an unfamiliar word by looking in the text for examples of what it is. (Words and phrases such as *for example, for instance, like, such as, in this case,* and *as if* sometimes signal that an example will follow.) In the sentence below, an example of what *lifesaving* means is underlined.

Ever since she saved a toddler from drowning years ago, Chloe has wanted a career that involves **lifesaving.**

Read each sentence below, and underline the example provided for each boldface word.

1. Everybody benefits from **recognition;** for instance, my father was so pleased when I praised his cooking that he decided to make my favorite meal the next night.
2. You can **enlist** classmates to work on your project by inviting them to write their names on a sign-up sheet.

LIFESAVING SERVICE

Eleanora E. Tate

IDENTIFY

Circle the name of the character this story is going to be about. Underline the details that help you understand where the story takes place.

PREDICT

Re-read lines 8–13. What do you think this story will be about?

IDENTIFY

Re-read lines 14–26. Circle the name of the character who is telling the story. What does this character have in common with Tucker?

I want to tell you about a boy I knew who lived in Morehead City, North Carolina, some years ago named Tucker Willis. He lived by Calico Creek where it narrows down to marsh grass, flounder, and fiddler crabs. It's not far from the back side of the Morehead City Port Terminal, where the big ships come in from the Atlantic Ocean.

Everybody liked him, and he was good at almost everything he put his hand to. But when Tucker turned eleven or twelve, he was still so short he looked like an elf. And you know how it is when you're a little different from other folks in even some harmless kind of way. Kids called him Tom Thumb, squirt, midget, inchworm, dwarf.

I thought Tucker was the cutest little thing in the world. But to him back then I was ole knock-kneed LaShana Mae, the girl who lived down the street. I was a couple years younger than him. We were friends, though, and went to the same church—St. Luke's Missionary Baptist—and the same school.

Back in those days, in the 1970s, young boys and girls didn't hang out as boyfriend and girlfriend like kids do now. Plus, I was just a skinny girl with braids and braces. Kids called me Wires because of those braces, and boy, did it ever make me mad! So Tucker and I had a lot in common, and lots of times we talked about the things kids called us, especially when we went fishing.

Even though being called those names hurt, Tucker gave up fighting the kids who said them. Fighting didn't help. The name-callers were all too big for him to beat up. So after a while, he learned to ignore the teasing. Most times he laughed it off. He was a tough little dude. But oh mercy, how he hated those names!

One day Tucker did something that made everybody stop calling him names he didn't like. I think it helped him grow a few inches, too.

You need to know a few things about this boy before I tell you what changed things around. Tucker could do almost anything that any other kid his age could do. He was a hotshot shortstop on the Little League baseball team. He could jump like a flea on the basketball court. He was smart in school. He was in the Boy Scouts. He could swim like a fish—and even surf!

He looked like a Tootsie Roll to me in that big ocean. Yeah, I had a name for him, too. I called him Tootsie Roll, but never to his face. I just kept it to myself. And when I called him that in my head, I didn't mean it in a bad way.

Tucker could do some fishing. He especially liked to fish his folks' little pier alongside their house. In the summertime he'd lie on his stomach on the pier and catch some of the biggest flounder to come out of Calico Creek. Instead of a rod and reel, he used a handful of fishing line, a hook baited with shrimp, and a sinker to keep the bait from floating on the surface.

He'd dangle that shrimp an inch or two off the bottom, right in front of a flounder's nose. Sometimes we'd fish together on his pier; and I wouldn't catch diddly-squat, not even a pinfish, not even a lizard fish, nothing. But ole Tootsie Roll could catch 'em.

CONNECT

Tucker tries fighting, ignoring, and laughing off the teasing he hates. What do you think is the best response to teasing? Explain.

PREDICT

In lines 36–42, underline the things Tucker is good at. Then, think about the title of the story. What do you think Tucker will do that makes people stop calling him names he doesn't like?

FLUENCY

Read aloud the boxed passage several times. Try to sound natural and casual, making the narrator's unique voice come through.

I tried fishing the way he did, but most of the time I used a rod and reel 'cause I thought the way Tucker did it was country. I still couldn't catch anything, not in Calico Creek. I did all right when I fished at the pier in Atlantic Beach.

That's how I'd see Tucker surfing. He even got teased about surfing, because not many black kids we knew surfed. Shoot, as much as we all loved the water, not a whole lot of us even knew how to swim. I didn't. Not until Tucker taught me later on.

He and his dad or mom would fish out on their own little pier all night sometimes with a Coleman lantern for light. His folks used regular rods and reels. I never fished out there at night with them because the mosquitoes and the gnats would about eat me up.

Plus, my momma liked to tell me that they used to do baptizing in that creek, which was okay. But then Momma'd say, "LaShana Mae, you watch out about being around that creek by yourself at night. The people who got baptized there and who've passed on come back to that creek as spirits in the middle of the night when the moon's full. They'll be singing and celebrating and shouting and praising, and they don't want to be disturbed. Unless you wanna join in with 'em."

Me being a scared little kid, you can believe that Momma didn't have to worry about me going out to *nobody's* Calico Creek by myself at night. But sometimes I'd go to my window at night and look out to see if anybody was celebrating the way she said. All I ever saw were grown folks fishing. Sometimes somebody would holler when they caught a big one. After I got grown I understood that Momma told me that story to try to help me stay out of trouble. She was worried I'd drown or get into

WORD STUDY

In line 62, LaShana Mae uses the word *country* as a slang term to refer to a way of doing things that seems backward and old-fashioned. This reflects a **stereotype,** or false generalization, about rural or country life.

WORD STUDY

The word *baptizing* (line 76) refers to a Christian ritual enacted when a person joins the church. In some churches, an adult who has accepted the faith is fully immersed in water.

RETELL

Re-read lines 75–83. Retell in your own words the story LaShana Mae's mother tells her to keep her away from the creek at night.

some kind of foolishness. Well, it worked. I knew that it was easy to get into trouble when you're out someplace where you're not supposed to be.

Anyway, what happened to change all the name-calling started when Tucker was on his pier trying to catch a flounder. He noticed a man standing on the Moten Motel dock just a few yards from him. The man had a thick white mustache and Vandyke beard and wore a blue-and-gold military-style jacket and cap. I wasn't there, so I didn't see him, but that's what Tucker told me.

When the man waved, Tucker, being a friendly kind of kid, waved back. They struck up a conversation. The man said his name was Richard and that he was staying at the motel for a few days. His home was in Manteo, on Roanoke Island, not far from the Outer Banks, where he worked with the U.S. Lifesaving Service.

Tucker figured what he meant was that he was with the U.S. Coast Guard. Tucker was pretty knowledgeable about the coast guard, but he had never heard of this life-saving service. Tucker asked the man if he liked to fish. Richard said yes. He'd been a **commercial** fisherman before he became a captain in the lifesaving service. As a lifesaver, he said, he and his men went into the ocean in the middle of hurricanes and nor'easters to save passengers and crew members whose ships were sinking.

Of course, anything about water fascinated Tucker, so he must have asked this Richard a million questions. Richard didn't seem to mind, though. He said he didn't get to talk to kids much anymore.

Richard said a good crewman had to be strong, an excellent swimmer, a quick thinker, and in good physical health, have good eyesight, and understand how dangerous

PREDICT

Lines 93–95 **foreshadow** later events in the story. What do you predict will happen?

INTERPRET

Pause at line 113. Why do you think Tucker knows about the Coast Guard but has never heard of the U.S. Lifesaving Service?

VOCABULARY

commercial (kə·mur′shəl) *adj.:* involving the buying and selling of goods.

What other meaning do you know for the word *commercial*?

Notes

VOCABULARY

enlist (en·list′) *v.:* join an organization or cause.

qualifications (kwôl′ə·fi·kā′shənz) *n.:* qualities or skills needed to do a job.

Based on the list of qualities Richard gives in lines 123–126, do you agree that Tucker has the **qualifications** to be a good crewman? Why or why not?

© BJ Formento/CORBIS

the sea can be. He told so many stories about lifesaving that Tucker wished he could **enlist** right away, and said so. He had the right **qualifications**—other than being too young, of course. And too short.

Richard told him it wasn't the size of a person that got the job done. It was how bad the person wanted to do it.

How were those huge ships two and more stories high able to move into the Morehead City port and back out to sea? Most couldn't do it without little tugboats pushing and pulling them in, Richard said. A tugboat could bring in a ship many times its size.

Richard said that Tucker would make a good tugboat and one day might even grow to be a big ship. He thanked Tucker for the conversation, said maybe they'd meet again, and then the man wandered off back toward the motel. Tucker said for the rest of the afternoon, he thought over what Richard had said.

A few days later, Tucker decided to go with his dad to the Atlantic Beach pier to fish. His daddy worked there as a cook. For some reason I couldn't go that day. I've always wished I had. Tucker said he took his surfboard, too, in case fishing got slow. It was early morning, but a hot July wind blew in from the southwest, making the waves choppy and sandy. The tide was going out. Hardly anybody was on the pier, which was another hint that the fish might not be biting. Tucker said only one guy was in the water, floating on a red raft like a huge jellyfish.

After a good hour had passed and he hadn't got a bite, Tucker left his rod and reel with his father in the pier restaurant's kitchen and went surfing. After he swam out far enough, he climbed onto his surfboard and rode a wave in. When he glanced back at the pier, guess who he saw? His new friend, Richard, on the pier, clapping for him. At least this time he had on shorts and a regular shirt. Tucker said he bet Richard had about burnt up in that heavy uniform the other day.

Richard hollered, "Do it, Tugboat! Pull that ole wave in!"

PREDICT

Re-read lines 130–138. What point is Richard making to Tucker? What might the comment about Tucker making a good tugboat **foreshadow**?

PREDICT

Underline details in lines 143–153 that might **foreshadow** what will happen at the pier.

CLARIFY

Circle words that describe Richard's relationship to Tucker in Line 159. Why does Richard call Tucker "Tugboat"? (Look back at lines 132–138.)

COMPARE & CONTRAST

What is the difference between Richard calling Tucker by the nickname "Tugboat" and the man on the raft calling him "squirt"?

PREDICT

Underline the details in lines 171–181 that build **suspense**—a feeling of tension or anxiety about what will happen next. What do you think these details **foreshadow**?

Tugboat? Tucker said he frowned until he remembered Richard's story about tugboats. So he waved back and swam out to pull in another one, passing the man on the raft. The man said, "You're kinda little to be way out here, ain't ya, squirt?" Tucker just shook his head and kept going.

Tucker pulled in four more waves until he noticed a tall purple thunderhead rising up on the southwest horizon. That cloud meant a storm was probably on its way, but Tucker figured he had at least half an hour before the wind kicked up the waves and blew the cloud in and the rain began. Tucker wasn't afraid of a thing, but his common sense and his folks had told him to always leave away from water when storms and lightning came along. It's hard to get grown without having common sense, because being stupid can get you killed sometimes.

Keeping an eye on the horizon, Tucker went on pulling in those waves until a huge one arched up behind his back and crashed down on him. Tucker disappeared.

Wipeout. No big deal for Tucker, though. He popped right up in the water and grabbed his board, which was tied to his ankle. He was all right. But the man on the raft wasn't. He thrashed around in the water screaming that he couldn't swim.

As that big black cloud spread across the sky toward them, the wind and waves grew rougher. Wanting to help the man, but concerned about his own safety, Tucker hesitated, then straddled his surfboard and, using his hands for oars, paddled toward the raft. He'd have time to get the guy's raft back to him and then head in. But as Tucker passed, the man lunged at the surfboard, knocking Tucker off.

And then this guy grabbed hold of Tucker! Wrapped up in that big bear's arms and legs, with the sea getting choppier, Tucker said he knew he was about to die. He began to pray.

But something lifted Tucker up through the water and onto his surfboard, where he was able to catch his breath. That's when he saw his friend Richard in the water, too! Have mercy! Richard was hauling that raft toward the man. With two big **heaves,** Richard snatched that guy straight up out of the water and onto the raft.

Richard yelled, "Let's push and pull it, Tugboat! Push and pull it in!"

Somehow Tucker and Richard pushed and pulled that raft—with the guy glued to it—close enough to shore that the man was able to wade in the rest of the way. Four or five people splashed into the water and helped them onto the beach and into the pier house. One of the helpers was a reporter on vacation.

As soon as everybody was inside the pier house, the rain poured down. An arrow of lightning whizzed across the pier into the water and lit up the whole ocean. That's when Tucker said he got scared, seeing that lightning. He'd have been fried alive, you know. The guy Tucker rescued was named Nibbles. Mr. Nibbles was so grateful that he gave Tucker a hundred dollars right on the spot.

The reporter interviewed everybody and took pictures of Tucker, Nibbles, and Tucker's dad, who almost had a heart attack when he heard what happened. When the reporter asked how such a small boy was able to rescue a big, grown man, Tucker said, "'Cause I'm a tugboat, like Richard said. We pull the big ones in."

But when Tucker turned around to point out Richard, he couldn't find him.

VOCABULARY

heaves (hēvz) *n.:* shoves or lifts performed with great effort.

RETELL

Re-read lines 202–215. Explain how Tucker is able to rescue the big man on the raft.

INTERPRET

Pause at line 222. When does Tucker realize how dangerous his situation really was?

INTERPRET

Re-read lines 231–245. Tucker has become a hero, but there is no mention of Richard's role in the rescue. Why do you think this is?

COMPARE & CONTRAST

What is the difference between the names Tucker used to be called and the new nickname—Tugboat—that he has been given?

PREDICT

Pause at line 259. No one saw Richard but Tucker. What might this detail **foreshadow**?

The reporter's story about Tucker's rescue was in the local paper, then got picked up by the Associated Press and went all over the world. CBS TV even flew him and his folks to New York to be on its morning show Afterwards, back home in Morehead City, strangers stopped Tucker on the street, in stores, even came to his home. They wanted to see the little "tugboat" that hauled in that big man, and get his autograph.

Businesses up and down Arendell Street put up WELCOME HOME TUGBOAT! posters in their windows. And there was a parade. Tucker was a hero! He and the mayor rode on the back of a big ole white Cadillac convertible and waved at everybody. I was so proud that I almost forgot and hollered out, "Way to go, Tootsie Roll!" but I caught myself in time.

Everybody—even local folks—called Tucker Tugboat after that, including us kids. We'd never seen a real live hero close up before, especially one our age. It wasn't cool anymore to tease him with those other names. Funny how things can turn right around, isn't it?

And you know what? Tucker grew to be six feet five. He played on the North Carolina Central University Eagles basketball team, joined the U.S. Coast Guard, and lives in Kill Devil Hills, North Carolina, on the Outer Banks.

But there's something Tucker never figured out. When he first told people that Richard was the real hero, nobody believed him. Apparently nobody but Tucker had seen Richard—not even Mr. Nibbles.

There's more. When Tucker went into the pier gift shop to spend some of his rescue money, he picked up a book about the coast guard. He was thumbing through it when he stopped at an old-timey picture of some black men wearing jackets like Richard's. They were standing in front of a building on the Outer Banks. Below it was a picture of—yes, Richard! Mustache, beard, jacket, everything!

Tucker read, "History of the Pea Island Lifesaving Service. Captain Richard Etheridge was Keeper of the Pea Island Lifesaving Service, a forerunner of part of what is now the U.S. Coast Guard. This unique, all African American, courageous lifesaving crew, and those who followed, saved hundreds of shipwrecked passengers' lives by plunging into the stormy seas and bringing their charges back to safety."

Tucker said he shot out of that gift shop toward the restaurant to show his dad the book to prove his case, but what he read next made him stop: "Captain Etheridge, born in 1844 on Roanoke Island in North Carolina, died in 1900."

Tucker said he read that date fifteen or twenty times before it started to sink in. Nineteen hundred? Richard Etheridge had been dead for almost one hundred years. How was it possible a dead man helped him save that guy? Unless Richard was a ghost. He'd been talking to, and swimming with—a ghost?

You can believe Tucker hit up the library that very next day and searched for as much information as he could find on Richard Etheridge. There wasn't much, but what he read was that Richard Etheridge was all those great things he had read about and that he still died in 1900.

A few years later, when Tucker's folks visited the North Carolina Aquarium on Roanoke Island, Tucker found Richard Etheridge's grave and monument. Etheridge's headstone was marked 1844–1900. That's

RETELL

Pause at line 280. Explain what Tucker learns about Richard.

INTERPRET

Tucker wonders how Richard could have helped him if he died in 1900. What is your explanation?

INFER

Why do you think Tucker stopped talking about Richard being involved in the rescue after he saw Richard's headstone?

CONNECT

Re-read lines 302–305. Do you agree that this is the most important lesson? What else might Tucker have learned?

CLARIFY

Circle the fact you learn about the narrator at the very end of this story. Does her identity make the events of the story more believable?

when Tucker stopped talking about Richard being involved in the rescue. Unless somebody asked.

So now, if you run into Tucker "Tugboat" Willis, ask him about the rescue, and he'll tell you. Then, real carefully, ask if he ever met Richard Etheridge. He'll tell you yes, he did, and what he learned. What he learned was that it pays to be polite to everybody you meet, like Tucker was to a man named Richard. You never know when that person might help you.

And every time Tucker tells me the story, he tells it to me the same way I told it to you. Seeing how Tucker turned out proves that some mighty things that help folks out in some mighty big ways can come in some mighty small packages.

It also proves that good things come to those who wait, like I did. I know, because I'm Mrs. LaShana Mae Willis, Tugboat's wife.

• • •

There really was a man named Richard Etheridge, a professional fisherman who was born in 1844 on Roanoke Island off North Carolina. A member of the Thirty-sixth U.S. Colored Troops of the Union Army, he fought at the Battle of New Market Heights in Virginia during the Civil War. And in 1880, Etheridge was hired as the Keeper of the Pea Island Lifesaving Station on the Barrier Islands (the Outer Banks) of North Carolina. The station continued to set a high standard of performance with its all-black personnel until 1947, when the Coast Guard closed down the facilities.[1]

1. **facilities** (fə·sil′ə·tēz) *n.:* buildings designed for a particular function or activity.

No one made any formal **recognition** of the Pea Island surfmen's daring sea rescues until 1996. In March of that year, Etheridge and his men were finally acknowledged posthumously[2] in formal ceremonies in Washington, D.C., with a Gold Lifesaving Medal from the United States Coast Guard. Etheridge and his wife and daughter are buried on the grounds of the North Carolina Aquarium in Manteo, which maintains an exhibit on these brave men.

---

2. **posthumously** (päs′cho͞o·məs·lē) *adv.:* after death.

MEET THE WRITER

Eleanora E. Tate (1948–) was born in Canton, Missouri, and spent her first year of school in a one-room schoolhouse for African American children in the first through eighth grade. She wrote her first short story when she was in third grade. She says she writes books and stories so that all people can read about the proud history and culture of African Americans. This story comes from her book *Don't Split the Pole: Tales of Down-Home Folk Wisdom.* Other books of hers you might enjoy include *The Secret of Gumbo Grove, Thank You, Dr. Martin Luther King, Jr.!* and *Front Porch Stories at the One-Room School.*

VOCABULARY

recognition (rek′əg·nish′ən) *n.:* acknowledgment; something done as an expression of appreciation.

Circle two examples of recognition in lines 328–333.

EVALUATE

What do you think of this addition of historical facts to the end of a fictional story? Does it add anything to the story, or is it unnecessary? Explain.

Lifesaving Service

Literary Skills Analyze the use of suspense and foreshadowing.

Suspense Boxes Writers keep your interest in a story by building suspense. One of the ways they do this is through **foreshadowing.** They drop hints about what will happen later on in the story. Skim through "Lifesaving Service" and the notes you took. Then, fill in the boxes below. For each box on the left, fill in an example of foreshadowing from the story. Then, for each box on the right, describe the event that was hinted at.

Foreshadowing Hints		Events Foreshadowed
1.	→	
2.	→	
3.	→	

Skills Review

Lifesaving Service

VOCABULARY AND COMPREHENSION

A. Clarifying Word Meanings: Examples Choose three words from the Word Bank. Then, write sentences in which you give an example of each.

Word Bank

- commercial
- enlist
- qualifications
- heaves
- recognition

1. ______________________________

____

____

2. ______________________________

____

____

3. ______________________________

____

____

B. Reading Comprehension Answer each question below.

1. Where does Tucker first meet Richard Etheridge? ______________

____

____

2. What does Richard do to help Tucker? ______________

____

____

3. What does Tucker later learn about Richard? ______________

____

____

Vocabulary Skills
Clarify word meanings by using examples.

Collection 2

Living Many Lives

© Cindy Charles/PhotoEdit

Academic Vocabulary for Collection 2

These are the terms you should know
as you read and analyze the selections in this collection.

Character A person or an animal who takes part in the action of a story.

Characterization The way a writer tells you about characters. Typically you learn about characters by observing their appearance and actions, "listening" to what they have to say, reading about their thoughts and feelings, and paying attention to how other characters react to them.

Direct Characterization Statements in a story that tell you directly what a character is like. Example: "Although Jason was tough, he was able to make friends easily."

Indirect Characterization Showing rather than telling what a character is like. You must observe the character and draw your own conclusions about the character.

Character Trait A quality that describes some aspect of a character's personality, such as kind, nervous, or generous. Character traits are revealed through a character's appearance, words, actions, thoughts, and effects on other characters.

Motivation The reasons characters do the things they do. Feelings, needs, wishes, and pressures from other story characters are all forces that can motivate a character.

Before You Read

Seventh Grade by Gary Soto

LITERARY FOCUS: CHARACTER TRAITS

What's your best friend like? Funny? A little impatient? A neat freak? The words you choose to describe your friend also describe his or her character traits. **Character traits** are the qualities that are revealed by a character's appearance, spoken words, actions, and thoughts. Character traits are also revealed by how a character affects other characters in a story.

Use the space below to list some character traits of your favorite book or television character.

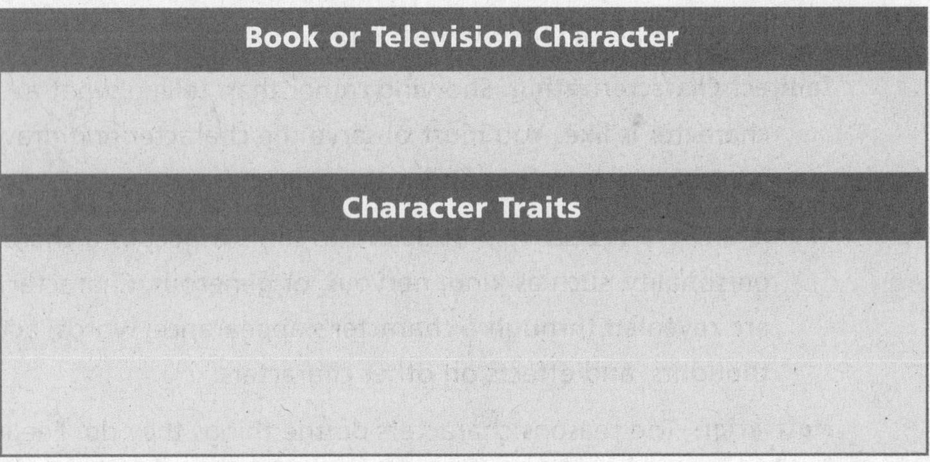

Book or Television Character
Character Traits

READING SKILLS: MAKING INFERENCES

Imagine that you are eating lunch in your backyard. You leave your sandwich on the picnic table and go into the house for a glass of water. When you return to your lunch, your sandwich is gone and your dog has peanut butter on his nose. What do you think happened? You can use the evidence you have to make an **inference**, or educated guess, that your dog swiped your sandwich. In the same way, you can use story details to make inferences about characters in a story.

As you read "Seventh Grade," collect story details to help you make inferences about the characters.

Literary Skills Understand character traits.

Reading Skills Make inferences.

Vocabulary Skills Understand word origins.

VOCABULARY DEVELOPMENT

PREVIEW SELECTION VOCABULARY

Take a few minutes to preview these words before you begin to read "Seventh Grade."

propelled (prə·peld′) *v.:* pushed onward.

Victor is propelled down the hall by the sight of Teresa in the distance.

conviction (kən·vik′shən) *n.:* firm belief.

When the girls don't notice him, Michael scowls and glares at them with greater conviction.

unison (yo͞o′nə·sən) *n.:* sounding the same note at the same time.

The teacher likes to hear a chorus of voices, so he asks his students to greet him in unison.

bouquets (bo͞o·kāz′) *n.:* bunches of cut flowers.

Victor handed Teresa a bouquet of flowers he picked from the field behind his house.

UNDERSTANDING WORD ORIGINS

A word's **etymology** (et′ə·mäl′ə·jē) tells you what language the word comes from and how the word has developed through different languages over many years. An etymology is usually listed in brackets or parentheses after its entry in a dictionary. Definitions of symbols and abbreviations in the front or back of the dictionary will help you read the etymology. For example, the common symbol < means "comes from" or "derived from." You will notice that many English words can be traced back to Latin, the language spoken by the ancient Romans.

Take a look at the etymology of *student* to understand the word's history. As you read the story that follows, look for sidenotes that help explain the etymology of words.

Etymology	Meaning
student < L *studere*, to study	*Student* comes from the Latin word *studere*, which means "to study."

Seventh Grade

Gary Soto

IDENTIFY

Underline the setting and circle the name of the character introduced in the first paragraph. How do you know what grade he is in?

INTERPRET

Re-read lines 4–13. Why does Victor want to study French?

On the first day of school, Victor stood in line half an hour before he came to a wobbly card table. He was handed a packet of papers and a computer card on which he listed his one elective, French. He already spoke Spanish and English, but he thought some day he might travel to France, where it was cool; not like Fresno,[1] where summer days reached 110 degrees in the shade. There were rivers in France, and huge churches, and fair-skinned people everywhere, the way there were brown people all around Victor.

Besides, Teresa, a girl he had liked since they were in catechism classes[2] at Saint Theresa's, was taking French, too. With any luck they would be in the same class. Teresa

1. **Fresno:** town in the San Joaquin Valley, in central California.
2. **catechism** (kat′ə·kiz′əm) **classes:** instruction in the principles of Christianity taken before joining the Catholic Church.

is going to be my girl this year, he promised himself as he left the gym full of students in their new fall clothes. She was cute. And good in math, too, Victor thought as he walked down the hall to his homeroom. He ran into his friend, Michael Torres, by the water fountain that never turned off.

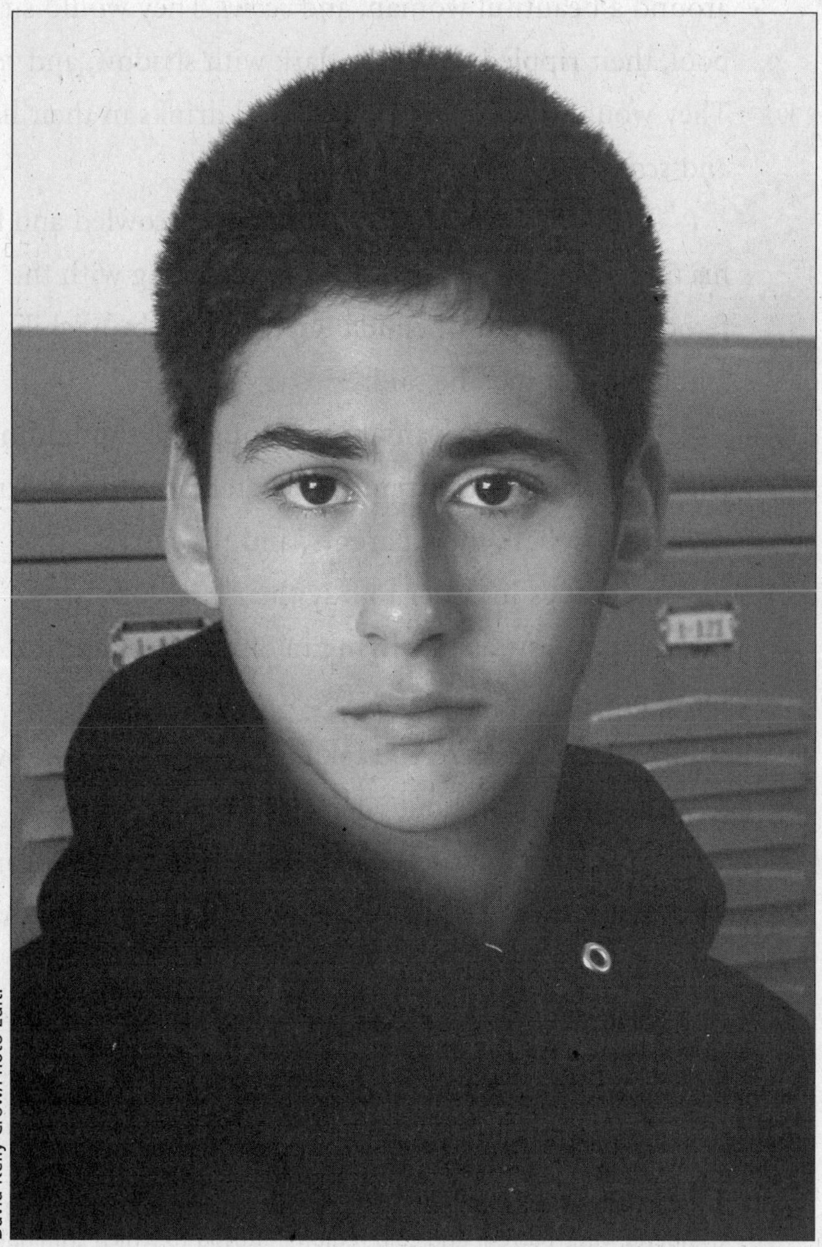

David Kelly Crow/Photo Edit.

INFER

Without directly describing Victor, the author gives us details about Victor's thoughts and actions on his first day of school. Underline the details in lines 1–19 that give you clues to Victor's **character traits.** List a few of these character traits.

VISUALIZE

Does this photograph look like Victor as you picture him so far? Why or why not?

INFER

Re-read lines 23–35. Think about what you can learn about Michael from the way he acts and what he says. What **character traits** are revealed by his words and actions?

IDENTIFY

In lines 36–41, underline the interests and activities that Victor and Michael share.

VOCABULARY

propelled (prə·peld′) *v.:* pushed onward.

This word is derived from the Latin word *propellere*, which is composed of *pro-*, meaning "forward," and *pellere*, meaning "to drive."

They shook hands, *raza*-style, and jerked their heads at one another in a *saludo de vato.*[3] "How come you're making a face?" asked Victor.

"I ain't making a face, *ese.* This *is* my face." Michael said his face had changed during the summer. He had read a *GQ* magazine that his older brother had borrowed from the Book Mobile and noticed that the male models all had the same look on their faces. They would stand, one arm around a beautiful woman, and *scowl.* They would sit at a pool, their rippled stomachs dark with shadow, and *scowl.* They would sit at dinner tables, cool drinks in their hands, and *scowl.*

"I think it works," Michael said. He scowled and let his upper lip quiver. His teeth showed along with the ferocity of his soul. "Belinda Reyes walked by a while ago and looked at me," he said.

Victor didn't say anything, though he thought his friend looked pretty strange. They talked about recent movies, baseball, their parents, and the horrors of picking grapes in order to buy their fall clothes. Picking grapes was like living in Siberia,[4] except hot and more boring.

"What classes are you taking?" Michael said, scowling.

"French. How 'bout you?"

"Spanish. I ain't so good at it, even if I'm Mexican."

"I'm not either, but I'm better at it than math, that's for sure."

A tinny, three-beat bell **propelled** students to their homerooms. The two friends socked each other in the arm

3. ***saludo de vato*** (sä·lo͞o′dō dā bä′tō): Spanish for "homeboy greeting."
4. **Siberia:** vast, barren, and cold region in Russia to which criminals and political prisoners were often sent as punishment.

and went their ways, Victor thinking, man, that's weird. Michael thinks making a face makes him handsome.

On the way to his homeroom, Victor tried a scowl. He felt foolish, until out of the corner of his eye he saw a girl looking at him. Umm, he thought, maybe it does work. He scowled with greater **conviction.**

In homeroom, roll was taken, emergency cards were passed out, and they were given a bulletin to take home to their parents. The principal, Mr. Belton, spoke over the crackling loudspeaker, welcoming the students to a new year, new experiences, and new friendships. The students squirmed in their chairs and ignored him. They were anxious to go to first period. Victor sat calmly, thinking of Teresa, who sat two rows away, reading a paperback novel. This would be his lucky year. She was in his homeroom, and would probably be in his English and math classes. And, of, course, French.

The bell rang for first period, and the students herded noisily through the door. Only Teresa lingered, talking with the homeroom teacher.

"So you think I should talk to Mrs. Gaines?" she asked the teacher. "She would know about ballet?"

"She would be a good bet," the teacher said. Then added, "Or the gym teacher, Mrs. Garza."

Victor lingered, keeping his head down and staring at his desk. He wanted to leave when she did so he could bump into her and say something clever.

He watched her on the sly. As she turned to leave, he stood up and hurried to the door, where he managed to catch her eye. She smiled and said, "Hi, Victor."

He smiled back and said, "Yeah, that's me." His brown face blushed. Why hadn't he said, "Hi, Teresa," or "How was your summer?" or something nice?

VOCABULARY

conviction (kən·vik′shən) *n.:* firm belief.

Conviction comes from the Latin *convictio*, meaning "proof" or "demonstration."

COMPARE & CONTRAST

In what ways are Victor and Michael alike and different?

IDENTIFY

Pause at line 81. Circle what Teresa says to Victor. Now circle Victor's response. What does Victor wish he had said?

As Teresa walked down the hall, Victor walked the other way, looking back, admiring how gracefully she walked, one foot in front of the other. So much for being in the same class, he thought. As he trudged to English, he practiced scowling.

In English they reviewed the parts of speech. Mr. Lucas, a portly man, waddled down the aisle, asking, "What is a noun?"

"A person, place, or thing," said the class in **unison**.

"Yes, now somebody give me an example of a person—you, Victor Rodriguez."

"Teresa," Victor said automatically. Some of the girls giggled. They knew he had a crush on Teresa. He felt himself blushing again.

"Correct," Mr. Lucas said. "Now provide me with a place."

Mr. Lucas called on a freckled kid who answered, "Teresa's house with a kitchen full of big brothers."

After English, Victor had math, his weakest subject. He sat in the back by the window, hoping that he would not be called on. Victor understood most of the problems, but some of the stuff looked like the teacher made it up as she went along. It was confusing, like the inside of a watch.

After math he had a fifteen-minute break, then social studies, and, finally, lunch. He bought a tuna casserole with buttered rolls, some fruit cocktail, and milk. He sat with Michael, who practiced scowling between bites.

Girls walked by and looked at him.

"See what I mean, Vic?" Michael scowled. "They love it."

"Yeah, I guess so."

INFER

Re-read lines 76–86. Underline the clues that tell you how Victor feels about Teresa. In your own words, describe his feelings. Are there any words or phrases that suggest Teresa's feelings for Victor? Write them below.

VOCABULARY

unison (yo͞o′nə·sen) *n.:* sounding the same note at the same time.

Unison is derived from the Latin words *unus*, meaning "one," and *sonus*, meaning "sound."

They ate slowly, Victor scanning the horizon for a glimpse of Teresa. He didn't see her. She must have brought lunch, he thought, and is eating outside. Victor scraped his plate and left Michael, who was busy scowling at a girl two tables away.

The small, triangle-shaped campus bustled with students talking about their new classes. Everyone was in a sunny mood. Victor hurried to the bag lunch area, where he sat down and opened his math book. He moved his lips as if he were reading, but his mind was somewhere else. He raised his eyes slowly and looked around. No Teresa.

He lowered his eyes, pretending to study, then looked slowly to the left. No Teresa. He turned a page in the book and stared at some math problems that scared him because he knew he would have to do them eventually. He looked to the right. Still no sign of her. He stretched out lazily in an attempt to disguise his snooping.

Then he saw her. She was sitting with a girlfriend under a plum tree. Victor moved to a table near her and daydreamed about taking her to a movie. When the bell sounded, Teresa looked up, and their eyes met. She smiled sweetly and gathered her books. Her next class was French, same as Victor's.

They were among the last students to arrive in class, so all the good desks in the back had already been taken. Victor was forced to sit near the front, a few desks away from Teresa, while Mr. Bueller wrote French words on the chalkboard. The bell rang, and Mr. Bueller wiped his hands, turned to the class, and said, *"Bonjour."*[5]

"Bonjour," braved a few students.

---

5. ***bonjour*** (bon·zhōōr'): French for "hello" or "good day."

EVALUATE

Pause at line 118. Do you think Michael's plan for attracting girls is actually working? Explain.

VISUALIZE

Underline the details in lines 119–137 that help you visualize this scene.

FLUENCY

Read the boxed passage aloud. Vary the tone and emphasis of your voice to help set the scene inside the classroom. Concentrate on pronouncing the French word correctly, and pay attention to the punctuation, especially the commas, at which you should pause.

VISUALIZE

Does the girl in this picture resemble your idea of Teresa? Why or why not?

WORD STUDY

The word *populace* (line 150) comes from the Italian word *popolaccio*, which means "mob." If Mr. Bueller had used *mob* instead of *populace*, how would the effect of his words have been different?

Corbis

"*Bonjour,*" Victor whispered. He wondered if Teresa heard him.

Mr. Bueller said that if the students studied hard, at the end of the year they could go to France and be understood by the populace.

One kid raised his hand and asked, "What's 'populace'?"

"The people, the people of France."

Mr. Bueller asked if anyone knew French. Victor raised his hand, wanting to impress Teresa. The teacher beamed and said, "*Très bien. Parlez-vous français?*"[6]

Victor didn't know what to say. The teacher wet his lips and asked something else in French. The room grew silent. Victor felt all eyes staring at him. He tried to bluff his way out by making noises that sounded French.

"La me vave me con le grandma," he said uncertainly.

Mr. Bueller, wrinkling his face in curiosity, asked him to speak up.

Great rosebushes of red bloomed on Victor's cheeks. A river of nervous sweat ran down his palms. He felt awful. Teresa sat a few desks away, no doubt thinking he was a fool. Without looking at Mr. Bueller, Victor mumbled, "Frenchie oh wewe gee in September."

Mr. Bueller asked Victor to repeat what he said.

"Frenchie oh wewe gee in September," Victor repeated.

Mr. Bueller understood that the boy didn't know French and turned away. He walked to the blackboard and pointed to the words on the board with his steel-edged ruler.

"*Le bateau,*" he sang.

"*Le bateau,*" the students repeated.

"*Le bateau est sur l'eau,*" he sang.

"*Le bateau est sur l'eau.*"[7]

Victor was too weak from failure to join the class. He stared at the board and wished he had taken Spanish, not French. Better yet, he wished he could start his life over.

6. ***Très bien. Parlez-vous français*** (Trā byen. Pär′lā voo frôn·sā′): French for "Very good. Do you speak French?"
7. ***Le bateau est sur l'eau*** (Loo ba·tō′ ā sür lō): French for "The boat is on the water."

INTERPRET

Pause at line 160. What **motivates** Victor to pretend he knows French?

INFER

Re-read lines 156–169. **Indirect characterization** occurs when the writer shows, instead of tells, you about a character. What can you infer about Victor based on his actions in this scene?

He had never been so embarrassed. He bit his thumb until he tore off a sliver of skin.

The bell sounded for fifth period, and Victor shot out of the room, avoiding the stares of the other kids, but had to return for his math book. He looked sheepishly at the teacher, who was erasing the board, then widened his eyes in terror at Teresa who stood in front of him. "I didn't know you knew French," she said. "That was good."

Mr. Bueller looked at Victor, and Victor looked back. Oh please, don't say anything, Victor pleaded with his eyes. I'll wash your car, mow your lawn, walk your dog—anything! I'll be your best student, and I'll clean your erasers after school.

Mr. Bueller shuffled through the papers on his desk. He smiled and hummed as he sat down to work. He remembered his college years when he dated a girlfriend in borrowed cars. She thought he was rich because each time he picked her up he had a different car. It was fun until he had spent all his money on her and had to write home to his parents because he was broke.

Victor couldn't stand to look at Teresa. He was sweaty with shame. "Yeah, well, I picked up a few things from movies and books and stuff like that." They left the class together. Teresa asked him if he would help her with her French.

"Sure, anytime," Victor said.

"I won't be bothering you, will I?"

"Oh no, I like being bothered."

"Bonjour," Teresa said, leaving him outside her next class. She smiled and pushed wisps of hair from her face.

INTERPRET

Pause at line 187. What is surprising about what Teresa says to Victor?

INFER

Re-read lines 193–199. Underline the words that tell you what Mr. Bueller is thinking and what he is doing. What **character traits** do these details reveal?

"Yeah, right, *bonjour,*" Victor said. He turned and headed to his class. The rosebushes of shame on his face became **bouquets** of love. Teresa is a great girl, he thought. And Mr. Bueller is a good guy.

He raced to metal shop. After metal shop there was biology, and after biology a long sprint to the public library, where he checked out three French textbooks.

He was going to like seventh grade.

VOCABULARY

bouquets (bo͞o·kāz′) *n.:* bunches of cut flowers.

This word comes from the Old French word *boschet,* meaning "small grove" or "thicket."

INFER

Characters' thoughts and actions reveal a lot about what they are like. Re-read lines 210–217. What does Victor think and do at the end of this story that shows his happiness and excitement about the future?

MEET THE WRITER

Gary Soto (1952–) grew up among Mexican American farmworkers in California's San Joaquin Valley. While studying geography at Fresno City College, Soto began reading poetry and soon tried his hand at writing his own. His first collection, *The Elements of San Joaquin,* was published in 1977. Eventually, he began writing novels, short stories, and essays. An award-winning writer of works for both children and adults, Soto often draws on his personal experiences to create vibrant characters.

Seventh Grade

Literary Skills Analyze character traits.

Character Traits Chart Writers bring characters to life by describing how the characters look, talk, act, and think. Sometimes a writer directly describes a character's traits. For example, a writer might tell you that so-and-so is kind, sympathetic, or tough. Often, however, you have to make inferences about the characters based on details the writer provides.

Select one of the characters from "Seventh Grade," and complete this chart with details you find in the story. Then, review those details and list the character's traits in the box.

Character:

Appearance

Speech

Actions

Thoughts and Feelings

Other Characters' Reactions

Character's Traits:

Skills Review

Seventh Grade

VOCABULARY AND COMPREHENSION

A. Word Origins The partial etymologies given below tell the story of three of the Word Bank words. Select the vocabulary word that matches each etymology, and write the word in the blank provided.

Word Bank

conviction
propelled
unison
bouquets

1. < L *unus*, meaning "one" ______________________
2. < F *boschet*, meaning "small grove" ______________________
3. < L *convictio*, meaning "proof" ______________________

B. Reading Comprehension Answer each question below.

1. What is Victor's personality like?

____

____

2. What is Michael's new strategy for attracting girls?

____

____

3. What does Victor do to try to impress Teresa?

____

____

4. What does Mr. Bueller do when he realizes Victor cannot really speak French?

____

____

____

Vocabulary Skills
Understand word origins.

The War of the Wall by Toni Cade Bambara

LITERARY FOCUS: THE NARRATOR

A **narrator** is the teller of a story. When you begin reading a story, look for clues about who the narrator is. A narrator who observes the action and is not a story character is called an **omniscient** (äm·nish′ənt) **narrator.** This type of narrator can tell you about the thoughts and feelings of all the story characters.

A **first-person narrator,** on the other hand, *is* a story character. A first-person narrator participates directly in the story's action. If the storyteller tells the whole tale using such first-person pronouns as *I, me,* and *mine,* then you know you're reading a story told by a first-person narrator.

READING SKILLS: MAKING INFERENCES

A story told by a first-person narrator usually gives you a lot of information about the character who is narrating the story. However, it is still important for you to take part in the story by making your own **inferences,** or educated guesses, about the characters. Use these tips to make inferences about the narrator of "The War of the Wall."

- Pay close attention to what the narrator says and does.
- Observe the way other characters respond to the narrator.
- Examine what you learn about the narrator's thoughts.
- Think about how the narrator is like, or not like, people you know.

Literary Skills Understand the narrator.

Reading Skills Make inferences.

Vocabulary Skills Use context clues.

VOCABULARY DEVELOPMENT

PREVIEW SELECTION VOCABULARY

Preview the following words from "The War of the Wall" before you begin reading.

courtesies (kurt′ə·sēz) *n.:* polite acts.

Because they were angry and late to school, the kids were rude and didn't bother with courtesies.

integration (in′tə·grā′shən) *n.:* bringing together equally people of all races in public spaces, such as schools, parks, and neighborhoods.

Things didn't get better right away when integration was introduced to the town.

drawled (drôld) *v.:* spoke slowly, drawing out vowel sounds.

Mama took her time and drawled her answer to the question.

liberation (lib′ər·ā′shən) *n.:* release from slavery, prison, foreign occupation, and so on.

Neighborhood residents were pleased to see African flags of liberation on the wall.

inscription (in·skrip′shən) *n.:* short written or spoken message dedicating something to someone as a sign of respect.

Even the angry kids finally had to change their minds when they saw the respectful inscription on the wall.

USING CONTEXT CLUES

When you come across an unfamiliar word, you can often figure out its meaning by using **context clues.** In the examples below the passages in italics provide context clues that will help you understand the boldface words.

Restatement	**Courtesies** enable people to live comfortably together, because *polite actions and ways of speaking* help everyone get along.
Definition	Mama **drawled,** *saying her words slowly, drawing out the vowels* in her beautiful southern accent.
Example	On the day of **liberation,** *jails were thrown open and the prisoners were set free.*
Contrast	When **integration** became the town's policy, *members of minority groups were no longer excluded from the schools and parks.*

The War of the Wall

Toni Cade Bambara

BACKGROUND: Literature and Social Studies
This story takes place in the South in the 1960s or 1970s during the civil rights movement and the Vietnam War. Although great strides toward equality were taken during the 1960s, not all people in the South were happy about the civil rights laws enacted at this time to enforce integration. Even as great leaders like Martin Luther King, Jr., spoke of nonviolence and equality, there was tremendous anger, strife, and conflict in the nation.

Me and Lou had no time for **courtesies**. We were late for school. So we just flat out told the painter lady to quit messing with the wall. It was our wall, and she had no right coming into our neighborhood painting on it. Stirring in the paint bucket and not even looking at us, she mumbled something about Mr. Eubanks, the barber, giving her permission. That had nothing to do with it as far as we were concerned. We've been pitching pennies against that wall since we were little kids. Old folks have been dragging their chairs out to sit in the shade of the wall for years. Big kids have been playing handball against the wall since so-called **integration** when the crazies 'cross town poured cement in our pool so we couldn't use it. I'd sprained my neck one time boosting my cousin Lou up to chisel Jimmy Lyons's name into the wall when we found out he was never coming home from the war in Vietnam to take us fishing.

VOCABULARY

courtesies (kurt'ə·sēz) *n.:* polite acts.

integration (in'tə·grā'shən) *n.:* bringing together equally people of all races in public spaces, such as schools, parks, and neighborhoods.

IDENTIFY

In lines 1–3, circle three different pronouns that indicate this story is told by a **first-person narrator.**

INFER

Why is Jimmy Lyons not coming home from the war in Vietnam?

© Richard Koek/Getty Images

"If you lean close," Lou said, leaning hip-shot against her beat-up car, "you'll get a whiff of bubble gum and kids' sweat. And that'll tell you something—that this wall belongs to the kids of Taliaferro Street." I thought Lou sounded very convincing. But the painter lady paid us no mind. She just snapped the brim of her straw hat down and hauled her bucket up the ladder.

"You're not even from around here," I hollered up after her. The license plates on her old piece of car said "New York." Lou dragged me away because I was about to grab hold of that ladder and shake it. And then we'd really be late for school.

When we came from school, the wall was slick with white. The painter lady was running string across the wall and taping it here and there. Me and Lou leaned against

Notes

IDENTIFY

In lines 1–24, underline the reasons the narrator and the other neighborhood kids consider the wall to be theirs.

INFER

What can you infer about the narrator's character from her words and actions in lines 25–29?

CONNECT

Pause at line 35. Do you think the narrator and Lou are overreacting to the woman painting the wall, or do you understand their anger? Explain.

COMPARE & CONTRAST

Re-read lines 42–44. How are the narrator's and Lou's reactions to the painter different? What do their reactions say about the **character traits** of each?

the gum ball machine outside the pool hall and watched. She had strings up and down and back and forth. Then she began chalking them with a hunk of blue chalk.

The Morris twins crossed the street, hanging back at the curb next to the beat-up car. The twin with the red ribbons was hugging a jug of cloudy lemonade. The one with yellow ribbons was holding a plate of dinner away from her dress. The painter lady began snapping the strings. The blue chalk dust measured off halves and quarters up and down and sideways too. Lou was about to say how hip it all was, but I dropped my book satchel on his toes to remind him we were at war.

Some good aromas were drifting our way from the plate leaking pot likker[1] onto the Morris girl's white socks. I could tell from where I stood that under the tinfoil was baked ham, collard greens, and candied yams. And knowing Mrs. Morris, who sometimes bakes for my mama's restaurant, a slab of buttered cornbread was probably up under there too, sopping up some of the pot likker. Me and Lou rolled our eyes, wishing somebody would send us some dinner. But the painter lady didn't even turn around. She was pulling the strings down and prying bits of tape loose.

Side Pocket came strolling out of the pool hall to see what Lou and me were studying so hard. He gave the painter lady the once-over, checking out her paint-spattered jeans, her chalky T-shirt, her floppy-brimmed straw hat. He hitched up his pants and glided over toward the painter lady, who kept right on with what she was doing.

1. **pot likker** (pät lik′ər) *n.:* left-over liquid from cooked meat and vegetables, often used to make a sauce.

"Watcha got there, Sweetheart?" he asked the twin with the plate.

"Suppah," she said, all soft and country-like.

"For her," the one with the jug added, jerking her chin toward the painter lady's back.

Still she didn't turn around. She was rearing back on her heels, her hands jammed into her back pockets, her face squinched up like the masterpiece she had in mind was taking shape on the wall by magic. We could have been gophers crawled up into a rotten hollow for all she cared. She didn't even say hello to anybody. Lou was muttering something about how great her concentration was. I butt him with my hip, and his elbow slid off the gum machine.

"Good evening," Side Pocket said in his best ain't-I-fine voice. But the painter lady was moving from the milk

INFER

In lines 68–76, the narrator and Lou have different interpretations of the painter's behavior. Underline Lou's interpretation. Why does the narrator get angry at Lou's reaction to the painter? What does this tell you about the narrator's **character**?

INFER

The narrator says the painter is giving a show. Underline details in lines 77–88 that help you visualize the painter's behavior. Do you think she is intentionally performing for her audience? Why or why not?

ANALYZE

What do you think the expression "full of sky" means (line 93)? Circle the word in the next sentence that gives you a clue to what this phrase might mean.

crate to the stepstool to the ladder, moving up and down fast, scribbling all over the wall like a crazy person. We looked at Side Pocket. He looked at the twins. The twins looked at us. The painter lady was giving a show. It was like those old-timey music movies where the dancer taps on the table top and then starts jumping all over the furniture, kicking chairs over and not skipping a beat. She didn't even look where she was stepping. And for a minute there, hanging on the ladder to reach a far spot, she looked like she was going to tip right over.

"Ahh," Side Pocket cleared his throat and moved fast to catch the ladder. "These young ladies here have brought you some supper."

"Ma'am?" The twins stepped forward. Finally the painter turned around, her eyes "full of sky," as my grandmama would say. Then she stepped down like she was in a trance. She wiped her hands on her jeans as the Morris twins offered up the plate and the jug. She rolled back the tinfoil, then wagged her head as though something terrible was on the plate.

"Thank your mother very much," she said, sounding like her mouth was full of sky too. "I've brought my own dinner along." And then, without even excusing herself, she went back up the ladder, drawing on the wall in a wild way. Side Pocket whistled one of those oh-brother breathy whistles and went back into the pool hall. The Morris twins shifted their weight from one foot to the other, then crossed the street and went home. Lou had to drag me away, I was so mad. We couldn't wait to get to the firehouse to tell my daddy all about this rude woman who'd stolen our wall.

All the way back to the block to help my mama out at the restaurant, me and Lou kept asking my daddy for ways to run the painter lady out of town. But my daddy was busy talking about the trip to the country and telling Lou he could come too because Grandmama can always use an extra pair of hands on the farm.

Later that night, while me and Lou were in the back doing our chores, we found out that the painter lady was a liar. She came into the restaurant and leaned against the glass of the steam table, talking about how starved she was. I was scrubbing pots and Lou was chopping onions, but we could hear her through the service window. She was asking Mama was that a ham hock in the greens, and was that a neck bone in the pole beans, and were there any vegetables cooked without meat, especially pork.

"I don't care who your spiritual leader is," Mama said in that way of hers. "If you eat in the community, sistuh, you gonna eat pig by-and-by, one way or t'other."

Me and Lou were cracking up in the kitchen, and several customers at the counter were clearing their throats waiting for Mama to really fix her wagon for not speaking to the elders when she came in. The painter lady took a stool at the counter and went right on with her questions. Was there cheese in the baked macaroni, she wanted to know? Were there eggs in the salad? Was it honey or sugar in the iced tea? Mama was fixing Pop Johnson's plate. And every time the painter lady asked a fool question, Mama would dump another spoonful of rice on the pile. She was tapping her foot and heating up in a dangerous way. But Pop Johnson was happy as he could be. Me and Lou peeked through the service window, wondering what planet the painter lady came from. Who ever heard of baked macaroni without cheese, or potato salad without eggs?

INFER

In line 118, the narrator calls the painter a "liar." On what evidence does the narrator base this judgment?

INFER

Reread lines 128–143. What can you tell about the painter's diet from the questions she is asking? What effect are all her questions having on Mama? (Why does Mama keep adding rice to Pop Johnson's plate?)

FLUENCY

Read the boxed passage aloud a couple of times to get comfortable saying the words. Then, read it with expression. Can you make your voice sound like the painter from the North? Can you capture Mama's angry southern tone?

INFER

Re-read lines 165–182. Lou and the narrator want Mama to "open fire" on the painter, but instead Mama seems to make excuses for the painter's behavior. Why does this make the narrator so angry? What does her repetition of the line "Me and Lou didn't want to hear that" tell you about the narrator's **character**?

VOCABULARY

drawled (drôld) *v.*: spoke slowly, drawing out vowel sounds.

"Do you have any bread made with unbleached flour?" the painter lady asked Mama. There was a long pause, as though everybody in the restaurant was holding their breath, wondering if Mama would dump the next spoonful on the painter lady's head. She didn't. But when she set Pop Johnson's plate down, it came down with a bang.

When Mama finally took her order, the starving lady all of a sudden couldn't make up her mind whether she wanted a vegetable plate or fish and a salad. She finally settled on the broiled trout and a tossed salad. But just when Mama reached for a plate to serve her, the painter lady leaned over the counter with her finger all up in the air.

"Excuse me," she said. "One more thing." Mama was holding the plate like a Frisbee, tapping that foot, one hand on her hip. "Can I get raw beets in that tossed salad?"

"You will get," Mama said, leaning her face close to the painter lady's, "whatever Lou back there tossed. Now sit down." And the painter lady sat back down on her stool and shut right up.

All the way to the country, me and Lou tried to get Mama to open fire on the painter lady. But Mama said that seeing as how she was from the North, you couldn't expect her to have any manners. Then Mama said she was sorry she'd been so impatient with the woman because she seemed like a decent person and was simply trying to stick to a very strict diet. Me and Lou didn't want to hear that. Who did that lady think she was, coming into our neighborhood and taking over our wall?

"Welllll," Mama **drawled**, pulling into the filling station so Daddy could take the wheel, "it's hard on an artist, ya know. They can't always get people to look at their work. So she's just doing her work in the open, that's all."

Me and Lou definitely did not want to hear that. Why couldn't she set up an easel downtown or draw on the sidewalk in her own neighborhood? Mama told us to quit fussing so much; she was tired and wanted to rest. She climbed into the back seat and dropped down into the warm hollow Daddy had made in the pillow.

All weekend long, me and Lou tried to scheme up ways to recapture our wall. Daddy and Mama said they were sick of hearing about it. Grandmama turned up the TV to drown us out. On the late news was a story about the New York subways. When a train came roaring into the station all covered from top to bottom, windows too, with writings and drawings done with spray paint, me and Lou slapped five. Mama said it was too bad kids in New York had nothing better to do than spray paint all over the trains. Daddy said that in the cities, even grown-ups wrote all over the trains and buildings too. Daddy called it "graffiti." Grandmama called it a shame.

We couldn't wait to get out of school on Monday. We couldn't find any black spray paint anywhere. But in a junky hardware store downtown we found a can of white epoxy paint, the kind you touch up old refrigerators with when they get splotchy and peely. We spent our whole allowance on it. And because it was too late to use our bus passes, we had to walk all the way home lugging our book satchels and gym shoes, and the bag with the epoxy.

COMPARE & CONTRAST

The narrator and Lou spend the weekend complaining about the painter. Do you think they are both equally angry? Why or why not? What do their actions tell you about their **characters**?

INFER

Pause at line 205. Why do the narrator and Lou buy a can of white epoxy paint?

CONNECT

Get together with a group of classmates and do some research to identify the people on this mural—clockwise from left, Sonny Rollins, Martin Luther King, Jr., Frederick Douglass, W.E.B. Du Bois, and Malcolm X.

PREDICT

Pause at line 211. Do you think the narrator and Lou will get a chance to use the epoxy?

A mural of famous African Americans, situated along Auburn Avenue in Atlanta, Georgia.

When we reached the corner of Taliaferro and Fifth, it looked like a block party or something. Half the neighborhood was gathered on the sidewalk in front of the wall. I looked at Lou, he looked at me. We both looked at the bag with the epoxy and wondered how we were going to work our scheme. The painter lady's car was nowhere in sight. But there were too many people standing around to do anything. Side Pocket and his buddies were leaning on their cue sticks, hunching each other. Daddy was there with a lineman[2] he catches a ride with on Mondays. Mrs. Morris had her arms flung around the shoulders of the twins on either side of her. Mama was talking with some of her customers, many of them with napkins still at the throat. Mr. Eubanks came out of the barber shop, followed by a man in a striped poncho, half his face shaved, the other half full of foam.

2. **lineman** (līn′mən) *n.:* worker whose job is to set up and repair telephone or electric power lines.

"She really did it, didn't she?" Mr. Eubanks huffed out his chest. Lots of folks answered right quick that she surely did when they saw the straight razor in his hand.

Mama beckoned us over. And then we saw it. The wall. Reds, greens, figures outlined in black. Swirls of purple and orange. Storms of blues and yellows. It was something. I recognized some of the faces right off. There was Martin Luther King, Jr. And there was a man with glasses on and his mouth open like he was laying down a heavy rap. Daddy came up alongside and reminded us that he was Minister Malcolm X. The serious woman with a rifle I knew was Harriet Tubman because my grandmama has pictures of her all over the house. And I knew Mrs. Fannie Lou Hamer 'cause a signed photograph of her hangs in the restaurant next to the calendar.

Then I let my eyes follow what looked like a vine. It trailed past a man with a horn, a woman with a big white flower in her hair, a handsome dude in a tuxedo seated at a piano, and a man with a goatee holding a book. When I looked more closely, I realized that what had looked like flowers were really faces. One face with yellow petals looked just like Frieda Morris. One with red petals looked just like Hattie Morris. I could hardly believe my eyes.

"Notice," Side Pocket said, stepping close to the wall with his cue stick like a classroom pointer. "These are the flags of **liberation**," he said in a voice I'd never heard him use before. We all stepped closer while he pointed and spoke. "Red, black, and green," he said, his pointer falling on the leaflike flags of the vine. "Our liberation flag. And here Ghana, there Tanzania. Guinea-Bissau, Angola,

CONNECT

Do you know who all the people are in the wall painting (lines 229–240)? If you don't, look in an encyclopedia or on the Internet for Martin Luther King, Jr., Malcolm X, Harriet Tubman, and Fannie Lou Hamer. You can also look up Louis Armstrong, the man with a horn; Billie Holliday, the woman with a white flower; Duke Ellington, the man in a tuxedo at the piano; and W.E.B. Du Bois, the man with a goatee and book.

VOCABULARY

liberation (lib'ər·ā'shən) *n.:* release from slavery, prison, foreign occupation, and so on.

INTERPRET

Underline what the narrator's and Lou's portraits look like. What do these new details tell you about their **characters**?

VOCABULARY

inscription (in·skrip′shən) *n.:* short written or spoken message dedicating something to someone as a sign of respect.

INFER

What **inferences** can you make about the significance of the inscription? Cite details from the first page of the story as well as from the description of the painting here in your response.

Mozambique."[3] Side Pocket sounded very tall, as though he'd been waiting all his life to give this lesson.

Mama tapped us on the shoulder and pointed to a high section of the wall. There was a fierce-looking man with his arms crossed against his chest guarding a bunch of children. His muscles bulged, and he looked a lot like my daddy. One kid was looking at a row of books. Lou hunched me 'cause the kid looked like me. The one that looked like Lou was spinning a globe on the tip of his finger like a basketball. There were other kids there with microscopes and compasses. And the more I looked, the more it looked like the fierce man was not so much guarding the kids as defending their right to do what they were doing.

Then Lou gasped and dropped the paint bag and ran forward, running his hands over a rainbow. He had to tiptoe and stretch to do it, it was so high. I couldn't breathe either. The painter lady had found the chisel marks and had painted Jimmy Lyons's name in a rainbow.

"Read the **inscription**, honey," Mrs. Morris said, urging little Frieda forward. She didn't have to urge much. Frieda marched right up, bent down, and in a loud voice that made everybody quit oohing and ahhing and listen, she read,

To the People of Taliaferro Street
I Dedicate This Wall of Respect
Painted in Memory of My Cousin
Jimmy Lyons

---

3. **Ghana, Tanzania, Guinea-Bissau, Angola, Mozambique:** countries in Africa.

MEET THE WRITER

Toni Cade Bambara (1939–1995) was born Miltonia Mirkin Cade. As an adult, the author added "Bambara," from a signature on a sketchbook belonging to her great-grandmother, to her name. She grew up in Harlem in the 1940s surrounded by vibrant literary, artistic, and political communities. She learned the power of the spoken word on "speaker's corner," where people preached and spoke about issues of community and national importance. She absorbed the rhythms of jazz and bebop that filled the New York City streets and clubs. She recorded the speech of her friends and neighbors, trying to capture the pulse of daily life. Even after moving to Atlanta and later Philadelphia, her early Harlem years continued to inspire her as a writer and community activist. Bambara is the author of two much-loved short story collections and an award-winning novel, *The Salt Eaters.* Later in her life, Bambara's focus shifted to film. She wrote screenplays, including one for Toni Morrison's *Tar Baby,* scripts for documentaries, and adapted her short story "Raymond's Run" for television.

ANALYZE

The author of this story never reveals if the **narrator** is a boy or a girl. Why do you think she doesn't say? Do you think the narrator is a he or a she? Does it matter? Explain your position.

The War of the Wall

Literary Skills Analyze the narrator.

Reading Skills Make inferences.

Narrator Detector Even though this story is told in the first person, the writer does not directly reveal very much information about the narrator—not even whether the narrator is male or female. Clues to the narrator's **character** can be found in his or her actions and thoughts and in how other people react to the narrator. Fill in the chart below. In the left-hand column, list some of the narrator's actions and thoughts and other characters' reactions (don't forget the painter's reaction). In the right-hand column, describe what these clues reveal about the narrator's character.

Clues from the Story	Narrator's Character
Narrator's actions: **1.** **2.**	
Narrator's thoughts: **1.** **2.**	
Reactions of other characters: **1.** **2.**	

Skills Review

The War of the Wall

VOCABULARY AND COMPREHENSION

A. Using Context Clues Fill in the blanks with the correct Word Bank word. Use context clues in the paragraph to help you.

Word Bank

- courtesies
- integration
- drawled
- liberation
- inscription

When students began chatting in the middle of her lesson, the teacher (1) ____________ a gentle complaint, "I hope y'all will extend to me the (2) ____________ I am owed as your teacher." As the students quieted, she continued teaching about Nelson Mandela. She compared his role in the (3) ____________ of South African black people from apartheid to Martin Luther King, Jr.'s role in ending the segregation of black and white people in the United States. Both men helped bring about (4) ____________, in which blacks and whites are able to participate jointly in the political processes of their countries. The students then worked together to write an (5) ____________ on the board expressing respect for each hero.

B. Reading Comprehension Answer each question below.

1. What are the narrator and Lou angry about at the beginning of the story? ____________

   ____

2. What does the painter do that annoys people in the restaurant?

   ____

3. What do members of the neighborhood see in the finished wall painting? How do they react? ____________

   ____

Vocabulary Skills
Use context clues.

Before You Read

Virtue Goes to Town by Laurence Yep

LITERARY FOCUS: CHARACTER TRAITS

We learn about characters in many different ways. Sometimes a writer will tell us directly what a character is like; for example, "Tommy had a cruel streak." More often, however, writers allow us to find out for ourselves what a character is like by describing his or her appearance, speech, thoughts, actions, and effect on other characters. These details reveal a character's qualities, or **character traits.**

As you read "Virtue Goes to Town," look for details that help bring its main character, Virtue, to life.

READING SKILLS: MAKING PREDICTIONS

One of the pleasures of reading is jumping right into a story and getting to know some new people as their story unfolds. You are about to meet Virtue, the main character in a folk tale from China. Pause from time to time as you read to think over Virtue's situation. Then, try to predict how he will deal with each of the problems he encounters. (A **prediction** is a guess based on the evidence in the text as well as on what you know about life and people.) Keep in mind that although not all your predictions will turn out to be correct, half the fun of reading a story is being surprised at how things turn out. If any of your predictions prove to be incorrect, simply adjust them as you go on.

As you read, you may want to fill out a chart like this one:

Literary Skills Identify character traits.

Reading Skills Make predictions.

Vocabulary Skills Use context clues.

My Predictions	What Really Happened

FOLK TALE

VOCABULARY DEVELOPMENT

PREVIEW SELECTION VOCABULARY

Get to know these words from "Virtue Goes to Town" before you read the folk tale.

destiny (des′tə·nē) *n.:* what will necessarily happen to a person; fate.

Virtue asks a wise woman to tell him what his destiny is.

braggart (brag′ərt) *n.:* person who brags; overly boastful person.

The foreman believes Virtue is a braggart who cannot do what he claims.

smirked (smurkd) *v.:* smiled in a knowing way.

The foreman smirked because he was certain Virtue would fail at the task.

grudgingly (gruj′iŋ·lē) *adv.:* resentfully; reluctantly.

The foreman grudgingly agreed to hire the rest of the crew as cooks.

USING CONTEXT CLUES

When you come across an unfamiliar word, you can often figure out its meaning by using context clues. In the examples below the words in italics provide context clues for the boldface words. Look for these types of context clues in "Virtue Goes to Town." They will help you figure out the meanings of unfamiliar words and phrases.

Restatement	Virtue boasted that he could *cook* any kind of meat, even **fricassee** a dragon.
Definition	Virtue's **cauldrons,** *large cooking pots,* were enormous; each of them was big enough to hold a handful of men.
Example	Virtue was *not* a **modest** man; he *considered himself to be the best at virtually everything and always seemed to be bragging.*
Contrast	*Instead of completely boiling* the rice, he just let it **simmer** over a low flame.

Virtue Goes to Town

Laurence Yep

VOCABULARY

destiny (des′tə·nē) *n.:* what will necessarily happen to a person; fate.

PREDICT

Pause at line 9. Virtue says he hates being bored. What do you think will happen to him when he goes to town?

INFER

Circle two **character traits** of Virtue that the writer states directly in lines 14–15. Why do you think the townsman calls Virtue "Turnip"? (A turnip is a hardy root vegetable; it is sometimes seen as "poor man's food" because it is often part of the diet of poor rural people.)

IDENTIFY

The writer states that Virtue became impatient. Underline the details that show Virtue's impatience.

After Virtue had buried his parents, he went to see the wise woman. "They say you can read a face like a page in a book. Tell me what my **destiny** is."

But the wise woman just kept sipping her tea. "What would you have? A quiet, happy life as a farmer? Or a life of sorrow and glory?"

"I hate being bored," Virtue said.

The wise woman studied his face a long time. She patted his shoulder sadly. "Then go into town."

When Virtue arrived there, he saw a long line of men. "I heard that town folk did the oddest things. Are you all practicing to be a fence?" he asked.

A townsman leaning against a wall looked at Virtue and then looked away again. But Virtue's voice was loud, and he was such a pest that the townsman finally said, "They're hiring workers, Turnip."

"The name's Virtue. And they can sign me up too. I left the farm to see the world and get rich." He got in line behind the townsman.

However, it was a hot summer day and Virtue quickly became impatient. As he wiped at the sweat on his forehead, he shouted, "Hey, can't you go any faster?"

The foreman sat at his table in the shade. He ignored Virtue and went on just as slowly as ever.

"Hey, we're not getting any younger," Virtue yelled. Still the foreman ignored him.

"Maybe he's deaf." Virtue started forward.

Bildarchiv Preussischer Kulturbesitz/Art Resource, NY

Young Chinese Man (1919) by Anita Rée (1885–1933). Oil on canvas, 75 x 60.5 cm. Inv. 1936.

The townsman stuck out his arm. "Hey, Turnip, wait your turn."

"I told you. My name's Virtue. So why don't I just take you right with me, friend?" Virtue tucked his arm into the townsman's. The others were too afraid to say anything else, but everyone watched as he stomped up to the foreman.

"I can outplow a water buffalo and can harvest more than twenty folk," Virtue said.

The foreman took an instant dislike to Virtue. "You may be strong; but you're not that strong. No one likes a **braggart.**"

Notes

ANALYZE

Other characters' reactions can reveal a **character's traits.** What do you learn about Virtue from the foreman's reactions to him?

VOCABULARY

braggart (brag′ərt) *n.:* person who brags; overly boastful person.

PREDICT

Do you think Virtue is just bragging, or will he prove he can work harder than twenty people? Explain your response.

ANALYZE

Notice the cooking term *fricassee* (to chop up and cook pieces of meat and make a sauce from their own juices) in line 52. Do you think Virtue is telling the truth or exaggerating to make a point? Explain.

INTERPRET

What do Virtue's words and actions in lines 58–71 reveal about his **character**?

"It's not bragging if you really can do it," Virtue said.

The foreman grunted. "I'm the boss here. I say how we do things. Get back there."

"Come on, friend." With a sigh, Virtue carried the townsman back to the end of the line.

It took most of the day before Virtue finally reached the table. Virtue made a muscle for the foreman. "No job's too hard for me."

The foreman put down his brush and folded his hands over his big belly. "I have all of my work crew already. All I need is a cook. Can you do that?"

Virtue frowned. He thought a cook's job was beneath him, but times were hard and jobs were scarce. "Can I cook?" Virtue said. "I could cook a whale and fricassee a dragon."

The foreman twiddled his thumbs. He would have liked to turn Virtue away, but he needed a cook. "You only have to cook rice, dried fish, and vegetables. I guess even you couldn't ruin that."

"Whatever I do, I always do well," Virtue promised. "I would make a better worker. But if you want me as a cook, then I'll be the best cook I can be."

The workers had to get up at sunrise, but Virtue had to get up even earlier to boil the water for their tea. Even so, he always had the tea poured and the cold rice served in bowls before the first man was up. He tried to have a friendly, cheerful word for each of the other workers. "Smile, friend," he would say to one. "We're keeping farm hours now—not town hours."

And to another, he would say, "We're all in this together, neighbor."

And to a third, he would grin. "Teamwork. That's how we do it on the farm."

But all the other men were from town. They never thanked him. In fact, they never spoke to him. Behind his back, they laughed and called him the loud-mouthed turnip.

Still, Virtue did not give up easily. "These townsfolk will come around once they get to know me."

At noon, he served them supper. Then, picking up a huge cauldron[1] in each hand, he went down to the river. Each of the cauldrons could have held a half dozen men, but Virtue dipped them into the water and lifted them out as easily as if they were cups.

After making several trips, he would set the cauldrons of water on big fires. By sunset, they would be bubbling. When the work crew came back, they would wash before they sat down to eat their dinner.

But one noon, the other workers were delayed. Virtue got hungrier and hungrier as he smelled the food. Finally, he ate his bowlful of rice. Still, there was no sign of anyone. Virtue was so bored that the only thing he could think of doing was to eat another bowlful of rice and wait.

When no one had shown up yet, he began to feel sorry for himself. "I do my job, but no one appreciates me. So maybe I'll just have another bowlful. That'll show them."

When he had finished his third bowl, he looked at the cauldron simmering on the big fire. "This rice is going to get burned. I shouldn't let it go to waste." Bored and lonely, Virtue began to eat right from the cauldron. Before he knew it, he had finished the whole cauldron of rice.

1. cauldron, also spelled **caldron** (kôl′drən) *n.:* large cooking pot.

PREDICT

Underline Virtue's prediction in lines 76–77. Do you think he will be right? Why or why not?

RETELL

Explain in your own words what Virtue does when the workers are late coming back for lunch.

Notes

© Bill Bachmann/PhotoEdit

A Chinese farmer at work in a rice paddy in Yangshou, China.

EVALUATE

Pause at line 109. Do you think the workers have the right idea about Virtue? Why or why not?

Tired and dirty, the work crew finally came back to camp. They were angry when they found the empty cauldron. "Where's our food, Turnip?" they demanded angrily. But no one went too close to Virtue.

Virtue gave an embarrassed cough. "My name's Virtue."

They glared at him. "You're nothing but a big sack of wind. How do you expect us to work on empty bellies?"

Virtue brightened. "Since I ate all your lunch, let me do all your work. It's only fair."

The foreman got ready to fire Virtue. "One person couldn't meet our goals by himself."

"We take turns back on the farm. I'll do their work and they can do mine," Virtue said.

"You'll kill yourself," one of the work crew objected.

The foreman thought for a moment and then **smirked.** "Let him."

So Virtue left the others back in camp and marched off to work with the foreman. The foreman set a hard pace, but Virtue did not complain. By the end of the day, he had done all the work and more—much to the surprise of the foreman.

When Virtue came back, he shook his head when he saw the one pot of hot water. "You're supposed to have hot water for me. That wouldn't wash a cat's tail." And then he saw the pot of rice they had cooked for him. "I've done the work of twenty men. I've got the hunger of twenty men. That wouldn't even feed a mouse."

"We don't have enough firewood," one of the work crew said.

"Then I'll take care of it myself this time." Picking up an ax in either hand, he marched up to the nearest tree. In no time, he had chopped it into firewood. Then, taking the huge cauldrons, he went down to the river and filled them.

One cauldron he used for his rice. The other he used for his bath.

When he finally sat on the ground, he wolfed down the whole cauldron of rice. The others just watched in amazement. Virtue laughed. "I work hard, I eat hard, friends."

VOCABULARY

smirked (smurkd) *v.:* smiled in a knowing way.

PREDICT

Pause at line 118. Why does the foreman smirk and agree to Virtue's proposal? What does he predict will happen? Do you think he will be right? Explain.

CLARIFY

How has Virtue proved that he wasn't just bragging when he said he could work harder than twenty men?

VOCABULARY

grudgingly (gruj′iŋ·lē) *adv.:* resentfully; reluctantly.

FLUENCY

Re-read the boxed passage aloud until you can read it smoothly. Try to use different voices for Virtue, the foreman, the worker, and the narrator.

COMPARE & CONTRAST

Pause at line 161. In the past in China, bowing was considered a sign of respect. What has Virtue done to change the workers' opinion of his **character**?

ANALYZE

Re-read the last paragraph of the folk tale. Based on Virtue's actions in this story, would you have predicted that this would be his destiny? Why or why not?

All this time, the foreman had been thinking. "You're not just bragging. You really can do the work of a whole crew." The foreman still didn't like Virtue, but it was more important to get the job finished. "Tomorrow you can do the work again."

But Virtue had learned a few things since he had left the farm. He winked at the rest of the crew. "We're all a team." He turned back to the foreman. "You're not going to fire them, are you?"

The foreman had been planning to do that very thing. Then he could pocket all the extra wages. But there was something in Virtue's look that made the foreman think again.

"No, they can be the cooks," the foreman said **grudgingly.**

One of the work crew grinned at Virtue. "No one will ever mistake you for a modest man, but your heart's in the right place." Then he bowed his head to Virtue. And one by one, the others did too.

And that was why there was only one worker but twenty cooks.

And even though Virtue went on to become a mighty warrior and general, he never lost his talent for making friends . . . and enemies.

MEET THE WRITER

Laurence Yep (1948–) knows what it feels like to be an outsider. Yep was born in San Francisco to a Chinese immigrant family and grew up in an African American neighborhood. Because of this, Yep felt torn between cultures. In high school he discovered science fiction and, when he was eighteen, published his first science-fiction story. In his twenties he became interested in his Chinese roots. He began to explore his heritage in his writing. The Newbery Award–winning *Dragonwings* is a historical novel that tells the story of a young Chinese American aviator living in San Francisco in the early 1900s. A varied and adventurous writer, Yep has produced stories, novels, and plays in many different forms—including science fiction, fantasy, and retellings of Chinese folktales. Yep believes that living on the border between cultures helps him as a writer by allowing him to be a better observer.

Notes

SKILLS PRACTICE

Virtue Goes to Town

Literary Skills Analyze character traits.

Character Traits Chart A **character trait** is a particular quality in a person. Generosity, kindness, and shyness are all character traits. When we read, we discover character traits by examining a character's appearance, speech, thought, actions, and the reactions of other characters. Fill in the following chart with examples of Virtue's words, thoughts, actions, and effects on others. Then, list a character trait that each item suggests. Finally, write a sentence describing Virtue's character.

Virtue's Words and Thoughts	Virtue's Actions	Reactions of Other Characters
↓	↓	↓
Character Trait	**Character Trait**	**Character Trait**

Virtue's character: ______________________________

____

Virtue Goes to Town

VOCABULARY AND COMPREHENSION

A. Using Context Clues Fill in the blanks with the correct Word Bank word. Use context clues in the paragraph to help you.

Word Bank

destiny
braggart
smirked
grudgingly

Louis thought it was his (1) ____________, his fate, to become a great inventor. When he described the wonderful machines he was building, his classmates (2) ____________ instead of smiled and thought he was a (3) ____________, an overly boastful person. When he won first prize at the science fair for his house-cleaning robot, though, they (4) ____________ admitted that he had been right all along, reluctantly acknowledging his genius at last.

B. Reading Comprehension Answer each question below.

1. Why does Virtue decide to go to town?

____

____

2. What do the townspeople think of Virtue?

____

____

3. What job does Virtue accept from the foreman? How does he feel about this job?

____

____

Vocabulary Skills
Use context clues.

4. How does Virtue get the townspeople to change their minds about him?

____

____

Collection 3

Living in the Heart

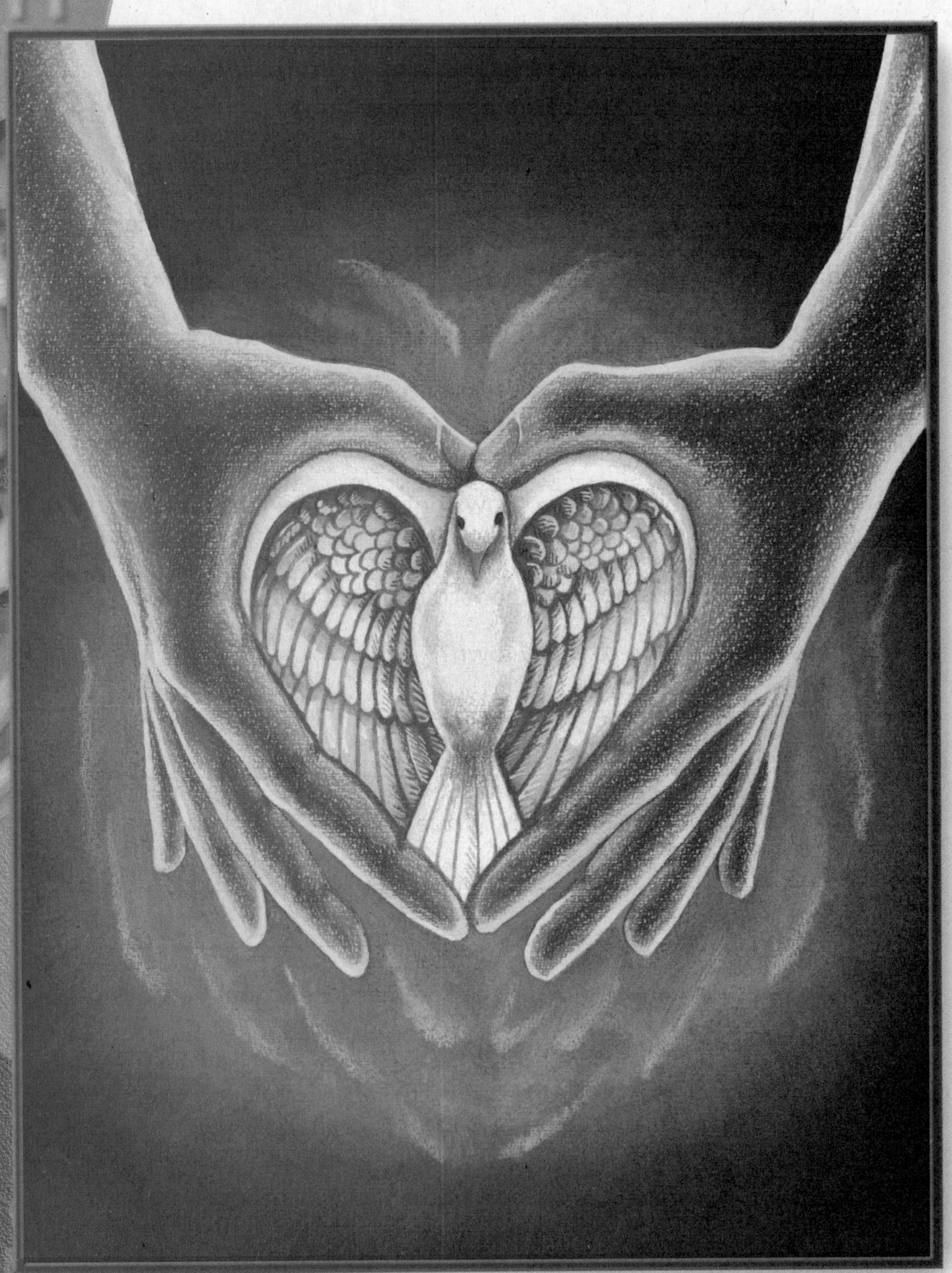

Academic Vocabulary for Collection 3

These are the terms you should know as you read and analyze the selections in this collection.

Topic or Subject What a story or poem is about. A story's topic may be friendship, for example. A **theme** goes a step further and comments on the topic; for example, "To be a good friend, you must like yourself first."

Theme A truth about life revealed in a work of literature. Theme is a key element of literature—of fiction, nonfiction, poetry, and drama.

Recurring Theme A theme that appears over and over again in literature. For example, a poem written in China one thousand years ago may have the same theme as a story that was written just last year. You may be familiar with such recurring themes as "love is powerful" and "honesty is the best policy."

Before You Read

Hum by Naomi Shihab Nye

LITERARY FOCUS: THEME

In the same way parents and teachers tell real-life stories to teach a lesson or make a point, writers often reveal insights about life through stories and poems. We call such insights **themes.** For example, you might read a story about a wooden boy whose nose grows long every time he tells a lie. But what's this story *really* about? What truth does it reveal about life? Maybe it reveals that lying is never without consequence. Or perhaps it reveals something else.

A theme is not generally spelled out by the writer. Rather, it is something you discover as you read. To help you identify the theme of a work, consider these questions:

- How has the main **character** changed over the course of the story?
- Which scenes or passages strike you as especially important?
- Does the story's **title** suggest anything special about the story?

READING SKILLS: IDENTIFY CAUSE AND EFFECT

If you trained for a marathon in the same pair of running shoes every day for a year, what would happen? You'd probably injure your leg muscles and joints. The **cause** of the injuries is *running in worn-out shoes*. The **effect** of running in worn-out shoes is *injuries*.

These same kinds of cause-effect patterns can be found in stories you read. As you read "Hum," identify causes and effects. Ask yourself, "Why did this happen?" and "What happened because of this?" You might want to record the cause-and-effect patterns you find in a chart like this one.

Literary Skills Understand and identify themes.

Reading Skills Identify cause and effect.

Vocabulary Skills Use context clues.

Cause: Why did this happen?	Effect: What happened because of this?

VOCABULARY DEVELOPMENT

PREVIEW SELECTION VOCABULARY

Preview these words from "Hum" before you begin to read.

dramatically (drə·mat′ik·lē) *adv.:* powerfully; vividly.

The sun set dramatically, leaving streaks of red, yellow, and purple in the sky.

jovial (jō′vē·əl) *adj.:* cheerful; joyful.

Celebrating his birthday with his new friends, Sami felt relaxed and jovial.

solitude (säl′ə·to͞od′) *n.:* state of being alone.

Sami's school waited in solitude for students to return.

anonymous (ə·nän′ə·məs) *adj.:* given or written by an unknown person.

Sami told Hugh the letter was anonymous because it was unsigned.

communicative (kə·myo͞o′ni·kā′tiv) *adj.:* able to communicate easily; talkative.

A communicative group of students founded the Dialogue Club.

quizzical (kwiz′i·kəl) *adj.:* puzzled; curious.

Sami wore a quizzical expression when he looked at his first corn dog lunch.

USING CONTEXT CLUES

As you read, you often use context clues to figure out the meanings of unfamiliar words. Context clues include *definitions, examples, restatements,* and *contrast words.* The chart below gives examples of context clues for one of your Vocabulary words. The context clues are in italics.

Definition	*Alone* on the prairie, Daniel felt that the **solitude**, or *lack of human contact,* was very difficult.
Example	I love the **solitude** that my country cabin provides. *There are no houses around for miles.*
Restatement	I enjoy the feeling of **solitude** when I read a book. *Spending time alone* with a good book is calming and peaceful.
Contrast	I could not find any **solitude** at my homecoming party because *everyone wanted to talk to me.*

Naomi Shihab Nye

BACKGROUND: Literature and Social Studies

Palestine is a historic region at the eastern end of the Mediterranean Sea. Its status as the Holy Land for Jews, Christians, and Muslims has made it a source of frequent conflict. In the twentieth and twenty-first centuries, Palestine has become a battleground for Jewish and Arab nationalist movements. This story describes the experiences of a Palestinian immigrant living in Texas at the time of the September 11, 2001, terrorist attack on the World Trade Center buildings in New York City and the Pentagon in Washington, D.C.

IDENTIFY

Pause at line 6. Underline the things that were improving in Sami's life.

CONNECT

Re-read lines 7–15. Circle the date Sami's family arrived in the United States. What connection can you make between this date and the reference in lines 1 and 2 that Sami's life in his new home was about to get worse?

Sami Salsaa thought things were improving in his new life, right before they got worse.

His classmates had stopped joking about his first name ending with "i," like a girl's name—Brandi, Lori, Tiffani. And about his last name, which they said sounded like hot sauce.

In a country where basketball stars had fish names—Kobe, Samaki—they could get over it. In a country where people poked silver posts through their tongues and shiny rings into their navels and the man at the auto body shop had a giant swan with a pink heart tattooed on his upper right arm, who cared?

His parents had taken his advice, which was rare.

"Don't call it 'America,'" Sami had said to them, after they unpacked their cracked suitcases on August 6, 2001,

David Young-Wolff/Photo Edit

and settled into putty-colored Apartment 276 with the tiny black balcony jutting out over a stained parking lot. The sign at the bank across the street flashed 98 degrees. Sami hadn't realized Texas would be so blazing hot.

"Call it 'the United States,'" he said soberly. "'America' means more, means North, South, and Central America, the whole thing. Don't you like it better when people say 'Palestine' instead of 'the Middle East'? We shouldn't sound dumb."

VISUALIZE

Does the boy in this picture reflect your impressions of Sami as you know him so far? Why or why not?

ANALYZE

Re-read lines 20–24. Where is Sami from? What do you know about this region of the world? Make a few notes below about your thoughts.

INTERPRET

What is Sami's reaction to his new country? Underline the details that tell you (lines 29–48).

INFER

Re-read lines 49–56. What do we learn about Sami and his background?

They stared at him.

His mom said, "I only said 'America' because it was shorter."

Both of them began saying "United States" right away.

School in Texas began in the middle of August. Sami got an easy locker combination—10-20-30—and the best mark in his eighth-grade class on the first pre-algebra test of the year. Algebra was one of those subjects that translated easily from country to country; Sami had started working with equations in his cousin Ali's textbook in Bethlehem[1] a year ago, during a curfew period,[2] so the concepts felt familiar.

The teacher singled him out for praise, mentioning his "neatness" and "careful following of directions." Though he had not yet raised his hand once in class, now he thought he might. Sami found himself wishing he were taking full-fledged algebra instead of pre-algebra, which sounded babyish.

There was so much to look at in this country. Girls in tight T-shirts and jeans, for one thing. Magazines with interesting covers fanned out on a neat rack next to soft blue couches in the library's reading corner. Fifty different kinds of bread in neat plastic wrappers lined up at the grocery store.

Two boys, Gavin and Jim, set their trays down next to his at lunch. They told him what a corn dog was. They showed him how to dip it into a small pool of mustard. A girl named Jenny laughed when he tried it.

"Do you have brothers and sisters?" they asked.

"No," Sami said. "I am probably the only Palestinian who doesn't have any brothers or sisters." All his cousins and friends back home had huge families.

---

1. **Bethlehem** (beth′lə·hem′): city located in the Middle East, five miles south of Jerusalem. According to the Bible, it is the birthplace of Jesus Christ.
2. A **curfew period** is a time during which everyone must stay indoors.

His history teacher asked him to stay after class during the third week of school and surprised him by saying, "I just want you to know I think our country's policy in your homeland has been very unfair. And more people than you might think would agree with me. Don't let the slanted press coverage get you down." The teacher clapped his hand on Sami's shoulder warmly and smiled at him.

Sami felt light walking the long sunny blocks between school and his apartment complex.

This might work out after all.

On top of that, his father flew to Los Angeles for the weekend to see his brother, Sami's uncle, and reported that hummus, Sami's favorite simple food from back home, was served on the plane. Incredible! Hummus, in a little plastic tub, with a shrink-wrapped piece of pita bread alongside it!

Next thing they knew, there might be a *falafel* stand in Lubbock.

It had been difficult for Sami's family to leave Bethlehem, the only town Sami and his mother had ever lived in, but the situation there had been so horrible recently, everyone was exhausted. Sami's school had been closed every other week and all citizens of Bethlehem put under curfew. His aunt Jenan had been gunned down in the street by Israeli soldiers as she returned from the market. When she died, it was the first time Sami ever felt glad she had no children. Always before, he had wished she had a boy just his age. His parents cried so much they said they used up all their tears.

So when his father, a professor at Bethlehem University, was offered a teaching position in the engineering department at Texas Tech in Lubbock, he accepted it. Sami had felt sad at first that his family wasn't moving to a community with lots of other Arab immigrant families, like Dearborn,

WORD STUDY

In line 61, *slanted* means "biased," or providing facts or information in a way that unfairly supports one opinion or one side of an argument. Circle the **context clues** that help explain the meaning of *slanted*. Explain what you think the teacher means by "slanted press coverage."

INTERPRET

Re-read lines 75–87. Why has Sami's family immigrated to the United States?

Michigan. Lubbock was a remote west Texas city with far fewer immigrants than Dallas or Houston. Someone on the plane told Sami's mother that a Middle Eastern bakery in Austin churned out spinach pies and *zaater* bread by the hour. That made Sami wish they were moving to Austin.

"Use this situation as an opportunity," his father said when Sami worried out loud about being too noticeable in Lubbock. His father always said things like that. "Let people notice you for how outstanding you are, not just how different."

A teacher at school told Sami there was an Arab family living far out on a ranch, raising cows. Their kids were in college already. This surprised Sami. Arabs knew about cows? He thought they only knew about sheep and goats. A famous Syrian eye surgeon had moved to Lubbock with his family long ago. Sami's father planned to go meet him soon.

Lubbock had a huge, straight horizon; it would be hard to find a larger horizon in the whole United States. You couldn't see a single hill in any direction. At night the stars glittered **dramatically** in the giant dark dome of sky. There were smooth streets in all directions with no Israeli tanks or armed soldiers in them, neat buildings and shopping centers, brilliant pink and orange sunsets, shiny pickup trucks with tires, and men in blue jeans wearing baseball caps that said COORS and RED RAIDERS.

"Hey, Sambo!" shouted one of his classmates outside the cafeteria a few weeks after school began. This made Sami feel familiar, **jovial**. He couldn't understand why the boy got in trouble for saying it.

Sami and his mother stood on the balcony and watched with pleasure as the sky swirled like milk in tea, one night before the dreadful day, when smoke poured from the

SUMMARIZE

Pause at line 99. Explain what Sami is worried about. Underline his father's advice. What **theme,** or insight about life, does this passage suggest to you?

VISUALIZE

Underline the words and phrases in lines 106–114 that help you visualize Lubbock. What impression does the passage give you of this small city?

VOCABULARY

dramatically (drə·mat′ik·lē) *adv.:* powerfully; vividly.

jovial (jō′vē·əl) *adj.:* cheerful; joyful.

buildings in New York and Washington and the buildings fell and the people died and no one was able to look at Sami in quite the same friendly way at school.

His parents had bought the television set just a few days before and kept checking out the different channels, so they had it turned on at breakfast when the news broke.

Sami wished he had never seen the images of the jets flying into the buildings.

He wished he had closed his eyes.

Before that morning, a soaring silver airplane had been Sami's favorite mental picture; he'd always dreamed of the plane that would lift him out of a hard and scary life into a happier one, even before their big journey. Planes were magic; you stepped on, then stepped off in a completely different world. Someday he thought he'd go to New Zealand, and other places too. The world was a deep pocket of wonders; he had barely stuck his hand in.

But now Sami's joy in watching and imagining jets in flight was totally ruined.

He did not go to school. His father went to the university to teach a ten o'clock class, but none of his students appeared, so he came home. Everyone was numb. Sami and his parents stared hard at the television all day. He knew his relatives and friends in Bethlehem would be watching too. Sami's eyes kept blurring. Each time the television voices said "Arabs," his heart felt squeezed. A reporter said Palestinians had been "celebrating" the disaster, and Sami knew that was a lie. Palestinians had practically forgotten how to celebrate anything.

He stood at the window staring out, feeling afraid some other terrible thing would drop from the sky and flatten everyone.

CONNECT

Pause at line 130. What "dreadful day" (line 121) is Sami referring to?

CONNECT

How does Sami's background affect his experience of that tragic day? What is one way your experience was similar to or different from Sami's?

INFER

What **inference** can you make about the man with the dog? Underline evidence in lines 154–164 to support your inference.

INTERPRET

Pause at line 175. What is surprising to Sami about his parents' reaction to the events of the day?

When it was eventually evening a tall man he had noticed before, walking slowly with a large blond dog on a leather harness, came around the corner on the level below, and paused.

The man turned and sat down in a green plastic chair next to a door on the ground floor. Was that his apartment? The dog stretched out beside him.

The man stared into the empty darkening sky and the empty blue water of the swimming pool. No one was swimming now. Why wasn't he watching television like everyone else?

That night Sami's mother forgot to cook. So Sami toasted bread in their new toaster oven and spread red jelly on top. It looked like blood. He offered bread to his parents, but they didn't want to eat.

He had never seen his parents so shocked before, not when Jenan died, not even when his own friends were beaten and shot by Israeli soldiers, or when his uncle's perfect stone house was bulldozed to the ground without any cause or recourse.[3] *Sad,* Sami had always seen them, forever and ever—sadness was their tribal legacy[4]—but this shocked? Never.

Although they had all been trying to speak only in English, to sharpen their English skills, they reverted to Arabic without even noticing it.

His parents stayed up almost all night, fixated on the screen, and Sami lay awake, shivering, staring at his ceiling. What made people do what they did?

---

3. **recourse** (rē′kôrs′) *n.:* source of assistance.
4. **tribal legacy:** something handed down from generation to generation in a particular group.

The next day, his father met him outside the school to walk him home. "Did anything bad happen today?" his father asked.

Sami shook his head. Some students had stayed home for a second day. Teachers turned on television sets in the classrooms. Everyone had been so shocked they forgot he was there.

A tight pressure in his chest made it hard to breathe.

Bad things started happening the *next* day, but Sami couldn't tell his parents.

"GO HOME," said a scribbled, unsigned note taped to his locker.

"Your people are murderers," Jake Riley whispered in homeroom.

Murderers? His people? No one had said the hijackers were Palestinian.

His family had always spoken out against the suicide bombings that killed Israeli civilians. Many Palestinians did. But who could hear them? They were regular people, not politicians. No one quoted them in the news.

All day Sami thought of things he might have whispered back.

Not true.

Just a few of them.

Some of yours are too.

A counselor came to take Sami out of class. She had a worried expression. "You realize that you are the only Arab student in this school at a very difficult time. If anyone gives you any trouble . . ."

Sami didn't think he could tell her what had already happened.

It would make him seem weak.

IDENTIFY CAUSE & EFFECT

Pause at line 197. How do some students' attitudes toward Sami change as a result of the September 11 attacks? Explain.

CLARIFY

Underline Jake Riley's accusation toward Sami. Circle Sami's reaction to it.

INFER

Why doesn't Sami tell the counselor about the bad things that have happened?

If anyone found out he told, they would hate him even more.

No one sat with him at lunch now. He tried sitting down next to some boys from his PE class and they stopped speaking and stared at him. "I feel very bad about what happened," Sami said, with difficulty, though his words were so true. "Very very bad." His tongue felt thick. But did saying that implicate[5] him in some way? As if all Arabs had done it? Still, what else could he say?

Nobody answered him. They finished eating in silence, exchanging glances with one another, and left the table.

The streets of Lubbock glistened in their **solitude** for days and days. It seemed no one was going out to shop. Restaurants were empty. Everyone stayed glued to their gloomy televisions.

In English class Sami and his classmates wrote responses to September 11 for more than a week and read them out loud, discussing them at length. The teacher even insisted they do second drafts. She said it would be good therapy.

Sami was the only one who mentioned that other people in the world also suffered from terrorism, all the time. Some of it, he said, was even governmentally sponsored and official. He did not mention his own family's bad experiences. He wrote this so that Americans wouldn't feel as if they were the only victimized people in history. But no one responded as if this had been a good thing to say.

Sometimes it seemed that a huge blanket had been spread over the vast and lumpy distant sorrows of the world—hushing them. Making them invisible. But weren't

EVALUATE

Pause at line 224. A **stereotype** is a widely held belief about a group of people that doesn't allow for individual differences. What stereotypes do the other students now have about Sami? Based on what you know about Sami, are these stereotypes true?

VOCABULARY

solitude (säl′ə·to͞od′) *n.:* state of being alone.

INTERPRET

Re-read lines 234–241. How is Sami's response to the September 11 attacks different from that of his classmates? How do you think his background affects his response?

---

5. **implicate** (im′pli·kāt′) *v.:* connect, as with a crime.

they still under there? Maybe people could only feel the things that touched *them*, the things at closer range.

One evening before sunset, Sami said to his parents, "I'm going out to take a walk."

"No!" his mother said. "It's almost dark!"

His father touched her hand to quiet her, and said, "Just around the apartments, yes? Don't leave the apartments."

His father looked so tired again, the way he had before they left Bethlehem. Some students had tried to drop his classes, though the deadline for that had passed.

A mysterious person had placed an ugly **anonymous** letter inside his faculty mailbox, but his father wouldn't tell Sami exactly what it said.

"Did you throw it away?"

"I burned it," his father said sadly. "In the outdoor ashtray."

Everyone had forgotten how to smile.

Sami's mother was working as an aide at a nursery school. She felt the eyes of the parents on her like hot buttons when they read her name tag, HANAN, even if they didn't know where she was from.

Sami stepped outside. He walked down the metal stairs toward the vacant swimming pool. Trash cans were spilling over next to the barbecue grills.

A little toddler stood on a couch inside a neighboring apartment, staring out. Sami fluttered his fingers at her. She ducked and covered her face. The baby was lucky. She could not understand the news.

Cars slept in their assigned spaces under the carport roof. It seemed strange, but Sami felt jealous of them. It might be easier to be a car.

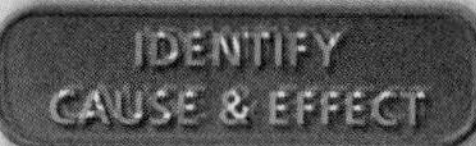

IDENTIFY CAUSE & EFFECT

Underline the details in lines 252–265 that describe the effect of the September 11 attacks on Sami's parents.

VOCABULARY

anonymous (ə·nän′ə·məs) *adj.:* given or written by an unknown person.

COMPARE & CONTRAST

Pause at line 275. Compare and contrast the way Sami is now feeling about his life in the United States to the way he was feeling before September 11.

CONNECT

Explain what Sami means when he says that the hijackers had "ruined his life" (line 292).

INFER

What does Sami's memory of his life in Bethlehem (lines 292–301) add to your understanding of Sami?

Another evening he asked his mother if he could make soup. She was surprised at his sudden interest in cooking. He rinsed lentils in a colander, as he had seen her do many times. He chopped an onion and fried garlic in a skillet.

As the soup was simmering, his mother remembered she had forgotten to pick up the mail downstairs when she came in from work. She asked if he would go get it and handed him the little key.

The mailbox was stuffed with bills and ads.

How could so many people have their address when they'd only been here two months?

Walking back toward the apartment with his hands full, Sami kicked a red balloon on the ground. It felt good to kick something sometimes. The balloon had a ribbon dangling from it—someone must have had a party. Today he had wished he could kick his backpack at school. Did those hijackers realize they had ruined his life too? He used to kick stones on the roads around Bethlehem. These were the same white stones that everyone was always getting in trouble for throwing. He only kicked them.

Once he had kicked a tin can all the way to Manger Square and his father passed him walking home from the bakery with a fresh load of steaming pita bread wrapped inside a towel. He spoke sharply to Sami for wasting his time.

"Find something useful to do," his father had said.

Today, so far away, after so much had happened, Sami thought of those long-ago words as the balloon snagged on a bush and popped. He spotted a thick unopened envelope on the ground. Had it fallen from someone's trash?

He stooped to pick it up, awkwardly, since his hands were full.

The envelope was addressed to Hugh Mason, Apartment 109.

Looking around, Sami realized that was the apartment where the tall man with the blond dog lived.

Sami pressed the buzzer. The man opened the door, dog at his side. He was staring straight ahead. Sami had finally understood, after watching him pass through the courtyard more than once, that he couldn't see. "Yes?"

The dog seemed to take a step forward to stand between his master and Sami.

"Mr. Hug Mason?" Sami pronounced it "hug"—he had never seen this English name before and did not know how to say it.

The tall man laughed. "Yes?"

"I have a letter for you with your name on it. I found it on the ground by the mailboxes. Maybe you dropped it?" He also wanted to ask, "How do you read it?" but was embarrassed to.

Mr. Mason put out his hand. "Thank you. I have dropped many things in my life. Very kind of you. You have an interesting accent. Where are you from?"

Sami hesitated. Could he lie?

Could he say Norway?

He knew his accent was not like a Mexican-American accent.

"I am," he said, in as American a voice as he could muster, "from Bethlehem."

Mr. Mason paused. "So you're Palestinian?"

"I am."

The dog seemed to have relaxed. He sniffed Sami's hand. His pale coat was lush and rumpled.

Mr. Mason's voice was gentle. "That must be harder than usual these days."

PREDICT

Pause at line 310. What is Sami going to do with the letter? What connection can you make between Sami's decision to pick up the letter and his memory of his father telling him to do something useful (line 301)?

FLUENCY

Read the boxed dialogue between Sami and Hugh. Try to capture the expressions of Sami's hesitation and Hugh's gratitude.

INFER

Re-read lines 327–341. What can you infer about Hugh based on his questions to Sami?

VISUALIZE

Does this picture help you visualize Tum Tum? Why or why not?

PREDICT

Do you think Sami and Hugh will become friends? Underline the words and phrases in lines 345–352 that give you clues.

© Jim Craigmyle/CORBIS

A seeing-eye dog guiding a blind person.

Sami felt startled when tears rose up in his own eyes. At least the man couldn't see them.

Sami whispered, "It is. Does your dog have a name?"

Half an hour later, Hugh and Sami were sitting on the green plastic chairs outside together, still talking. Tum Tum lay calmly beside them. They had discussed Lubbock, school, the troubles of Bethlehem, and the recent disaster. It was amazing how fast they had each talked, and how easily they had moved from subject to subject. They had not mentioned Hugh Mason's blindness, though Sami felt curious about it.

But they *had* discussed Tum Tum's job. Hugh had flown to California to be trained, alongside Tum Tum, four years ago. Training lasted twenty-eight days and was very "intense." Sami liked that word. He had never used it. This was Hugh's second dog. He'd had his first one for twelve years after his wife was killed. Killed? Crossing a street. "Hit-and-run."[6] Sami didn't know the phrase. Hugh had to explain it.

Tum Tum had been trained for "intelligent disobedience." If, for example, he saw Hugh getting ready to do something dangerous, like fall off a cliff (were there any cliffs in Lubbock?) or into the swimming pool, he would stand up on his hind legs, put his huge paws on Hugh's shoulders, and knock him over backward.

Later, thinking about it, Sami wished all people had dogs to guide their behavior if they were about to get into trouble.

When Tum Tum needed to go outside the apartment to pee behind a bush, he would hum.

Hum? What was "hum"? Hugh demonstrated, making a low smooth sound in his throat. Not all guide dogs did this—it was something particular to this one.

Tum Tum's ears perked up straight when he heard Hugh humming. Hugh said that if Tum Tum was just sitting on the grass right next to him, the dog would sometimes hum or make little talking sounds to let Hugh know what he was doing. Now he hummed in response to Hugh's hum. Tum Tum was a very **communicative** dog.

Hugh said that when a guide dog died, the loss for a blind person was nearly as hard as the loss of a human being, you were so used to each other by then. But had he always been blind? Why was this such a hard question to ask?

6. **hit-and-run:** accident in which a driver hits a person or animal and then immediately flees the scene.

WORD STUDY

Intense (line 356) means "existing in a powerful degree." Circle any context clues that help you understand Hugh's use of the word *intense.* In your own words, explain what he means by calling his training "intense."

ANALYZE

Re-read the example Hugh gives of "intelligent disobedience" in lines 361–366. Then, write your own definition of the term.

VOCABULARY

communicative (kə·myo͞o′ni·kā′tiv) *adj.:* able to communicate easily; talkative.

IDENTIFY

Pause at the bottom of the page. Underline the things you have learned about Tum Tum. What is the most surprising thing you learned?

INFER

Pause at line 391. Why is Sami's mother upset?

INTERPRET

Pause at the end of the page. Why is Sami upset about his mother's attitude toward Hugh? Recall the unfair suspicions people have had toward Sami and his family. What message might the writer be trying to communicate about people and the judgments they make about each other?

Sami heard his mother's worried call. The soup! He had forgotten it completely. He jumped up.

His mother walked anxiously toward them with her hands raised. What had happened to him?

Sami answered in Arabic.

This was a good man, he'd found a letter . . . but his mother only said in Arabic, "*Come home.*"

Sami said to Hugh, "Excuse me, we will visit another day?"

Hugh stood up and shook his hand as if Sami were a school principal.

"Anytime! I enjoyed the visit very much." He held out his hand in the general direction of Sami's mother and said, "Good evening, pleased to meet you, I am Hugh Mason, you have a very nice son."

The lentils were too soft. Sami measured cumin and salt into the pot. He squeezed lemons. His mother was anxiously waiting for his father to come home. She was fretting and dusting things. At dinner Sami's mother told his father, he *had been with a man,* as if it were a big mistake to talk to a neighbor!

Sami couldn't believe it.

"Did you go in his house?"

Sami knew better than to go in his house.

"No."

"What did he want from you?"

"Nothing! To talk! He can't even see!" For the second time that afternoon, tears rose into Sami's eyes. "He offered me a job."

"A JOB?"

A fork fell off the table.

"To read to him. He is very smart. He works at a hospital answering telephones. The phone board has a Braille[7] panel so he can connect the calls. Someone drives him there. The dog goes too. Tum Tum. But he needs some reading help at home."

His father said, "You need to focus on your studies."

Sami said, "But he would pay me! I need some money too! Also, I learned new words. He has an excellent vocabulary, like a professor. I would read the newspaper, his mail, some magazines, and maybe even books. PLEASE?"

His father closed his eyes and shook his head. "Some days I wish we had never come here."

Sami started reading to Hugh on Tuesday and Thursday evenings. He read for two hours. Sometimes his throat felt hoarse afterward. He and Hugh sat outside when the weather was warm. When the "northers" came—Hugh told Sami that was the word everyone used for the cold winds from the north—they sat inside, Sami on the flowered couch and Hugh in a wooden chair at the table. Tum Tum sprawled happily between them and seemed to listen.

Sami would read the newspaper headlines and ask Hugh if he wanted to hear the stories. Whenever it was a sad story about Palestine and Israel, Hugh would say, "No. Don't read it. Tell me a story about Bethlehem instead."

So Sami would put the paper down and find himself describing little details he had never mentioned to anyone before. The way the stones were stacked to make a wall outside his old school. Crookedly, if you looked at it from the side. But the wall felt smooth along the top.

CLARIFY

Pause at line 427. Underline the duties of the job Hugh has offered Sami. Why is Sami excited about this job?

INFER

Pause at line 439. Why do you think Hugh is more interested in Sami's stories about Bethlehem than in the newspaper stories?

7. **Braille** (brāl):. writing and reading system for the blind in which characters are represented by raised bumps that are felt by the fingers.

VISUALIZE

Re-read lines 445–458. Underline details that help you picture Sami's life in Bethlehem.

INTERPRET

What might Hugh mean when he says that in some ways he can "see better than people who aren't blind" (lines 466–467)?

EVALUATE

In lines 468–472, underline the reasons why Sami likes the word "dialogue" more than "debate." Do you agree with his way of thinking? Explain.

The olive-wood carvers who shaped elegant nativity sets[8] and doves of peace from hunks of wood and served mint tea to traveling nuns, hoping they would buy presents to take home.

The teacher whose jacket was so old and raggedy he had long threads trailing down his back. Everyone whispered that he lived alone, had no one to take care of him. This was rare in Bethlehem. Few people lived alone. (Sami felt bad after telling this, since Hugh lived alone. No, not alone. He had Tum Tum.)

Sami told about the ancient wrinkled grandma-lady who made small date pies and kept them warm in her oven. She gave them to any student who stopped to visit her, even for two minutes, on the way home from school.

Hugh said he could visualize all these things with his "inner eyes."

"Does everyone have inner eyes?" Sami asked. "Even people who can see?"

"Of course," said Hugh. "You know whenever you remember something? You use them then. But some people don't use them enough. They forget about them. But they're all I have. In some ways, I think I can see better than people who aren't blind."

The teachers at school had urged Sami to join the Debate Club, but he didn't want to debate anyone. Debate involved winning and losing. Sami felt more attracted to "dialogue," a word he had heard Hugh use frequently, because dialogue was like a bridge. The teachers said, "In that case, you'll have to start your own club."

"Okay," he said. Why did he say that? he thought later. He didn't know how to start a club!

---

8. nativity sets: sets of small figures used to represent a scene from the birth of Jesus.

His history teacher printed up a set of "Guidelines for Dialogue Groups" off the Internet. It said things like: (1) Never interrupt; (2) Try to speak in specifics and stories, instead of generalities;[9] (3) Respect varying opinions. Everyone does not have to agree, but everyone needs to respect everyone else.

A Korean girl named Janet approached Sami in the gym and said she had heard about the club from the art teacher and wanted to join it. "The art teacher is my good friend," Janet said. "Let's go to her room tomorrow after school and make some posters on those big tables."

Sami was glad Janet was so artistic since he was *not.* She designed the posters and he colored in the letters and graphics with fat felt-tip markers. Janet chattered freely as they worked. Adopted at birth, she had been brought to west Texas by her parents. Everyone was always asking her if she was Chinese.

The new club met on a Wednesday after school in the English classroom. Three students from Mexico City appeared at the meeting, looking **quizzical.** They said their English teacher had told them to come, to work on their language skills. They were happy to talk about anything. A tall Anglo American who had lived in Saudi Arabia with his oil engineer dad, an African-American girl named Hypernia, a very large girl in overalls, and a boy with a prosthetic leg appeared. Sami would never have known about the leg until the boy sat down and his pants revealed a bit of hardware at his ankle. There was also a Jewish boy who went by his initials, L. B.

For the first meeting, people just introduced themselves and told a bit about their lives. The boy who had lived in Saudi Arabia said he felt personally grieved by

9. **generalities** (jen'ər·al'ə·tēz) *n.:* statements that apply to all members of a group.

EXTEND

Re-read the guidelines for the Dialogue Club in lines 476–481. How might the guidelines for a debate club differ from these guidelines?

INFER

What facts do you learn about Janet in lines 482–492? Why might she be interested in the Dialogue Group?

VOCABULARY

quizzical (kwiz'i·kəl) *adj.:* puzzled; curious.

IDENTIFY

Write a number next to each of the members of the Dialogue Club. How many are there so far?

COMPARE & CONTRAST

Re-read lines 505–518. Despite their obvious differences, what do the students in the Dialogue Club have in common?

EXTEND

Pause at line 524. Underline the reason the club decides to visit the mechanic. What do you think they will say to the mechanic when they see him?

CLARIFY

Re-read lines 532–542. Circle what Sami learns about the girl in overalls. Underline why he is surprised.

September 11, since the Arabs he had known were always so "nice." Hypernia said she had felt very lonely since her parents moved to Lubbock from Dallas, where she'd attended a school that was 80 percent African-American. "I feel like an alien or something. Like everyone is staring at me. I never felt this way before."

L. B. said he was really tired of explaining about the Jewish holidays. Sami asked if he had ever been to Israel and he said no, but his grandmother had. He stared at Sami hard and said, "I really wish people could get along over there. I mean, it's terrible, isn't it?"

Sami said, "*Really* terrible." He liked the boy just for saying that.

The club ended up talking about the Pakistani auto mechanic on the east side of town whose shop windows had been broken after September 11. It had been in the newspaper. They decided to go visit him, take him a card.

Janet suggested "On Not Fitting In" as a topic for their next meeting. She had brought a poem by James Wright, an American poet, to read. It said, "Whatever it was I lost, whatever I wept for / Was a wild, gentle thing, the small dark eyes / Loving me in secret. / It is here."

Sami found it mysterious, but it made him think of Tum Tum.

He mentioned to the group that he worked for a man who could not see in usual ways, but who might be a nice guest speaker for their group someday. He had interesting ideas, Sami said, and he liked to listen. "I'm visually impaired too," said the large girl in overalls. "Bring him. I'd like to meet him." Sami looked at her, surprised. He had seen her tilt her head to other people as they spoke, but had no indication she was blind. Suddenly he noticed the white cane on the floor at her side. She said softly, as if in answer to a question he didn't ask, "I only see shades of light and dark. But I can't see any of your faces."

Weeks went by. The Dialogue Club was featured on the morning announcements at school. Gavin, who had once, so long ago, eaten lunch in the cafeteria with Sami, came to the club to write a story for the school paper, and he didn't get a single fact or quote wrong, which amazed the club members. They said the school paper was famous for getting everything wrong.

Sami's parents invited Hugh to dinner. They had stopped worrying about Sami's job when they discovered how nice and smart Hugh was. Sami's father seemed to feel a little embarrassed about having acted so negative in the beginning. So he took care to ask Hugh many questions, including the one Sami was most curious about himself.

Hugh had lost his sight at the age of four to hereditary glaucoma,[10] a disease that could have been partially averted if he'd had surgery earlier. His mother always blamed herself afterward for not realizing what was happening to her son. No one she had known in her family or his father's family had this condition. But she had known that Hugh, as a tiny boy, had vision troubles, and had gotten him thick glasses and fussed at him for stumbling instead of taking him to medical experts when something could still have been done. This great sorrow in the family eventually led to a divorce between Hugh's parents.

"So you went to college—when you were already blind?" Sami's father asked gently.

"Yes, I did. And there I met the woman who eventually married me, my wife, Portia. She was African-American, and her parents never forgave her for marrying someone

---

10. glaucoma (glô·kō′mə) *n.:* disorder of the eye that can lead to loss of vision.

INTERPRET

Pause at line 542. Consider what you have learned about the Dialogue Club—both its membership and its guidelines. What point might the writer be making about the value of acceptance and learning to appreciate differences among people?

CONNECT

Re-read lines 556–570. Underline the new information you have learned about Hugh. How does this information add to or change your understanding of him?

white *and* blind—it was too much for them. But we had nine wonderful years together. You would have liked her, Sami."

Sami's eyes were wide open. How many kinds of difficulties there were in the world that he had not even imagined yet!

His parents played soft Arabic flute music on their little tape player in the background for the first time in months, and served grape leaves, cucumber salad with mint and yogurt, and *ketayef*—a crescent-shaped, nut-stuffed pastry with honey sauce. Hugh ate a lot, and said it was the best meal he had tasted in *years*. Sami had seen the cans of simple soup lined on his kitchen counter, the hunks of cheese in the refrigerator, the apples in a bowl. He watched Hugh eat with gusto now and noticed how his fork carefully found the food, then his mouth, without any mishap or awkwardness.

Tum Tum kept sniffing the air as if he liked the rich spices.

Once he hummed loudly and Sami's father laughed out loud, for the first time since September 11. "What is that? Is he singing?"

Sami rose proudly to open the door to the courtyard. "It's his language," Sami said. "He needs to be excused for a moment."

He knew Tum Tum would walk to his favorite bush and return immediately, scratching on the door to be let back in. And he would not get the apartment doors confused, though they all looked alike—Tum Tum always knew exactly where Hugh was, instinctively. Sami's dad shook his head. "In this country, even dogs are smart."

ANALYZE

Pause at line 577. What does Sami learn from Hugh's story about his wife? What **theme**, or insight about life, is suggested by Hugh's story?

VISUALIZE

Re-read lines 578–602. Underline the details that help you picture the scene with Hugh and Sami's family at the dinner table. Write those words and phrases that describe the scene most powerfully for you.

Hugh said, "Friends, my stomach is full, my heart is full. Sami, come over here so I can pat your black hair! I'm so happy we're neighbors!"

Now Sami laughed.

"Hugh," he said, "my hair is red."

INTERPRET

The last line of "Hum" is humorous; however, the writer is also making a serious point and addressing the story's **theme.** What might Hugh's mistake and Sami's correction be saying about the power of stereotypes and the value of communication?

MEET THE WRITER

Naomi Shihab Nye (1952–) started writing at the age of six. She was addicted to writing from the moment she wrote her first poem, which she published at age seven. Nye was born in the United States, but she spent a year of her childhood living in Jerusalem, a part of Jordan at the time. She now lives in San Antonio, Texas, with her husband and son. The daughter of a Palestinian father and an American mother, it's not surprising that Nye often celebrates the diversity of American culture in her writing. Her Palestinian grandmother, or "Sitti" in Arabic, is a special influence in her life. She writes frequently of her grandmother, who influenced Nye through her love of peace and appreciation for differing cultures and religions. Nye's writing is also known for focusing on ordinary daily occurrences and the interactions between people of differing cultures. A well-known poet, Nye often runs workshops in schools to help students find the poetry hidden in their imaginations.

Hum

Literary Skills
Analyze theme.

Theme Chart A truth about life revealed in a story is its **theme.** One way to find a story's theme is to examine what we and the characters discover in the course of the story. That discovery usually points to the story's theme. Complete the graphic organizer below with details from "Hum."

Main character(s):

____

↓

Key experiences:

____

____

____

____

↓

What we discover from those experiences:

____

____

____

____

↓

Statement of theme:

____

____

____

____

Skills Review

Hum

VOCABULARY AND COMPREHENSION

A. Using Context Clues Fill in the blanks of the paragraph below with words from the Word Bank. Use the context clues to help you.

Word Bank

- dramatically
- jovial
- solitude
- anonymous
- communicative
- quizzical

Though he hadn't made any friends yet, Sami was enjoying his (1) ________________. He walked home alone after school. Sometimes, he read to Hugh. Since his dinner at Sami's place, Hugh wore a smile and appeared more (2) ________________. One day, an (3) ________________ letter with no return address arrived for Hugh. Sami was puzzled and looked at it with a (4) ________________ expression. Hugh was normally (5) ________________, but now he was strangely silent. Hugh opened the letter and took out the card inside, then exclaimed (6) ________________. The musical card reminded him it was his birthday!

B. Reading Comprehension Answer each question below.

1. Where is Sami's family from? Why did they leave?

   ____

   ____

2. What major historical event occurs after Sami moves to Texas? What effect does this event have on Sami and his new life?

   ____

   ____

3. How does Sami meet Hugh? What job does Hugh offer Sami?

   ____

   ____

Vocabulary Skills
Use context clues.

Before You Read

POEM

in the inner city by Lucille Clifton

LITERARY FOCUS: UNIVERSAL THEMES

No matter where or when they live, people seem to share the same kinds of dreams, feelings, and needs. And people all over the world and throughout history have written poems to express those dreams, feelings, and needs. That is why similar **themes**—insights about life—come up again and again. Themes in literature that reflect these common human experiences are called **universal themes.**

As you read the poem "in the inner city," think about what makes its theme universal.

READING SKILLS: READING POETRY

Poetry without punctuation, like "in the inner city," can be hard to understand at first. Here are some tips to get you started.

- Pay attention to units of thought. Where does each idea end and another begin?
- Think about line lengths. Why does the poet sometimes put only one or two words on a line? Why are other lines longer?
- Read the poem aloud. How does the sound of your voice help you to understand the meaning of the poem?

Literary Skills
Understand universal themes.

Reading Skills
Use strategies to read poetry.

© Royalty-Free/CORBIS

in the inner city

Lucille Clifton

in the inner city
or
like we call it
home
we think a lot about uptown
and the silent nights
and the houses straight as
dead men
and the pastel lights
and we hang on to our no place
happy to be alive
and in the inner city
or
like we call it
home

VISUALIZE

Underline the words the speaker uses to describe "uptown" (lines 5–9). What kind of place do you imagine uptown to be?

____

____

INFER

How do you think the speaker feels about the "inner city"?

____

____

____

____

____

ANALYZE

One way to identify the **theme** of a work of literature is to look for the most important word. What word in the poem do you think points to a theme? State what that theme is. How might this theme be considered a **universal theme**?

MEET THE WRITER

Lucille Clifton (1936–) writes poetry that honors life. Her poems celebrate the remarkable human ability to find hope and joy in the face of difficult circumstances. In addition to her poetry, Clifton has written more than sixteen children's books, including the Everett Anderson series, which features a young boy growing up in the inner city. Clifton's writing, both her poetry and her books for children, often highlights the African American experience. Clifton is known for using a spare form and simple language to express powerful ideas, a style known as minimalism. Clifton went to college at Howard University at only sixteen years old and has received numerous awards, including the National Book Award, for her poetry.

in the inner city

Literary Skills
Analyze a universal theme.

Theme Chart A good strategy for discovering the theme of a poem is to look for the most important word. In the chart below, identify a key word. Then, state the theme you think that word points to. Finally, describe why you think this could be a **universal theme.**

Most important word:
Theme the word points to:
Why this is a universal theme:

in the inner city

COMPREHENSION

Reading Comprehension Answer each question below.

1. What is the speaker's attitude toward "uptown"?

2. What details in the poem reveal the speaker's attitude toward "uptown"?

3. What is the speaker's attitude toward the "inner city"?

4. What details in the poem reveal the speaker's feelings about the "inner city"?

Before You Read

My Father's Song by Simon J. Ortiz

LITERARY FOCUS: DISCOVERING THEME

Here are some tips that can help you find the **theme**—or insight about life—revealed in a poem.

- Decide what the **characters** learn or discover in the course of the poem. Often that discovery can be written as a theme statement.
- Think about the **title** and what it might mean. Not all titles have significance. Some just tell you the topic, but others offer a clue to the theme.
- Consider the **topic** of the poem. What the poem says about the topic may reveal its theme.

Although "My Father's Song" is not a very long poem, you may be able to find more than one theme in it.

READING SKILLS: MAKING INFERENCES ABOUT THEME

A poet seldom states the theme of a poem directly. You have to make **inferences,** or educated guesses, to figure out a poem's theme. You base your guesses on both the information in the poem and your own experiences. You can also use the tips listed above to help you make inferences that will lead you to the poem's theme. Most works of literature reveal more than one theme, and those themes can be expressed in more than one way. What makes reading a poem especially valuable is the insights you, the reader, gain from the poem.

Literary Skills
Discover themes.

Reading Skills
Make inferences about theme.

My Father's Song

Simon J. Ortiz

© 1996 Lawrence Migdale.

INFER

Re-read the first stanza of this poem (lines 1–7). How do you think the speaker feels about his father? Underline the words that support your answer.

IDENTIFY

A colon, the punctuation at the end of line 7, indicates that the speaker is about to give an example of his father's song. What event is the speaker describing in lines 8–12?

Wanting to say things,
I miss my father tonight.
His voice, the slight catch,
the depth from his thin chest,
the tremble of emotion
in something he has just said
to his son, his song:

We planted corn one Spring at Acu—
we planted several times
but this one particular time
I remember the soft damp sand
in my hand.

My father had stopped at one point
to show me an overturned furrow;
the plowshare had unearthed
the burrow nest of a mouse
in the soft moist sand.

Very gently, he scooped tiny pink animals
into the palm of his hand
and told me to touch them.
We took them to the edge
of the field and put them in the shade
of a sand moist clod.

I remember the very softness
of cool and warm sand and tiny alive mice
and my father saying things.

MEET THE WRITER

Simon J. Ortiz (1941–) is a Native American poet and writer who lives in New Mexico. He was born in an Acoma Pueblo community in Albuquerque, New Mexico, and grew up speaking Keresan, the language of the Acoma Pueblo. "My Father's Song" comes from Ortiz's book of poetry *Going for the Rain,* a collection inspired by Acoma myths and songs. Though he learned English only later in school, Ortiz chooses to write in English because today it is the language most commonly spoken among Native Americans. In addition to speaking out about the struggles of Native Americans, Ortiz's poetry often celebrates the natural world and the human relationship to this world. He believes that Americans have lost an essential connection to nature, a relationship that is necessary for our survival.

RETELL

Retell what the speaker of the poem and his father find in the field and what they do about it (lines 13–26).

INFER

Think back to the **title** of the poem. What do you think is the father's song? What is the father teaching his son? What **theme** does this information reveal to you?

My Father's Song

Literary Skills Analyze theme.

Reading Skills Make inferences about theme.

Thematic Graph Details in a work of literature can point to its **theme.** For example, if a speaker in a poem suffers a loss, the theme might have something to say about how losses affect people. The chart below lists a possible theme from "My Father's Song." Fill in the boxes below with details from the poem that support that theme. Finally, list any other works you can think of that share the theme.

Theme of "My Father's Song"

We are all connected to each other and to other living things.

Supporting Detail 1	Supporting Detail 2	Supporting Detail 3

Other Works with the Same Theme

Skills Review

My Father's Song

COMPREHENSION

Reading Comprehension Answer each question below.

1. Why does the speaker of the poem miss his father?

2. What do the speaker and his father do together in the poem?

3. Why do you think the memory of finding and moving the mice is so important to the speaker?

Collection 4

Point of View: Can You See It My Way?

Bond of Union (1956) by Maurits Cornelius Escher. Lithograph.

The Granger Collection, New York

Academic Vocabulary for Collection 4

These are the terms you should know as you read and analyze the selections in this collection.

Narrator Character or voice who is narrating, or telling a story.

Point of View Vantage point from which a story is told. A story can be told from the point of view of one of its characters or from the point of view of an outsider, a person who simply observes the action.

Omniscient Point of View The all-knowing point of view, in which the narrator stands outside the action. This type of narrator can tell you everything about all the characters, even their most private thoughts.

First-Person Point of View When a story's character tells the story, we say the story is written from the first-person point of view. In this point of view, we know only what the one character can tell us.

Third-Person-Limited Point of View In this point of view, the narrator is not part of the story but has the ability to zoom in on the thoughts and feelings of just one story character.

● ● ●

Subjective Writing Type of writing in which the author shares his or her own feelings, thoughts, opinions, and judgments.

Objective Writing Unbiased writing that presents facts and figures rather than the writer's private feelings.

Before You Read

That October by D. H. Figueredo

LITERARY FOCUS: POINT OF VIEW

When a story's narrator is a character in the story who tells about his or her personal thoughts, feelings, and experiences, we say the story is told from the first-person point of view. In the **first-person point of view,** a narrator uses the pronouns *I, me, my,* and *mine* to refer to himself or herself. The boldface words in the following passage are clues that it's written from a first-person point of view.

> Just as the band turned the corner in front of the judges' stand, one of the baton twirlers tripped. Her baton sailed wildly toward the back of the band, and she crashed headlong into the drum major. **I** didn't know whether to laugh or cry. **I** bit down so hard on **my** saxophone mouthpiece that **my** reed split in two.

READING SKILLS: MAKING PREDICTIONS

Nothing ruins a movie more than having someone who's seen it tell you what will happen next. Much of the fun of watching a movie or reading a story is **making predictions,** or guessing at what is going to happen.

Use the tips below to make predictions.

- Look for clues that **foreshadow,** or hint at, what will happen next.
- Predict possible outcomes. Guess where the writer is heading, and revise your predictions as you go.
- Base predictions on your personal experiences, including your reading experiences.

Literary Skills. Understand first-person point of view.

Reading Skills Make predictions.

Vocabulary Skills Clarify word meanings by recognizing word parts.

VOCABULARY DEVELOPMENT

PREVIEW SELECTION VOCABULARY

Preview the following words from the story before you begin reading.

illegal (i·lē′gəl) *adj.:* against the law; unlawful; not legal.

Bebo thinks it is illegal for two baseball players to fill one position.

combination (käm′bə·nā′shən) *n.:* union or joining together of two or more things.

People flocked to ballgames to see the new combination player on the field.

unbeatable (un·bēt′ə·bəl) *adj.:* unable to be defeated.

After winning two games, the Leopards thought they were unbeatable.

wheezing (hwēz′iŋ) *v.* used as *adj.:* breathing hard with a rasping sound.

Rudy ran as fast as he could, wheezing loudly, around the bases.

CLARYIFYING WORD MEANINGS: WORDS AND WORD PARTS

Many readers use strategies to figure out the meanings of unfamiliar words. One good strategy is to look for a word or word parts within the unfamiliar word for a clue to its meaning. Practice using this strategy as you read the story that follows. Here are some examples.

Unfamiliar Word	Meaning
uncontrollable	"not able to be controlled"
fashionista	"person who works in the fashion industry"
globalize	"organize or establish worldwide"

That October

D. H. Figueredo

BACKGROUND: Literature and Social Studies

That October takes place in Cuba in 1962. On January 1, 1959, Fidel Castro took power in Cuba and soon established a communist government. Between 1960 and the late 1980s, Cuba relied on aid from the Soviet Union, a communist superpower formed from Russia, Ukraine, and other nations. The Soviet Union gave Cuba economic and political support and maintained a military presence on the island. The relationship between the two countries weakened in the late 1980s and early 1990s as the Soviet Union underwent major reforms and eventually collapsed.

IDENTIFY

Circle the pronouns in the first paragraph that let you know this story is written from the **first-person point of view.**

WORD STUDY

Comrade (line 7) means "friend, or person who shares an interest or activity" and was a common form of address in communist countries like Cuba and the Soviet Union. Circle the Spanish and Russian words that mean the same thing.

The Russian soldier came out of the building on the edge of the baseball field. He had a ball with him. When he noticed I was holding a bat, he started walking toward me.

Pointing at the broken window, he said, "It's against the law to damage government property."

My father was standing beside me. "*Camarada,*" he said, using the Spanish word for comrade. "You can't take my son to jail."

"*Tovaritch,*" the soldier said, using the Russian for comrade. "This building is used by the army for important research."

"The boy just forgot how strong he is," my father said.

The Russian looked at the orthopedic shoes[1] I was wearing and the metal braces that went from my right foot to the top of my thigh. "Did you hit the ball during the game?" he asked me.

"No," I answered.

"You did it on purpose?"

The baseball team had formed a circle around us. The parents had formed a circle around the players. There were Russian soldiers on the other side of the fence that surrounded the building. They were looking at us.

"*Camarada*, I can explain," my father said.

"I need an explanation, but not from you," the Russian said. "You talk," he ordered me.

"Go ahead, son," my father said.

This is what I told the Russian.

The Tigers were the best team in Havana and I wanted to play with them. But they didn't let me. Why? Because when I was little, I was sick with a virus called polio. I got better but I ended up with a very thin leg. Also, I moved in a funny way, like a puppet, and I limped and fell a lot.

The captain of the team, Alfredo, told me that he couldn't afford a weak player. The pitcher, Bebo, said that the team didn't need a bad player. But I knew I was neither. "I practice every day in my back yard," I told them. "Am always losing balls because I smack them so hard, they fly over the fence and disappear."

"But you can't run," said Alfredo.

"But I'm a good hitter," I said.

"So?"

1. **orthopedic** (ôr'thə·pē'dik) *adj.:* for treatment of diseases and injuries to bones, joints, and muscles.

PREDICT

Re-read the description of the confrontation in lines 19–23. What do you think will happen next?

EVALUATE

Circle the **simile**—the comparison using a word such as *like, as,* or *similar*—that the narrator uses in line 33 to describe how he moves. What does this simile tell you about his movement? Do you think he could be a good ballplayer? Explain.

VOCABULARY

illegal (i·lē′gəl) *adj.:* against the law; unlawful; not legal.

combination (käm′bə·nā′shən) *n.:* union or joining together of two or more things.

RETELL

Pause at line 59. The narrator tries to convince Alfredo and Bebo to let him join the Tigers. Circle the arguments for and against his joining the team.

INFER

Alfredo and Bebo are not convinced by the narrator's arguments. What do you think his father says to convince them?

IDENTIFY

The narrator is not the only addition to the team. Circle the other additions (line 72).

"We can work together," I said. "You and I are pretty good hitters. You're also a fast runner. You and I could play as a duo. I bat and you run."

He shook his head. "The team won't go for that," he said.

"The team does what you tell them to do," I said.

Bebo spoke up. He said that it wouldn't work and that it was **illegal.** But I told him it wasn't, because the Tigers were not an official team, didn't wear uniforms, and didn't have a book of rules. "So there are no rules to break," I said.

Alfredo then said that it would not be fair. "The team would be getting an extra player."

I told him that was not so, that the two of us together made up one person. "It's an experiment," I said.

But they were not convinced.

That evening, I didn't feel like eating. When I went to bed, my father massaged my foot, something he did every night. He could tell I was sad and wanted to know what was wrong. I told him and he asked me, "Is it okay if I talk with Alfredo?"

The next day my father went to the field to see Alfredo. Later on, Alfredo came by the house. He told me he had changed his mind and that I could play with the team. Right after he said so, I made myself a sandwich and poured a big glass of chocolate milk.

I was happy to be a Tiger. And I wasn't the only addition to the team. For the first time ever, the players were wearing real jerseys and baseball caps. People began to say that the team was different, that not only did the players look better but that there was also a new **combination** on the

baseball field. Friends and their friends came to see that combination. They said maybe it was a new creature, something like a centaur, the half-person half-horse from long ago. But they were soon disappointed. For what they saw was me batting and Alfredo running.

As the season went on, fewer fans came to the field. We played against teams from the neighborhoods of Miramar and Marianao, La Lisa and Los Pasos, losing some games but winning most. By October, we were ready for our World Series. This was when the two top teams played against each other. The winner was the first to win three out of five games.

Our opponents were the Leopards from the town of La Lisa. We won the first game. Then, the Leopards won the next two. By the time the fourth encounter came along, the Leopards were sure they were **unbeatable** and were boasting that a team with a boy wearing braces was no match for them.

ANALYZE

Line 77 contains a reference to a centaur, a mythical beast. Do you think the combination of Alfredo and the narrator playing one position is anything like a centaur? Why or why not?

VOCABULARY

unbeatable (un·bēt′ə·bəl) *adj.:* unable to be defeated.

RETELL

Re-read lines 99–104. What happens in the seventh inning that changes everything?

PREDICT

What do you think Alfredo's injury (line 119) will mean to the narrator and to the team?

At this game, the Leopards were the first to bat. But they didn't score. We did and at the end of the first inning, we were leading 1 to 0. For a long while, the score remained the same. The parents started to say that either both teams were really good or really tired. Then everything changed.

It happened in the seventh inning. The Leopards had a player on second. A batter bunted the ball and as we scrambled to catch it, the batter ran to first and the player on second made it to third. Then, the next player at the plate delivered a home run. The Leopards were ahead 3 to 1.

It was our turn at bat. Alfredo pulled me aside and told me to hit a homer with so much force that the bat would break in two. He planned to run so fast that his legs would turn into wheels, just like in the cartoons on television.

But I failed him. Instead, my bat made a "thud" sound and the ball whirled toward first. Running as hard as he could, Alfredo crash-landed on the base, but the first baseman shouted, the ball inside his glove, "You're dead, pal."

Alfredo cried out. From the stands, his father came out to help him. Leaning on him, Alfredo limped away from the base.

"I won't be able to run," he told me, sitting down on the bench. He had twisted his ankle.

We went into the final inning with Bebo in charge. He told us that we couldn't let the Leopards get in any more runs. He concentrated on his pitching and struck out the Leopards. But they were still winning by two runs.

Now, it was our turn to bat. One player directed a line drive into left field. He made it to first base. While the

Leopards' pitcher was pitching, our player stole second. The next hitter shot the ball over the pitcher's head. The pitcher jumped up, caught the ball but dropped it, giving the Tiger on second enough time to reach third and allowing the batter to get to first.

We had a chance to recover the game. My teammates stopped feeling sorry for themselves. They said that we could score. But the high hopes vanished when the following two batters struck out.

I was next. But Bebo stopped me. "Somebody else will bat, not you." He said, "This time, Alfredo can't help you."

"I'm a Tiger and the team expects me to play," I said.

"You're not a Tiger," he said. "The only reason you're playing is because your father has money."

"What?"

"See our new shirts? Your father bought them for us. He also gave money to the other teams."

"That's not true," I said.

"Are you calling me a liar?" Bebo asked.

From the bench, Alfredo shouted, "Let him play." He made a fist and opened the palm of his hand and punched it. "Let him play."

Bebo stepped aside. Was he right? Was I allowed to play only because my father was paying for me to play? I wanted to leave. But Alfredo said, "Do it. We need a homer."

I waited a few seconds. My father looked at me in silence. The team looked at me in silence. Bebo had a smirk on his face.

I stepped up to the plate. I nodded to let the pitcher know I was ready. The pitcher eyed the catcher.

Strike one.

FLUENCY

Read the boxed passage aloud by yourself a few times. Then, read only the dialogue with a partner. One reads the part of Bebo, and the other reads the part of the narrator. Let your voices express the characters' feelings.

INTERPRET

Bebo says the only reason the narrator is on the team is because his father has money (lines 139–140). Do you think he is right? Support your answer with evidence from the text.

INFER

How does the narrator feel about Bebo's accusation? Underline details in lines 149–152 that support your response.

Notes

INFER

What does the **simile** in line 167 tell you happens when the narrator swings the bat?

PREDICT

Pause at line 177. Why do you think everyone is looking at the narrator?

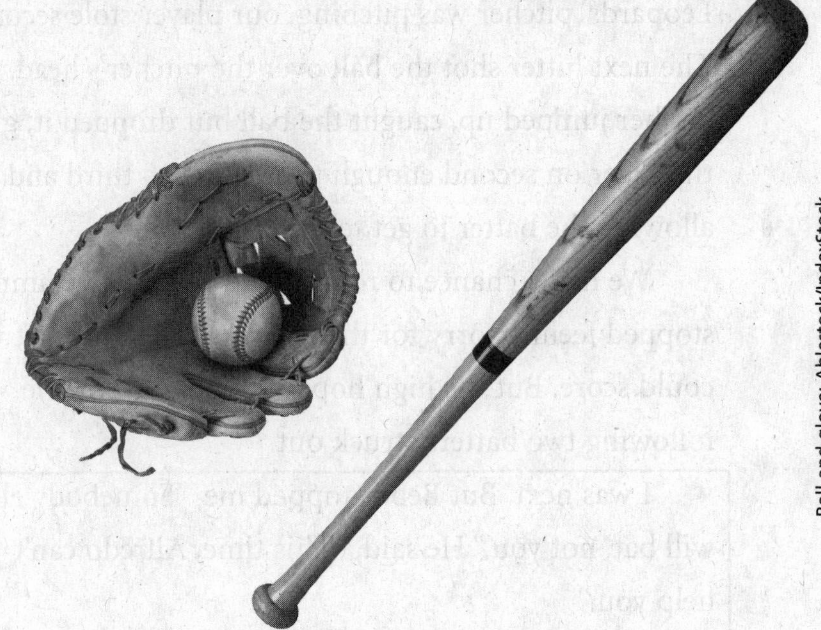

Ball and glove: Ablestock/IndexStock
Bat: © Royalty-free/CORBIS

Bebo looked at Alfredo. He said, "I told you he's no good. I told you."

Strike two.

Bebo threw his cap in the dirt.

I turned to Alfredo. He mouthed, "You can do it." I turned to my father who gave me thumbs up.

The pitcher stretched his arm back and thrust it forward. The ball curved. I lowered the bat and swung.

It sounded like the wind had banged a door shut. The bat shook in my hands. I stood still for a moment before throwing it backwards. Turning into a minirocket, the bat almost hit Bebo who had to duck. In the meantime, the ball was rising higher and higher, becoming one with the sun before falling to the ground.

The Leopards didn't try to catch the ball. They weren't even looking at it. The parents weren't looking at the ball either. Neither were Bebo, Alfredo, nor the rest of my teammates. Instead, they were all looking at me.

They were looking at me, running. Yes, running in a funny way, like a robin with a broken leg. Running and **wheezing,** like an old sugarcane mill. Running and making so much noise it sounded as if it were raining pots and pans. But running.

To first base.

To second.

To third.

By the time the Leopards figured that I could run and make it to the plate, it was too late. For the Tigers who had been on first and third had already reached home. And I was right behind them.

My father cheered. The parents said, "What a game, what a game." The Tigers congratulated each other. I picked up a ball from the ground and threw it high into the air. As it came down, I whacked it with the bat, whacked it so hard that the ball rose over the fence and the electric posts, heading right for the building.

"And that's how I broke your window," I told the Russian.

He didn't say anything. He noticed that my knees were bleeding and that there were scratches on my right leg.

"Sometimes the braces scratch him," my father said.

The Russian said, "The window is still broken. And it still belongs to the Cuban government. And it's still illegal to damage government property." He loomed over me. Was he going to arrest me?

"Don't do it again," he said, tossing me the ball.

As he started to walk away, my father called him. When the Russian faced him, my father extended his hand. "Thank you, *tovaritch.*"

The Russian shook his hand. "You're welcome, *camarada.*"

VOCABULARY

wheezing (hwēz′iŋ) *v.:* used as an *adj.:* breathing hard with a rasping sound.

RETELL

Pause at line 189. How have the Tigers won the game?

INTERPRET

Do you think the Russian soldier is really angry about the broken window? Explain why or why not.

IDENTIFY

We first learn the narrator's name in line 211. What is it?

IDENTIFY

Circle the date in line 226 that tells you when this story takes place.

INFER

After the successful ending of both the ballgame and the confrontation with the Russian soldier, the narrator describes three additional events in lines 225–235. What does the final sentence tell you about the narrator's feelings about the events he has described?

Then my father said, "My name is Rodolfo." He pointed at me. "His name is Rudy."

"Mine is Andrei," said the Russian. Joining the soldiers on the other side of the fence, the Russian went inside the building.

As the baseball players and their parents left the field, my father placed his arm around my shoulder. He said, "I bought the shirts with one condition: that you were allowed to play one game. But just one. The rest was up to you and the team."

From inside his father's car, Alfredo called out my name. "Rudy, you saved the team today," he shouted. "You're definitely a Tiger. And you know who said so?"

I shook my head.

"Bebo."

Later that October, the Tigers and the Leopards finished Havana's 1962 Little League World Series. The Leopards won the final game and were the league champions.

Later that October, the Cuban government told the Russian soldiers that the research they were doing in the building was over. The Russians left the island and went back home.

Later that October, the Cuban government gave my parents and me permission to leave Cuba. We left the island and moved to Miami.

I took the ball with me.

MEET THE WRITER

D. H. Figueredo (1951–   ) was born in Cuba and immigrated to the United States when he was fourteen. A lifelong book lover, Figueredo decided to become a librarian because he wanted to be surrounded by books every day. Figueredo fell in love with children's books while reading them to his own children. Eventually he began creating his own bedtime stories. After hearing one such story, his son told him that he should write it down. This was the start of Figueredo's writing career. He is known for creating children's books that offer a vivid picture of Latino culture and history. His children's book *When This World Was New* is based on the story of the first time his father walked in the snow.

Notes

That October

Literary Skills Analyze first-person point of view.

Narrator Chart **A first-person narrator** takes part in the story he or she tells. Identify the narrator of "That October" in the top box. Then, give three details from the story that reveal the narrator's thoughts or observations.

Narrator		

Narrator's Thoughts	Narrator's Thoughts	Narrator's Thoughts

Whose Point of View? Think for a moment about how "That October" would differ if it were told by another person in the story. Pick one story character, such as Bebo or the Russian soldier, and explain how the story would be different if it were told by that character.

____

____

____

____

____

____

____

Skills Review

That October

VOCABULARY AND COMPREHENSION

A. Clarifying Word Meanings: Words and Word Parts Match words and definitions. Write the letter of the correct definition next to each word. Then, circle familiar word parts in the Word Bank words. (Not all words will contain a familiar word part.)

Word Bank

illegal
combination
unbeatable
wheezing

_______ **1.** illegal **a.** union

_______ **2.** combination **b.** unlawful

_______ **3.** unbeatable **c.** breathing loudly

_______ **4.** wheezing **d.** undefeatable

B. Reading Comprehension Write **T** or **F** next to each statement to tell if it is true or false.

_______ **1.** Rudy breaks a window while hitting a home run in an important game.

_______ **2.** The Russian soldier threatens to arrest Rudy for breaking the window.

_______ **3.** Rudy wears a leg brace and limps because of a childhood disease.

_______ **4.** Rudy is invited to join the Tigers because he is such a good hitter.

_______ **5.** Rudy's home run wins a crucial game for the Tigers.

_______ **6.** The Tigers go on to win Havana's 1962 Little League World Series.

Vocabulary Skills
Clarify word meanings by recognizing word parts.

Before You Read

POEM

Identity by Julio Noboa Polanco

why some people be mad at me sometimes by Lucille Clifton

LITERARY FOCUS: SPEAKER AND FIRST-PERSON POINT OF VIEW

Poems written in the **first-person point of view** express the personal feeling, thoughts, opinions, and judgments of the narrator or **speaker,** as the narrator of a poem is called. You can tell that a work is written in the first person when the speaker uses the pronouns *I, me, mine, we, us,* and *our*. Sometimes the speaker is identical to the poet, but often the speaker and the poet are not the same. The poet may be speaking as a child, a woman, a man, an animal, or even an object.

As you read "Identity" and "why some people be mad at me sometimes," notice the very personal reactions of the speakers in the poems.

READING SKILLS: FINDING UNITS OF MEANING—STANZAS

A **stanza** is a group of lines that form a single unit of a poem. Similar to a paragraph in prose, a stanza often expresses a unit of thought. Some stanzas have a fixed number of lines. Stanzas in free-verse poems such as "Identity," however, vary in length. Short poems like "why some people be mad at me sometimes" may have only one stanza.

As you read "Identity" (or any poem with stanzas), ask yourself, "What thought or idea is conveyed in each stanza?"

Literary Skills Understand speaker and first-person point of view.

Reading Skills Find units of meaning—stanzas.

Identity

Julio Noboa Polanco

© Sven Martson/The Image Works

Let them be as flowers,
always watered, fed, guarded, admired,
but harnessed to a pot of dirt.

I'd rather be a tall, ugly weed,
clinging on cliffs, like an eagle
wind-wavering above high, jagged rocks.

To have broken through the surface of stone
to live, to feel exposed to the madness
of the vast, eternal sky.

INTERPRET

The **speaker** of the poem uses **extended metaphors**—comparisons that are developed over several lines of text—in the first two **stanzas** (lines 1–6) to express a strong opinion. Why would he rather be a "tall, ugly weed" than a flower?

COMPARE & CONTRAST

Explain in your own words what the speaker dislikes about being a flower and what he likes about being a weed.

CONNECT

Would you rather be a weed or a flower as the speaker describes them? Explain.

To be swayed by the breezes of an ancient sea,
carrying my soul, my seed, beyond the mountains of time
or into the abyss of the bizarre.°

I'd rather be unseen, and if
then shunned° by everyone
than to be a pleasant-smelling flower,
growing in clusters in the fertile valley
where they're praised, handled, and plucked
by greedy, human hands.

I'd rather smell of musty, green stench°
than of sweet, fragrant lilac.
If I could stand alone, strong and free,
I'd rather be a tall, ugly weed.

---

12. abyss (ə·bis′) *n.:* deep crack in the earth's surface. **bizarre** (bi·zär′) adj. used as *n.:* weird; strange.
14. shunned (shund) *v.:* avoided.
19. stench (stench) *n.:* awful smell.

MEET THE WRITER

Julio Noboa Polanco (1949–) was born in the Bronx, a section of New York City, and now lives in San Antonio, Texas. His best-known poem, "Identity," was written when he was in eighth grade. He had just broken up with his girlfriend, an event that marked a turning point in the young poet's life. Polanco continued to write poetry for many years until he decided to focus on writing essays and articles. Since then, he has written regular columns for Texas newspapers, commenting on educational and cultural issues.

why some people be mad at me sometimes

Lucille Clifton

they ask me to remember
but they want me to remember
their memories
and i keep on remembering
mine.

INTERPRET

Keeping the title in mind, explain in your own words what you think is the most important message of this short poem.

ANALYZE

What do the speakers of the two poems have in common?

To learn about Lucille Clifton, read Meet the Writer on page 108.

Identity / why some people be mad at me sometimes

Reading Skills
Analyze stanzas.

Stanza Chart In many poems, **stanzas**—groupings of lines—function as paragraphs in prose do: They supply units of meaning. Analyze the stanzas in "Identity" and "why some people be mad at me sometimes" by filling in the chart below with what you think is the meaning of each stanza.

"Identity"
Stanza 1 (lines 1–3)
Stanza 2 (lines 4–6)
Stanza 3 (lines 7–12)
Stanza 4 (lines 13–18)
Stanza 5 (lines 19–22)
"why some people be mad at me sometimes"
Stanza 1 (lines 1–5)

Skills Review

Identity / why some people be mad at me sometimes

COMPREHENSION

Reading Comprehension Answer each question below.

Identity

1. What qualities does the speaker of the poem dislike about flowers?

___

___

___

2. What qualities of weeds does he or she like?

___

___

___

why some people be mad at me sometimes

3. What do "they" want the speaker of the poem to do?

___

___

___

4. What does the speaker of the poem do?

___

___

___

Before You Read

Madam C. J. Walker by Jim Haskins

LITERARY FOCUS: BIOGRAPHY AND THIRD-PERSON POINT OF VIEW

A **biography** is the story of a person's life told by someone else. Well-written biographies consist mainly of **facts** that can be proved. The events they describe have been carefully researched using reliable sources. However, biographers cannot learn everything about their subjects, so they often add inferences and opinions of their own. Biographers may guess what their subjects were thinking, for example, or state an opinion about the social conditions of the time period.

Since biographers have not generally participated in the events they describe, they write from the **third-person point of view.** They use such third-person pronouns as *he, she, they,* and *it.* As you read "Madam C. J. Walker," notice the biographer's point of view.

READING SKILLS: FINDING THE MAIN IDEA

The **main idea** is the most important idea in a work of nonfiction. Sometimes the writer states the main idea directly. In an essay arguing a particular position, for example, the writer will usually state the main idea in the opening paragraph. At other times the writer only suggests the main idea. In a biography the reader generally has to **infer,** or make an educated guess about, the main idea. These tips can help you find the main idea.

- Look for important details or key events.
- Think about the point these details or events make.
- State the main idea in your own words.

Be aware that there may be more than one main idea in a work of nonfiction, especially in a biography like "Madame C. J. Walker."

Literary Skills Understand biography and third-person point of view.

Reading Skills Find the main idea.

Vocabulary Skills Clarify word meanings using context clues.

VOCABULARY DEVELOPMENT

PREVIEW SELECTION VOCABULARY

Get to know these words before you read "Madam C. J. Walker":

provisions (prə·vizh′ənz) *n.:* arrangements made to meet a person's needs.

After the Civil War few provisions were made to help freed slaves survive.

embarked (em·bärkd′) *v.:* started something new.

When her husband lost interest, Madame C. J. Walker embarked in business by herself.

institutions (in′stə·to͞o′shənz) *n.:* large organizations with a particular purpose, such as churches.

Institutions in the black community were the best outlets for her products.

recruited (ri·kro͞ot′id) *v.:* hired.

Wanting to help black women, Madame C. J. Walker recruited many to work in sales.

expectations (ek′spek·tā′shənz) *v.:* beliefs or hopes that something will happen.

Madame C. J. Walker always had high expectations for her own success.

CLARIFYING WORD MEANINGS: CONTEXT CLUES

You can often figure out what an unfamiliar word means from the context in which it is used. Context clues can be in the form of *definitions, examples, restatements,* and *contrast words.* Here are examples of how each type of context clue can help clarify the meaning of an unfamiliar word. The context clues are in italics.

Definition	An **aggressive** person, *someone who tends to fight a lot,* doesn't make the best friend.
Example	If you *continually argue with the coach,* she might begin to think you're too **aggressive.**
Restatement	You are too **aggressive.** You *constantly disrupt* our class discussions.
Contrast	Our debate team is **aggressive,** *unlike* our team coach, who *never gets into arguments.*

Madam C. J. Walker

Jim Haskins

The Granger Collection, New York

Sarah B. Walker (1867–1919), American businesswoman, also known as Madam C. J. Walker.

IDENTIFY

Underline Madam C. J. Walker's achievements. What is unusual about these achievements?

Madam C. J. Walker was the first American woman to earn a million dollars. There were American women millionaires before her time, but they had inherited their wealth, either from their husbands or from their families. Madam Walker was the first woman to earn her fortune by setting up her own business and proving that women could be financially independent of men. The company she started in the early 1900s is still in operation today.

Madam C. J. Walker was born Sarah Breedlove on December 23, 1867. She grew up in the South under very racist conditions. Her parents, Owen and Minerva Breedlove, had been slaves until President Abraham Lincoln's Emancipation Proclamation and the Union victory in the Civil War had freed the slaves.

After the war, few **provisions** were made to help former slaves become independent. They did not receive money to help them get started in their new lives. They were uneducated, they had few skills except the ability to grow crops, and many were unaware of what freedom meant. Like the majority of former slaves, the Breedloves remained on the Burney family plantation in Delta, Louisiana. They had little choice but to stay on the same land where they had been slaves, only now they were sharecroppers.

Sharecroppers farm land for a landowner. In return, they receive a place to live and part of the crop. But since they must buy what they cannot grow from the landowner, when they harvest the crop they find themselves owing whatever is their share to the landowner anyway.

The Breedloves sharecropped cotton. Like her brothers and sisters, Sarah was working in the cotton fields by the time she was six. By the time she was seven, both her parents were dead, and she moved in with her older sister, Louvenia. A few years later, they moved across the river to Vicksburg, Mississippi.

Sarah had little schooling. Like other sharecroppers' children, she had a chance to go to school only when there were no crops to be planted or harvested, which totaled about four months out of the year. She also had little happiness in her childhood. Not only was she an orphan, but she also suffered at the hands of her sister's cruel

IDENTIFY

In lines 10–15, underline Madam C. J. Walker's name at birth, and circle her date of birth. Where did she grow up?

VOCABULARY

provisions (prə·vizh′ənz) *n.:* arrangements made to meet a person's needs.

Underline in line 18 an example of a provision that was not met.

IDENTIFY

Circle three difficulties freed slaves faced after the Civil War (lines 19–21).

IDENTIFY

Number the four **facts** that you learn about Sarah in lines 31–36.

INFER

What do the details in lines 57–65 tell you about Sarah's **character**?

IDENTIFY

Circle the pronoun in line 58 that indicates this **biography** is told from the **third-person point of view.**

CAUSE & EFFECT

Re-read lines 66–69. What problem does Sarah experience after she moves to St. Louis? Underline the likely cause of this problem.

husband. Sarah was just fourteen when she married a man named McWilliams to get away from her sister's household.

By the time Sarah got married, conditions in the South for blacks were actually worse than they had been during slavery. This was the time when Jim Crow laws were passed, segregating southern blacks from whites in nearly every area of life. It was the time when white supremacy groups like the Ku Klux Klan achieved their greatest power, and lynchings of blacks were common.

Sarah and her husband lived with the terror of being black as best they could. In 1885 their daughter, Lelia, was born, and her parents dreamed of making a better life for their little girl. Then, when Lelia was two, McWilliams was killed by a lynch mob.

Sarah was a widow at the age of twenty, and the sole support of a two-year-old daughter. She took in laundry to earn a living and was determined to leave the South. With Lelia, she made her way up the Mississippi River and settled in St. Louis, where she worked fourteen hours a day doing other people's laundry. She enrolled Lelia in the St. Louis public schools and was pleased that her daughter would get the education that had been denied to her. But she wanted more for her daughter and for herself.

Not long after they moved to St. Louis, Sarah McWilliams realized that her hair was falling out. She did not know why, but it is likely that the practice of braiding her hair too tightly was part of the cause. At the time, few hair-care products were available for black women. The ideal was straight, "white," hair, and to achieve this effect black women divided their hair into sections, wrapped string tightly around each section, and then twisted them. When the hair was later combed out, it was straighter. But this procedure pulled on the scalp and caused the hair to fall out.

Sarah was not the only black woman to suffer from hair loss. But she was one who refused to accept the idea that there was nothing she could do about it. For years she tried every hair-care product available. But nothing worked.

Then one night she had a dream. As she told the story many years later, in her dream "a black man appeared to me and told me what to mix up for my hair. Some of the remedy was grown in Africa, but I sent for it, mixed it, put it on my scalp, and in a few weeks my hair was coming in faster than it had ever fallen out." Sarah never publicly revealed the formula of her mixture.

Sarah's friends remarked on what a full and healthy head of hair she had, and she gave some of her mixture to them. It worked on them, too, so she decided to sell it. She later said that she started her "Hair Grower" business with an investment of $1.50.

She had not been in business long when she received word that a brother who lived in Denver, Colorado, had died, leaving a wife and daughters. Her own daughter, Lelia, was attending Knoxville College, a private black college in Tennessee, and did not need her around all the time. Sarah decided to go to Denver to live with her sister-in-law and nieces.

In Denver, Sarah began to sell her special hair-care product and did well. But she realized she needed to advertise to get more customers. Six months after arriving in Denver, she married C. J. Walker, a newspaperman who knew a lot about selling by mail order. With his help, she began to advertise her product, first in black newspapers across the state and later in black newpapers nationwide, and to make more money.

RETELL

Pause at line 92. Explain how Madam C. J. Walker first got started in business.

INFER

Pause at line 99. Why do you think Madam C. J. Walker decided to move to Denver? What does this decision tell you about her **character**?

Notes

VOCABULARY

embarked (em·bärkd′) *v.:* started something new.

CLARIFY

Pause at line 115. Why did Madam C. J. Walker go into business by herself?

INFER

Affectation (line 119) means "behavior or attitude deliberately chosen to impress others." Why do you think Madam C. J. Walker thought this name would help her business?

A'Lelia Bundles

But soon her marriage was in trouble. As Sarah Walker later said of her husband, "I had business disagreements with him, for when we began to make ten dollars a day, he thought that amount was enough and that I should be satisfied. But I was convinced that my hair preparations would fill a long-felt want, and when we found it impossible to agree, due to his narrowness of vision, I **embarked** in business for myself."

In addition to helping her learn about advertising, her marriage gave Sarah Breedlove McWilliams Walker the name she would use for the rest of her life—Madam C. J. Walker. The "Madam" part was an affectation, but Sarah liked the way it sounded. She thought it would be good for her business. By 1906 her business was so good that she was able to stop doing laundry for a living and devote all her time to her hair-care company. Her products by this time included "Wonderful Hair Grower," "Glossine" hair oil, "Temple Grower," and "Tetter Salve" for the scalp.

Madam Walker was very proud of being a woman, and she was convinced that she could make it in the business world without the help of men. Almost from the start she determined that her business would be run by women. In 1906 she put her twenty-one-year-old daughter, Lelia, in charge of her growing mail-order business. She herself started traveling throughout the South and East selling her preparations and teaching her methods of hair care. She was so successful that two years later she and Lelia moved to Pittsburgh, Pennsylvania, and started Lelia College, which taught the Walker System of hair care.

Once again, Lelia ran the business while her mother traveled thousands of miles to spread the word. Madam Walker realized that the normal outlets for her products—white department stores and pharmacies—were not open to her. These stores would not stock black products because they did not want black customers. In addition to advertising, mostly in black newspapers, Madam Walker had to depend on the **institutions** in the black communities, the black churches, and the black women's clubs.

Madam Walker's lectures on hair culture were widely attended. She was an excellent speaker and a commanding woman, nearly six feet tall, who was always beautifully dressed and coiffed. She made a lasting impression wherever she went.

Her travels, and her personality, brought her into contact with many important black people. She joined the National Association of Colored Women and through that organization met the educator Mary McLeod Bethune. She also met Ida B. Wells-Barnett, who worked for the right of women to vote, and against lynching in the South. She formed friendships with these women, who helped her spread the word about her business.

Although she lacked the formal education that most of these women had, Madam Walker never felt ashamed of

IDENTIFY

Pause at line 145. What did Madam C. J. Walker do to make her business a success? What obstacles did she have to overcome in building her business?

VOCABULARY

institutions (in′stə·to͞o′shənz) *n.:* large organizations with a particular purpose.

Circle two examples of institutions.

VISUALIZE

Underline details in lines 146–150 that help you picture Madam C. J. Walker. (*Coiffed* means that her hair was carefully styled.)

INTERPRET

Based on the details in lines 151–164, what is your impression of Madam C. J. Walker?

her shortcomings in that area. She taught herself as much as she could and was not afraid to ask someone to define a word she did not know or explain something she did not understand.

There were other black hair-care companies in business at this time. A couple of companies were owned by whites. But they stressed hair straightening. Madam Walker emphasized hair care. Most of the products she developed were aimed at producing healthy hair, not straight hair. She did design a steel comb with teeth spaced far enough apart to go through thick hair, but its main purpose was not hair straightening.

Madam Walker also wanted black women to go into business. Why should they toil over hot laundry tubs and clean white people's houses when they could be in business for themselves? Helping other black women also helped the Walker Company, and with this goal in mind Madam Walker **recruited** and trained scores of women to use and sell Walker products. Many of them set up salons in their own homes. Others traveled door-to-door selling Walker products and demonstrating the Walker System. Madam Walker insisted that her agents sign contracts promising to abide by her strict standards of personal hygiene—long before various states passed similar laws for workers in the cosmetics field. By 1910 the Walker Company had trained around 5,000 black female agents, not just in the United States but in England, France, Italy, and the West Indies. The company itself was taking in $1,000 a day, seven days a week.

That same year, Madam Walker's travels took her to Indianapolis, Indiana, a city that impressed her so much that she decided to move her headquarters there. She put a man in charge of her operations, which was a departure

COMPARE & CONTRAST

Re-read lines 165–172. How were Madam C. J. Walker's products different from those of other black hair-care companies?

VOCABULARY

recruited (ri·kro͞ot′id) *v.:* hired.

INTERPRET

Pause at line 189. What business activities indicate that Madam C. J. Walker was ahead of her time?

from her usual philosophy, but Freeman B. Ransom was, in her opinion, an unusual man.

She had met him in her travels when he was working as a train porter summers and during school vacations, while working his way through Columbia University Law School. He impressed her with his ambition and with his vision of progress for blacks. When he finished school, she put him in charge of her Indianapolis headquarters.

In 1913 Lelia moved from Pittsburgh to New York to expand the Walker Company's East Coast operations. Madam Walker built a lavish town house in Harlem at 108–110 West 136th Street and installed a completely equipped beauty parlor.

Lelia had become an astute businesswoman herself, although she did not have the drive of her mother. Lelia, who changed her name to A'Lelia, liked to enjoy the fruits of their success. The Walker town house soon became the "in" place for parties in Harlem, attended by wealthy and artistic people, black and white.

Madam Walker also enjoyed spending the money she made. In 1917 she built a $250,000 mansion on the Hudson River in upstate New York. She hired the black architect Vertner Tandy to design it and named it Villa Lewaro. She drove around in an electric car, dressed in the finest clothing, and was said to have spent $7,000 on jewelry in a single afternoon.

Madam Walker also gave generously to charity. She had a strong interest in education and took time out of her busy schedule to be tutored by Booker T. Washington, founder of Tuskegee Institute in Alabama. She became an avid reader of literature and American history. She encouraged her friend Mary McLeod Bethune and later gave money to Mrs. Bethune to establish her Daytona Normal

COMPARE & CONTRAST

Pause at line 201. Why did Freeman B. Ransom impress Madam C. J. Walker? How are his qualities similar to those of Madam C. J. Walker? How are they different?

INFER

Re-read lines 213–231. What point is the biographer making about Madam C. J. Walker?

EVALUATE

Madam C. J. Walker gave generously to charity both during her lifetime (lines 220–231) and, through bequests—money left in a will—after her death (lines 244–252). What do these **facts** add to your impression of her **character**?

CLARIFY

How did A'Lelia fulfill one of Madam C. J. Walker's dreams (lines 253–259)?

and Industrial Institute for Negro Girls in Daytona, Florida. When the National Association of Colored Women decided to pay off the mortgage on the home of the late black abolitionist Frederick Douglass, Madam Walker made the largest single contribution.

Madam Walker did not have much of a private life. She spent her time thinking of new ways to increase her business. The friends she had were people who could help her.

By 1917 the years of traveling and overwork began to take their toll on her. She developed high blood pressure, and in 1918 her doctors warned her that she had to slow down. She turned over her responsibilities in the business to her daughter, to Freeman B. Ransom, and to other trusted associates, and retired to her mansion, Villa Lewaro. There, she tried to relax, but her mind was always on her business. She died quietly of kidney failure resulting from hypertension[1] in May 1919.

In her will, Madam Walker left the bulk of her estate and the business to her daughter, A'Lelia. But she also provided generously for a variety of educational institutions run by black women, including $5,000 to Dr. Bethune's school. She established a trust fund for an industrial and mission school in West Africa and provided bequests to Negro orphanages, old people's homes, and Negro YWCA branches. In addition, she made bequests to many friends and employees.

Also in her will, Madam Walker insisted that the Madam C. J. Walker Company always be headed by a woman, and her wishes were carried out. Her daughter, A'Lelia, became president of the company after her death and presided at the dedication of the new company headquarters in Indianapolis in 1927, fulfilling a long-held dream of her mother's.

1. **hypertension** (hī′pər·ten′shən) *n.:* abnormally high blood pressure.

Times have changed greatly since Madam C. J. Walker made her millions. Drugstores and department stores owned by both whites and blacks now stock hair- and skin-care products for black women. Many more companies, white and black, manufacture such products. In the midst of all that competition, the Walker Company is not as active as it once was, although it still sells some of the products Madam developed. The Walker Building is being renovated as part of the rejuvenation[2] of downtown Indianapolis. Now called the Madam Walker Urban Life Center, it houses professional offices and a cultural center.

Madam C. J. Walker, the daughter of former slaves, with little education, overcame the barriers of being black and a woman and succeeded beyond everyone's **expectations** but her own.

FLUENCY

Read the boxed passage silently, and think about how the tone differs in the two paragraphs. Then, read the passage aloud. Can you change your voice to reflect the tone in each paragraph?

EVALUATE

What do you think is Madam C. J. Walker's legacy? What message does her life story have for people today?

MEET THE WRITER

Jim Haskins (1941–2005) is the author of over one hundred books and is well-known for his biographies of influential African Americans. Haskins has chronicled the lives of singer Stevie Wonder, comedian Bill Cosby, Supreme Court Justice Thurgood Marshall and army general and statesman Colin Powell. Haskins grew up in Demopolis, Alabama, in a house full of children. He went to high school in Boston, Massachusetts, and to college at Alabama State University in Montgomery during the historic bus boycott by African Americans. This boycott was sparked by Rosa Parks's now-famous refusal to give up her seat to a white man. Years later Haskins met Rosa Parks when he worked with her on her autobiography for young adults, *Rosa Parks: My Story.* Always surrounded by people when he was young, the writer says that books gave him privacy by allowing him to escape into other worlds.

VOCABULARY

expectations (ek′spek·tā′shənz) *v.:* beliefs or hopes that something will happen.

2. **rejuvenation** (ri·jo͞o′və·nā′shən) *n.:* restoration; renewal.

Madam C. J. Walker

Literary Skills Analyze a biography.

Reading Skills Find the main idea.

Main Idea Chart In a biography the main idea often has to do with the subject's **character** or place in history. Jot down key details from "Madam C. J. Walker" in the chart below. Then, in the space provided, describe the main idea the biographer presents about his subject.

Subject: Madame C. J. Walker
Detail ↓
Detail ↓
Detail ↓
Detail ↓
Detail ↓
Main Idea

Madam C. J. Walker

VOCABULARY AND COMPREHENSION

A. Clarifying Word Meanings: Context Clues Circle the context clues that help you figure out the meaning of each boldface word.

provisions
embarked
institutions
recruited
expectations

1. When the hurricane hit, **expectations** were that aid would be prompt—that is, the people looked forward to a rapid response from their government.
2. Instead, residents of the island discovered no **provisions** had been made for their safety. There were no plans for providing transportation, housing, or food.
3. The **institutions,** or public organizations, that should have helped failed in their duty to the people they were expected to serve.
4. Officials should have **embarked** on a massive rescue mission; instead, they hesitated, unable to decide what to do.
5. Finally, rescue workers were **recruited.** Many people were hired to supply food, clothing, and temporary shelter and to begin rebuilding the damaged homes.

B. Reading Comprehension Answer each question below.

1. What kind of childhood did Madam C. J. Walker have? ____________

____

2. What made her decide to move north? ____________

____

3. What kind of business did she establish? ____________

____

4. Whom did she mostly employ in her business? ____________

____

Vocabulary Skills
Clarify word meanings by using context clues.

Collection 5

Worlds of Words: Prose and Poetry

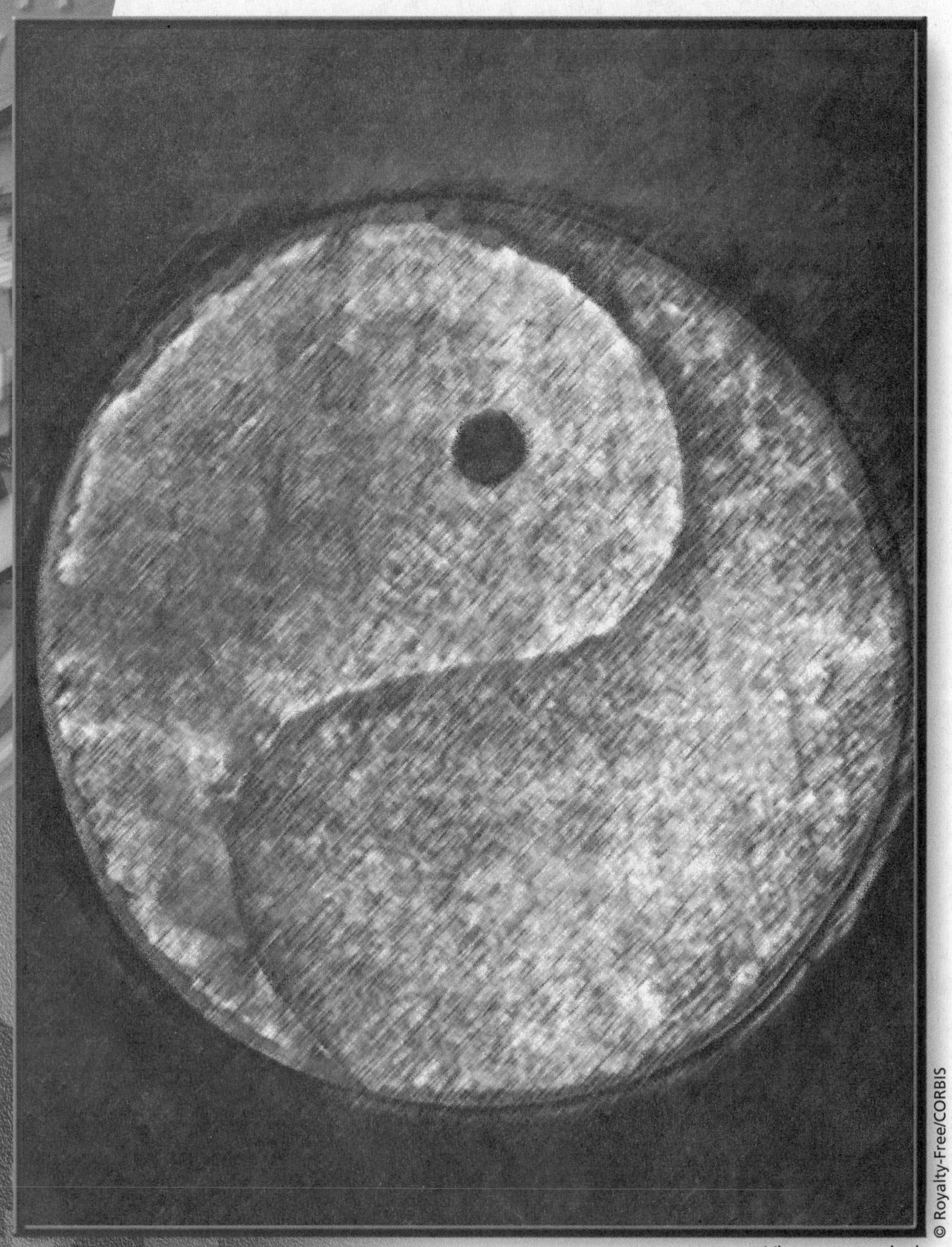

© Royalty-Free/CORBIS

Yin-yang symbol.

Academic Vocabulary for Collection 5

These are the terms you should know
as you read and analyze the selections in this collection.

Prose Writing that isn't poetry. Prose is generally divided into **fiction,** which consists of made-up stories, and **nonfiction,** which relates facts about real people, places, things, and events.

Novel A long work of fiction. Novels are much longer than **short stories.** Short stories usually feature one main character and his or her conflict. Novels may feature several main characters and several intertwining plots, conflicts, and themes.

Essay A work of nonfiction that examines a single topic. Some essays are personal and express the writer's feelings about a subject. Other essays are more **formal** and treat a subject in a serious, impersonal way.

• • •

Poetry A kind of rhythmic, compressed language that uses figures of speech and images that appeal to our emotions and imaginations.

Stanzas Groups of lines in a poem. Each stanza usually expresses a unit of thought, much as a paragraph does in a work of prose.

Rhythm A musical quality produced by the repetition of stressed and unstressed syllables or by the repetition of certain other sound patterns. A regular pattern of stressed and unstressed syllables is called **meter.**

Rhyme The repetition of accented vowel sounds and all sounds following them in words close together in a poem ("Once upon a midnight dreary, while I pondered, weak and weary").

Figure of Speech A word or phrase that describes one thing in terms of something very different. A figure of speech is not literally true. There are two common figures of speech: **similes,** which make a comparison using words such as *like* or *as* ("My heart is like a singing bird"), and **metaphors,** which make a comparison without using words such as *like* or *as* ("The road was a ribbon of moonlight").

How the Alvarez Girl Found Her Magic by Julia Alvarez

LITERARY FOCUS: FORMS OF PROSE—ESSAY

Essays are works of nonfiction prose that examine a single topic. Essays can contain both subjective (personal) details and objective (factual) details. **Subjective** details express the writer's personal feelings, thoughts, opinions, and judgments. **Objective** details, on the other hand, present facts in an unbiased manner. Writers sometimes combine subjective and objective details within the same essay.

Which of these passages contains subjective details? Which contains objective details?

Passage	Point of View
A warehouse burned to the ground Thursday morning. Investigators say the fire was caused by a short in the electrical wiring.	Subjective ☐ Objective ☐
Although some would disagree with me, I have to say that science writing is the most rewarding career a person could choose.	Subjective ☐ Objective ☐

Literary Skills Understand forms of prose: the essay; understand objective and subjective points of view.

Reading Skills Find the main idea.

Vocabulary Skills Clarify word meanings through synonyms.

READING SKILLS: DISCOVERING THE MAIN IDEA

The **main idea** is the idea that is central to the entire essay, not to part of it. Sometimes the main idea is stated directly in an essay; most of the time the main idea is **implied,** or suggested. When a main idea is not stated directly, you must look at all the key details in the essay and **infer,** or guess at, the main idea that the writer wants to share with you.

Use these tips to help you infer the main idea.

- Identify the important details in the essay.
- Think about the idea that all the details point to.
- State the main idea in your own words.

VOCABULARY DEVELOPMENT

PREVIEW SELECTION VOCABULARY

Preview the following words before you read "How the Alvarez Girl Found Her Magic."

bland (bland) *adj.:* dull; tasteless.

The stories about Dick and Jane seemed bland to Julia.

ruthless (ro͞oth′lis) *adj.:* having no regard for the rights of others; pitiless; cruel.

The dictator was ruthless in his efforts to take control of his country.

mesmerized (mez′mər·īzd′) *v.:* fascinated; hypnotized; held spellbound.

The stories mesmerized Julia.

tormented (tôr·ment′id) *v.:* tortured; annoyed; teased.

The boys tormented Julia on the playground because she spoke English with an accent.

transform (trans·fôrm′) *v.:* change from one form or function to another; convert.

The stories were so powerful they could transform the king.

CLARIFYING WORD MEANINGS: USING SYNONYMS

Synonyms are words that have the same or nearly the same meaning. You can clarify (or "make clear") the meaning of some words by thinking about their synonyms. Some synonyms have very important differences in meaning, while some synonyms mean pretty much the same thing. Each sentence below uses the word *bland.* Which synonym listed in parentheses in sentence l could be substituted for *bland*? Which synonym could be substituted for *bland* in sentence 2?

1. Julia found the Dick and Jane stories *bland* (synonyms: dull; tasteless).
2. Food without salt is *bland* (synonyms: dull; tasteless).

How the Alvarez Girl Found Her Magic

Julia Alvarez

BACKGROUND: Literature and Social Studies

The Dominican Republic is a country located on the island of Hispaniola, in the Caribbean Sea. The explorer Christopher Columbus landed on Hispaniola in 1492. The Dominican Republic has been ruled mostly by dictators or by other countries throughout its history. In 1930, the dictator Rafael Leonidas Trujillo Molina seized power. He was assassinated in 1961, one year after Julia Alvarez and her family were forced to leave the country.

VOCABULARY

bland (bland) *adj.:* dull; tasteless.

INFER

Dick and Jane are characters in elementary school readers. Dick and Jane live in a pretty town in the United States with Spot and Puff, a dog and cat. Tarantulas (line 11) are poisonous spiders. Why do you think Alvarez found the readers bland, or dull?

Perhaps you think that because I became a writer, I was one of those born bookworms who kept a diary and read Cervantes[1] by the time she was nine. I'm afraid I was definitely in the non-reading tradition of my family. I didn't care much for books. In part it was that I was surrounded by non-readers; there weren't many books around. At the American school where I was sent in hopes that it might turn me into a well-behaved young lady who spoke English, I was introduced to books: Dick and Jane, and their tame little pets Spot and Puff. Just that morning we had trapped tarantulas in the yard. Believe me, the Dick-and-Jane readers seemed **bland** in contrast to the world I was living in.

1. **Miguel de Cervantes** (1547–1616): Spanish writer; author of the great novel *Don Quixote.*

Julia Alvarez.

Besides, these books were written in that impossible marbles-in-your-mouth language of English. In my first self-motivated piece of writing, I scratched out a note for my teacher, a note that eventually found its way home to my mother. "Dear Mrs. Brown," my note read, "I love you very much. But why should I read when I can have fun?"

Although I was not a lover of the written word, I loved a good story or a catchy rhyme or the rhythmic lyrics of a merengue.[2] I just didn't think of these treasures as anything I'd find between the covers of a book. I was growing up in the '50s on a little island in the Caribbean, a basically oral culture where the most interesting information was passed around by word of mouth. I was also growing up in a **ruthless** dictatorship within which key information could *not* be written down. So, I never trusted books as places

2. **merengue** (mə·reŋ′gā) *n.:* rural folk dance popular in the Dominican Republic and Haiti.

Notes

IDENTIFY

In lines 19–30, underline the **subjective** details. Circle the **objective** details. Remember that *subjective* means "personal; resulting from feelings" and that *objective* means "real; actual; factual; without bias."

VOCABULARY

ruthless (ro͞oth′lis) *adj.:* having no regard for the rights of others; pitiless; cruel.

where I could find out anything I really needed to know. Instead I went to the people around me to find out the things I wanted to find out about.

But then I *read* my first book, read in the sense of being carried away by a narrative to a world I had not known before. It was *A Thousand and One Nights,* and it was given to me by a maiden aunt who read books and knew Latin and had not married by the time she was an old lady of 26. *A Thousand and One Nights* was the story of a young girl who lived in a kingdom where the sultan was killing all the women. This young girl's father kept her hidden away in his library. There, she spent the day reading books and learning all the stories in the world. Finally, this young girl volunteered to go to the sultan and try to save all the women in her kingdom. For 1,001 nights, she told the sultan story after story she had read in the books in her father's library. Ali Baba and the 40 thieves. Sinbad the sailor. Aladdin and his magic lamp. The merchant and the genie. Wonderful stories that **mesmerized** me as well as the sultan. In fact, he was so happy with this young storyteller that he spared her life and stopped killing women altogether. He also made her the queen of his kingdom.

Wow! I was impressed. I hadn't known stories had this kind of power. They could save lives. Reading could lead to becoming a queen. I became curious about books, books with bright, colorful pictures that were not part of school, books that began with a smart girl about to do something exciting—like Scheherazade[3] in *A Thousand and One Nights.*

Looking back, it strikes me as curious that this was the book that made the biggest impression on me as a young child. Here we were living in a dictatorship, surrounded by

---

3. **Scheherazade** (shə·her′ə·zäd′): name of the girl who tells the enchanting stories to the sultan.

COMPARE & CONTRAST

How is the young Julia's attitude about women and marriage (lines 34–36) different from the attitude of most people in the United States today?

IDENTIFY

Underline the detail that tells you why the story is called *A Thousand and One Nights* (lines 36–44).

VOCABULARY

mesmerized (mez′mər·īzd′) *v.:* fascinated; hypnotized; held spellbound.

ANALYZE

Re-read lines 50–55. Underline a sentence that you think states the **main idea** of this paragraph.

secret police and disappearances. It makes me wonder if part of my affection for the young girl of *A Thousand and One Nights* was that she had found a way to escape a situation not unlike the one we were in.

We left the Dominican Republic on August 6, 1960. My father had become involved in a plot against the dictator, and the secret police were on his trail. Overnight we lost everything: a homeland, an extended family, a culture and, most important, the language I felt at home in. The classroom English I had learned at the American school had very little to do with the English being spoken on the streets and in the playgrounds of New York City. I could not understand most things the Americans were saying to me.

One thing I did understand: Boys at school chased me across the playground, calling me names, telling me to go back where I came from.

"No speak English," I lied, taking the easy way out, instead of being brave and speaking up like Scheherazade.

But my silence was only strategy. I knew where to go when the world was unfriendly: the portable homeland of the imagination. From Scheherazade, I had learned where the real power lay. I read and read and read. My teachers began to encourage me to write down the stories of where I had come from.

Looking back now, I can see that my path as a writer began in that playground. Somewhere inside, where we make promises to ourselves, I told myself I would learn English so well that Americans would sit up and notice. I told myself that one day I would express myself in a way that would make those boys feel bad they had **tormented** me. Yes, it was revenge that set me on the path to becoming

COMPARE & CONTRAST

Re-read lines 58–62. How is the situation of the girl in *A Thousand and One Nights* similar to the situation in which the Alvarez family is living?

INTERPRET

Underline the sentence that states the new **motivation,** or reason, Alvarez has discovered for reading (lines 78–80). Explain in your own words what Alvarez means by "the portable homeland of the imagination."

VOCABULARY

tormented (tôr·ment′id) *v.:* tortured; annoyed; teased.

VOCABULARY

transform (trans·fôrm′) *v.:* change from one form or function to another; convert.

INTERPRET

Re-read lines 92–96. What does Alvarez hope to do with her writing?

FLUENCY

Read the boxed passage aloud until you are able to express the writer's enthusiasm with your voice. Before you read aloud, underline the words that you want to emphasize.

ANALYZE

What point is Alvarez making in lines 103–108? State that **main idea** in your own words.

a writer. At some point, though, revenge turned into redemption.[4] Instead of pummeling[5] those boys with my success, I began to want to save them. I wanted to change those looks of hate and mistrust, to **transform** the sultan's face into the beautiful face of the reclining prince on the cover of my childhood storybook.

Where did I get the idea that stories could do that? That *I* could do that?

At the end of her 1,001-night ordeal, Scheherazade has not only saved herself and the women in her kingdom, but she has transformed the sultan from a cruel tyrant into a loving man by the power of her stories.

That first book not only made me a reader, it gave me a powerful model of what I might want to do with my life. Stories had power: to save a life, to transform a king, to redeem the past, to protect a country and to while away night after night with the enchantments of narrative. I wanted to learn how to use that magic.

4. redemption (ri·demp′shən) *n.:* saving from sin or error.
5. pummeling (pum′əl·iŋ) *v.* used as *n.:* beating or hitting with the fists.

MEET THE WRITER

Julia Alvarez (1950–) was born in New York City to immigrants from the Dominican Republic. Shortly after her birth, her family moved back to the Dominican Republic. When Alvarez was ten years old, her family fled again to the United States, this time permanently. Struggling to find a foothold in a new culture, Alvarez began to write. At first she found it odd to write down stories, because she comes from an oral storytelling tradition. However, it did not take her long to figure out that she had found a new kind of home in literature. Throughout high school and college, Alvarez worked feverishly on her craft. The author has published four novels, one of which, *In the Time of the Butterflies,* has been made into a movie. Alvarez is known for her vibrant, energetic descriptions of the Latino immigrant experience in the United States.

Notes

How the Alvarez Girl Found Her Magic

Reading Skills
Find the main idea.

Main Idea Chart Fill in the following chart with at least five key details from "How the Alvarez Girl Found Her Magic." Then, review those details and state in your own words the **main idea** of the essay. Be sure to consider the meaning of the essay's title in your statement of the main idea.

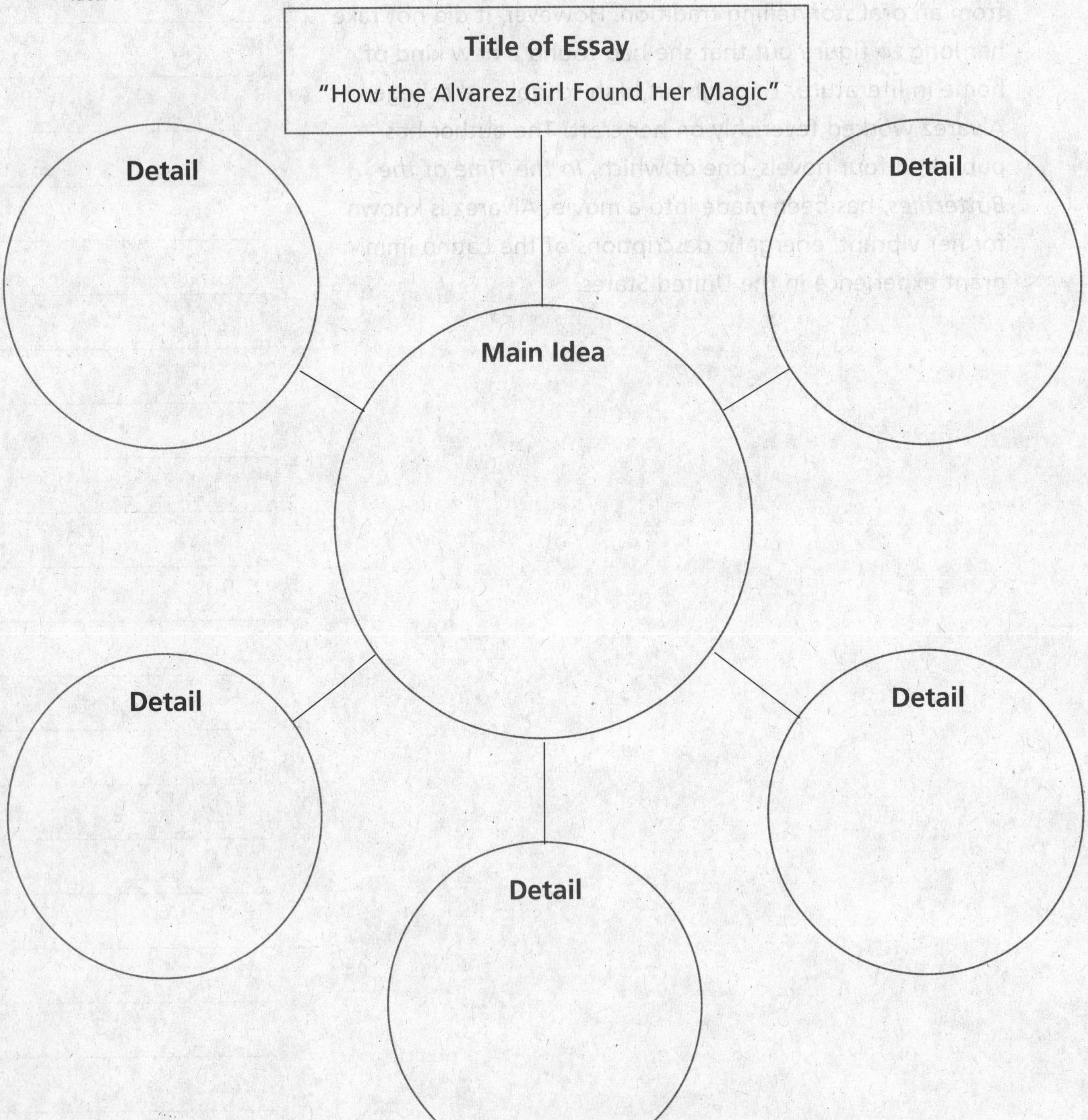

Title of Essay

"How the Alvarez Girl Found Her Magic"

Detail

Detail

Main Idea

Detail

Detail

Detail

How the Alvarez Girl Found Her Magic

VOCABULARY AND COMPREHENSION

A. Clarifying Word Meanings: Using Synonyms Fill in the blank following each sentence below with the Word Bank word that is a synonym for the word in italic.

Word Bank

bland
ruthless
mesmerized
tormented
transform

1. Juanita was *fascinated* by the beautiful ballet performance.

   ____

2. Harvey added hot sauce to the *tasteless* food at the diner.

   ____

3. Whenever her little sister *teased* the kitten, Carol stopped her.

   ____

4. Kindness can sometimes *change* a bully into a friend. ______________

5. The *cruel* movie villain had no pity for anyone. ______________

B. Comprehension Answer each question below.

1. What was life like in the Dominican Republic during Alvarez's childhood?

   ____

   ____

2. Why doesn't Alvarez like to read as a child?

   ____

   ____

3. How does the book *A Thousand and One Nights* turn Alvarez into a reader?

   ____

   ____

SKILLS FOCUS

Vocabulary Skills
Clarify word meanings through synonyms.

Before You Read

The Smartest Human I Ever Met: My Brother's Dog Shep

by Victor Villaseñor

LITERARY FOCUS: FORMS OF PROSE—ESSAY

An **essay** is a work of nonfiction prose that examines a single topic. Essays can be formal or informal. A **formal essay** is factual; its subject is usually something from history, science, politics, or literary criticism. A formal essay does not express the writer's personal feelings. An **informal essay** (sometimes called a personal essay), on the other hand, is about a personal experience and expresses the writer's feelings. Many personal essays, such as the one you are about to read, tell about incidents from the writer's own life.

The first thing that might strike you about the personal essay that follows is its unusual title. As you read, think about the **main idea** the writer wants to share with you.

READING SKILLS: COMPARISON AND CONTRAST

You compare and contrast things all the time without even thinking about it. When buying sneakers, for example, you may discover that although two pairs both lace up, are nylon, and are designed for running (points of comparison), you like the blue pair better than the white pair (point of contrast). This everyday skill can also help you in your reading. You can compare and contrast characters, events, settings, and ideas in all kinds of literary works.

Use the comparison-and-contrast strategy when you read "The Smartest Human I Ever Met: My Brother's Dog Shep." Note how the reactions of the characters are alike and different.

Literary Skills Understand forms of prose: essay.

Reading Skills Understand comparison and contrast.

Vocabulary Skills Use context clues.

VOCABULARY DEVELOPMENT

PREVIEW SELECTION VOCABULARY

Most of the words in this selection will probably be familiar to you, but here are three you may not yet know, even though context clues should help you understand what they mean.

internally (in·tur′nəl·lē) *adv.:* on the inside.

He seemed okay on the outside, but the accident left Joseph damaged internally.

level-headed (lev′əl hed′id) *adj.:* sensible.

Shep was usually a very smart and level-headed dog.

intercept (in′tər·sept′) *v.:* seize, stop, or meet along the way.

They said that Shep had gone to intercept Joseph's soul on its journey to heaven.

USING CONTEXT CLUES

When you come across an unfamiliar word in your reading, look for context clues that might help you figure out what the word means. Context clues are often found in the words and phrases surrounding an unfamiliar word. When you are looking for context clues, ask yourself the following questions:

- Is there a familiar word in the context that might help me figure out this difficult word?
- Is there a **synonym** (a word that means the same thing) in the word's context?
- Is there an **antonym** (a word that means the opposite) in the word's context?
- Does the meaning I guess at fit the sense of the sentence?

The Smartest Human I Ever Met: My Brother's Dog Shep

Victor Villaseñor

© Stan Osolinski/Oxford Scientific/PictureQuest

IDENTIFY

Circle what you learn about the author in the first paragraph, and draw one line under what you learn about his brother. Draw two lines under what you learn about the doctor.

VOCABULARY

internally (in·tur′nəl·lē) *adv.:* on the inside.

From "The Smartest Human I Ever Met: My Brother's Dog Shep" from *Walking Stars: Stories of Magic and Power* by Victor Villaseñor. Copyright © 1994 by Victor Villaseñor. Reproduced by permission of the **University of Houston & Arte Publico Press, c/o Margaret McBride Literary Agency.**

I was eight years old the night my brother's dog went crazy-*loco*[1] and started racing around the house, howling to the heavens. It was late at night, I was sound asleep, and my parents were down in San Diego at Scripps Hospital seeing my brother, who'd been sick for nearly a year. Joseph was sixteen years old, and he'd been hit in a football game and just bruised a little bit **internally,** but our local doctor—a drunk—hadn't attended to him correctly, and his liver was ruined and he developed leukemia.[2]

I could hear his dog Shep racing around the house, howling like crazy. Quickly, I got up to go see what was the matter. Shep was a very smart dog and didn't bark for just

1. *loco* (lō′kō) *adj.:* Spanish for "crazy."
2. **leukemia** (lo͞o·kē′mē·ə) *n.:* cancer of the blood-forming organs, resulting in an abnormal increase of white blood cells.

any reason. I pulled on my boots and got my BB gun and went out the front door. There was a half-moon and the stars were out by the thousands. We lived on a ranch in north San Diego County not far from the sea, and often animals came down the canyon behind our home on their way to the ocean. I looked around but saw nothing. As far as I could see, the dog was just chasing around after himself, acting crazy. I called him.

"Shep!" I shouted to him. "It's all right. Just come in. Nothing's the matter."

I wanted him to come to me so I could pet him and calm him down, but he wouldn't come near me. No, he just kept racing around and howling like he was *loco*. And Shep was a smart, **level-headed** dog, too. He was half coyote and half Shepherd and I'd been hunting and going horseback riding with him for as long as I could remember. He'd always listened to me before, so I couldn't figure out what was going on. He was acting really strange. He just kept racing around and around the house, howling something fierce.

My little sister Linda woke up and came outside to see what was the matter, too. Then, the Mexican-Indian woman, Rosa, who was taking care of us while my parents were gone, came outside to check on us.

"Is everything all right?" asked Rosa in Spanish. We all spoke Spanish on the ranch. English wasn't a language any of us spoke unless we went out the gates of the property.

"Yes," I said in Spanish, "it's just that our dog has gone crazy. He's barking at nothing and won't come to me."

"He's not barking at nothing," Rosa said to me. "He's barking because your brother is dying."

I was stunned. I didn't know what to think. "But my brother isn't dying," I said. "He's getting well. That's why my parents have him in the hospital."

PREDICT

Pause at line 31. Why do you think the dog is acting so strange?

VOCABULARY

level-headed (lev′əl hed′id) *adj.:* sensible.

EVALUATE

Pause at line 42. What do you think of the way Rosa breaks this news to the author?

EVALUATE

Pause at line 59. Do you think animals can know things that people don't know? Explain.

FLUENCY

Read the boxed passage aloud. Try to use your voice to express Emilio's gentleness at the beginning and the author's confusion and anger at the end.

COMPARE & CONTRAST

Read to the end of this page, and then tell how the author's interpretation of Shep's behavior differs from Rosa's and Emilio's.

Rosa's husband, Emilio, suddenly came out of the dark, and I now saw that several other of the farmhands were all sitting quietly under the huge pepper tree.

"Rosa is right," he said gently. "Your brother is dying. That's why his dog is going crazy; he loves your brother very much."

"Yes, he loves my brother, but, well," I stopped. I didn't know what to say. My parents had told my sister and me that they had the best doctors money could buy attending to my brother, and that he was getting well. I glanced from Emilio to Rosa and then back again. "But how can this dog know that my brother is dying? My brother is more than thirty miles away! You're wrong! You're wrong! You just don't know what you're talking about!"

"All right," said Emilio, putting his arm about his wife's shoulders, "have it your way. But understand, the soul knows no distance, and love speaks through the heart. And that dog is telling us of his heart breaking for your brother."

"No!" I yelled. "My brother isn't dying! Shep has got to stop howling!"

But no matter how much I yelled at him, Shep wouldn't stop. I began to cry, too. I was scared now, and my heart was breaking, just like Shep's.

The workmen never said a thing. They just sat there under the huge pepper tree, poking at the ground with sticks and being very quiet. Rosa finally took my sister and me back inside.

All that night, my brother's dog kept howling, and then, in the early morning, he suddenly stopped, just like that. When I went outside to see what had happened, I was told that he'd taken off for the hills.

My parents came home later that day and informed my sister and me that our brother Joseph had died. They said that the doctors had done all they could with their modern medicine, but still he was gone.

I could see that mother's whole face was swollen from crying when she went into the house. My father stayed outside with my sister and me. I wanted to tell my father that we'd found out about my brother's death the night before because of his dog, but I just didn't know how to say this without sounding stupid.

Later that day, I went to tell Emilio and Rosa that they were right, that my brother had died, but they said they already knew.

"We saw his dog take off this morning for the hills to **intercept** his soul," said Rosa.

I'll never forget the chills that went up and down my spine on hearing those words "to intercept his soul," and I got this powerful image of my brother's dog running up to the highest hilltop he could find and leaping into the sky to join with my brother's soul as it made its way to heaven.

We never saw my brother's dog after that. And when I asked Rosa and her husband what had happened to Shep,

INFER

Re-read lines 83–86. Why do you think the author decides he would sound stupid telling his father about Shep?

VOCABULARY

intercept (in'tər·sept') *v.:* seize, stop, or meet along the way.

How is this word used in sports?

EVALUATE

Do you think this photograph is a good illustration for the essay? Why or why not?

INFER

Re-read lines 105–110. Why do you think Rosa and Emilio return to Mexico?

COMPARE & CONTRAST

How is the father's attitude about Joseph's death different from Rosa's and Emilio's?

ANALYZE

What do you think is the author's **main idea** in this essay? Be sure to consider the essay's **title**.

they explained to me that he'd left his body up in the hills somewhere so he could travel to the other side of life with my brother, whom he'd loved very much. Animals, she'd explained to me, could do that at will, much easier than humans, because they hadn't learned how to talk and question yet, and love was still their basis for living life.

Shortly after that, Rosa and Emilio returned to Mexico. They left a couple of days after I told my father of the things that they'd told me about Shep and my brother. My dad got real angry and said, "Your mother and I got the finest doctor we could find for your brother, and no stupid old Indian beliefs are going to create doubt of my word!"

But, no matter how much my father raged and shouted, I still knew that I'd seen my brother's dog go crazy-*loco* with his love for my brother and then disappear the next day to never be seen again.

MEET THE WRITER

Victor Villaseñor (1940–) captured readers' attention with his bestselling book, *Rain of Gold,* an account of his parents' journey from Mexico to the United States. Villaseñor was born in Carlsbad, California. For years as a child, Villaseñor struggled in school. He felt insecure and shy about the difficulty he had with reading. Eventually, he was diagnosed with severe dyslexia, a condition that makes it difficult for someone to read. The doctors marveled that he ever learned to read at all. As a young man, Villaseñor traveled to Mexico and explored his homeland's culture and history. When he returned to California, he decided to celebrate Mexican and Mexican American culture through writing.

The Smartest Human I Ever Met: My Brother's Dog Shep

Comparison-and-Contrast Chart In "The Smartest Human I Ever Met: My Brother's Dog Shep," the characters all react in some way to Joseph's death. Fill in their reactions in the chart below. At the bottom, state what the characters' reactions have in common. Then, describe how their reactions are different.

Reading Skills
Compare and contrast.

Character	Reaction
Shep	
The author	
Rosa and Emilio	
The father	

How the reactions are similar: ______________________________

____

____

How the reactions are different: ______________________________

____

____

The Smartest Human I Ever Met: My Brother's Dog Shep

VOCABULARY AND COMPREHENSION

Word Bank

internally
level-headed
intercept

A. Using Context Clues In each of the following sentences, underline the words that contain context clues that point to the meaning of each italicized Word Bank word. Then, write the meaning of the Word Bank word.

1. Joseph was not injured on the outside; he was hurt *internally*.

____

2. Shep was usually *level-headed;* he was a very sane and sensible dog.

____

3. Shep wanted to *intercept* Joseph's soul on its journey; he wanted to meet Joseph's soul and join it on the way to Heaven.

____

B. Reading Comprehension Answer each question below.

1. How is Shep behaving at the beginning of the essay? ______________________________

____

2. How do Rosa and Emilio explain the dog's behavior? ______________________________

____

3. According to Rosa and Emilio, why does Shep leave for the hills?

____

____

Vocabulary Skills
Use context clues.

Before You Read

Dreams/Dream Variations by Langston Hughes

LITERARY FOCUS: FIGURES OF SPEECH

Have you ever thought of a poem as a rainbow? Langston Hughes did. He once wrote, "Poems are like rainbows: they escape you quickly." Comparisons like this—of things that seem very different—are called **figures of speech.** Poets use such imaginative comparisons to help us think about our world in a new way.

Two common figures of speech are similes and metaphors. **Similes** compare unlike things by using words such as *like* or *as*. Hughes's comparison of poems and rainbows is a simile because the comparison uses the word *like*. **Metaphors** compare unlike things without using a specific comparison word. The chart below provides a few examples of similes and metaphors.

Similes	Metaphors
The track star ran faster *than* a speeding bullet.	The track star was a bullet, speeding past the other racers.
Our neighbor's St. Bernard is *as* big *as* an elephant.	Our neighbor's St. Bernard is an elephant.

READING SKILLS: PUNCTUATION CLUES

When you read poetry, it is important to pay attention to punctuation. Follow these tips as you read "Dreams" and "Dream Variations."

- Make a full stop after periods and exclamation points. Pause at commas.
- Pause at ellipses (e·lip′sēz′)—three dots used to indicate a thought that is broken off.
- Look for sudden shifts in thought after dashes.
- Do not come to a full stop if a line does not end with punctuation. Continue reading until you come to a punctuation mark.

Literary Skills Understand similes and metaphors.

Reading Skills Use punctuation clues in poetry.

Dreams

Langston Hughes

INTERPRET

Underline the two metaphors in this poem.

INTERPRET

What kind of "dreams" do you think the speaker is referring to in this poem?

Hold fast to dreams
For if dreams die
Life is a broken-winged bird
That cannot fly.

Hold fast to dreams
For when dreams go
Life is a barren field
Frozen with snow.

© Rubberball/age fotostock

Dream Variations

Langston Hughes

To fling my arms wide
In some place of the sun,
To whirl and to dance
Till the white day is done.
Then rest at cool evening
Beneath a tall tree
While night comes on gently,
    Dark like me—
That is my dream!

To fling my arms wide
In the face of the sun,
Dance! Whirl! Whirl!
Till the quick day is done.
Rest at pale evening . . .
A tall, slim tree . . .
Night coming tenderly
    Black like me.

© Photo Lois Greenfield

IDENTIFY

The word *variation* in music means the repetition of a theme with some changes. Hughes uses these two stanzas to describe variations on a theme involving his dream. In each stanza, draw one line under what the speaker dreams of doing during the daytime. Then, draw two lines under what he dreams of doing at night.

IDENTIFY

Circle the two **similes** that describe night. Whom or what is the speaker comparing night to?

FLUENCY

Read the poem aloud. Pay close attention to punctuation clues to guide your reading.

Notes

MEET THE WRITER

Langston Hughes (1902–1967) was born in Joplin, Missouri, but lived most of his adult life in Harlem, in New York City. A writer from a young age, Hughes studied engineering during college to satisfy his father. Eventually, he made a break with his father and decided to pursue a writing career. While working as a busboy in a hotel restaurant, he left some of his poems at the poet Vachel Lindsay's table. Lindsay was impressed, and this was the start of Hughes's long, fruitful career as a writer. Hughes remains one of the most significant artists to come out of the Harlem Renaissance, a great flowering of African American writing and art during the 1920s. Best known as a powerful poet, he also wrote articles, shorts stories, and plays. His work is known for celebrating the lives—as well as the hopes and dreams—of African Americans.

Hughes says this about how, in the eighth grade, he began writing poetry:

"I was the Class Poet. . . . The day I was elected, I went home and wondered what I should write. Since we had eight teachers in our school, I thought there should be one verse for each teacher, with an especially good one for my favorite teacher, Miss Ethel Welsh. And since the teachers were to have eight verses, I felt the class should have eight, too. So my first poem was about the longest poem I ever wrote—sixteen verses, which were later cut down. In the first half of the poem, I said that our school had the finest teachers there ever were. And in the latter half, I said our class was the greatest class ever graduated. So at graduation, when I read the poem, naturally everybody applauded loudly. That was the way I began to write poetry."

Dreams/Dream Variations

Literary Skills
Analyze similes and metaphors.

Figures of Speech Figures of speech are imaginative comparisons of things that are basically not alike. There are two major types of figures of speech: the **simile,** which compares two things using words such as *like* or *as,* and the **metaphor,** which compares two things directly without using *like* or *as.* When you read a poem, it is important to interpret its figures of speech. Ask yourself, "What is the poet suggesting in these figures of speech? What feelings are evoked by the figures of speech?"

In the chart below in the first column, write out the metaphors and similes used in "Dreams" and "Dream Variations." In the second column, explain in your own words what you think each figure of speech means or suggests about the poet's feelings.

Figures of Speech	
"Dreams"	
1. Metaphor	**1. Interpretation**
2. Metaphor	**2. Interpretation**
"Dream Variations"	
1. Simile	**1. Interpretation**
2. Simile	**2. Interpretation**

Dreams/Dream Variations

COMPREHENSION

Reading Comprehension Answer each question below.

1. In "Dreams," the speaker compares a life without dreams to two things. What are they?

2. In your own words, describe what the speaker of "Dreams" thinks the world would be like without dreams.

3. In "Dream Variations," which do you think the speaker identifies with: the whirl of day or the gentleness of night? Explain.

4. In line 9 of "Dream Variations," the speaker says, "That is my dream!" What is this dream? Describe it using your own words.

Before You Read

A Poem for Langston Hughes

by Nikki Giovanni

LITERARY FOCUS: POETRY—RHYTHM AND RHYME

Like songs, most poems have rhythm. **Rhythm** in songs and poetry is created by repetition. Poems create rhythm by repeating various sound patterns, including refrains. Some poems create rhythm by using a regular pattern of stressed and unstressed syllables. We say that such poetry is written in **meter.**

Like most songs, many poems also use rhyme. **Rhyme** is the repetition of accented vowel sounds and all sounds following them in words close together: *writing* rhymes with *fighting; pale* rhymes with *hail; mister* rhymes with *sister.*

To help children remember them, and for fun, nursery rhymes use a great deal of rhythm and rhyme. In the example here the stressed syllables are marked **'** and the rhymes are underlined. (In case you are wondering, a "tuffet" is a tuft of grass; "curds and whey" are curdled, or soured, milk, which English children seemed to enjoy once upon a time.)

> Little Miss Muffet
> Sat on a tuffet,
> Eating her curds and whey.
> Along came a spider,
> Who sat down beside her,
> And frightened Miss Muffet away.

Read "A Poem for Langston Hughes" aloud to hear its rhymes and to feel its rhythm.

Literary Skills
Understand poetry; understand rhythm and rhyme.

A Poem for Langston Hughes

Nikki Giovanni

Carl Van Vechten photographer/the Van Vechten Trust, National Portrait Gallery, Smithsonian Institution/ Art Resource, NY

Langston Hughes, 1902–1967 (1932) by Carl Van Vechten.
Photograph, gelatin silver print, 14.1 x 21.4 cm. Gift of Prentiss Taylor.
National Portrait Gallery, Smithsonian Institution, Washington, DC.

COMPARE & CONTRAST

In lines 1–2, how are thoughts different from diamonds, oil, and gold? In lines 3–4, how are words different from weaving?

diamonds are mined . . . oil is discovered
gold is found . . . but thoughts are uncovered

wool is sheared . . . silk is spun
weaving is hard . . . but words are fun

highways span . . . bridges connect
country roads ramble . . . but i suspect

if i took a rainbow ride
i could be there by your side

metaphor has its point of view
allusion and illusion . . . too

meter . . . verse . . . classical . . . free
poems are what you do to me

let's look at this one more time
since i've put this rap to rhyme

when i take my rainbow ride
you'll be right there at my side

hey bop hey bop hey re re bop

MEET THE WRITER

Nikki Giovanni (1943–) was born in Knoxville, Tennessee, and comes from a long line of storytellers. Giovanni was especially influenced by her outspoken grandmother, who taught her to respect her African American heritage. As a college student in the 1960s, Giovanni became politically active. Her first books of poems were a response to the assassinations of civil-rights leaders Martin Luther King, Jr., Malcolm X, and Robert Kennedy. A powerful poet who speaks in many voices, Giovanni has published twenty collections of poetry, as well as essays and an autobiography. Her poems are known for being funny, wise, and a proud celebration of the African American tradition.

INTERPRET

What do you think the speaker means by "rainbow ride" in lines 7–8 and 15–16? (Hint: Look back at page 173 to see what Hughes once wrote about rainbows.)

FLUENCY/ANALYZE

Read the poem aloud to feel its **rhythm.** Notice the way strongly **stressed** syllables alternate with **unstressed** syllables. Then, put a ′ mark above each syllable that is strongly stressed.

INTERPRET

Why do you think Nikki Giovanni wanted to write a poem for Langston Hughes?

A Poem for Langston Hughes

Literary Skills Analyze poetry; analyze rhymes.

Rhyme List In the chart below, list all the rhyming words you can find in "A Poem for Langston Hughes." (It helps to read aloud when you're looking for rhymes.) Record the line numbers in the left-hand column and the rhyming words in the right-hand column. An example is provided for you.

Lines	Rhymes
1 and 2	discovered / uncovered
____ and ____	
____ and ____	
____ and ____	
____ and ____	
____ and ____	
____ and ____	
____ and ____	

A Poem for Langston Hughes

COMPREHENSION

Reading Comprehension Answer each question below.

1. In lines 3–4, how are "words" contrasted with the making of fabric?

2. Where will the rainbow take the speaker in lines 7 and 15?

3. Explain what you think the speaker is saying to Langston Hughes.

María in School from *Call Me María*

by Judith Ortiz Cofer

LITERARY FOCUS: FORMS OF PROSE—NOVEL

A **novel** is like a short story, only much longer. A novel has plot, setting, characters, point of view, and theme. Because a novel is long, it can have many characters and settings, a long, complicated plot, and even several subplots. Sometimes novels are told from more than one point of view; usually they have several themes.

"María in School" comes from the novel *Call Me María.* Most novels are written in prose (as opposed to poetry). *Call Me María,* however, is unusual: It combines prose, letters, and poems.

As you read "María in School," notice when the story is told in poetry and when it is told in prose. What do the poems and letters reveal about María and her English teacher?

READING SKILLS: MAKING INFERENCES

Writers don't tell you everything about their characters or about the events in their stories. That would spoil part of the fun of reading. Instead, you must make educated guesses, or **inferences,** about the story based on what the writers tell you and on your own life experience. As you read the excerpts that make up "Maria in School," note your inferences in the lines provided for each page of the story.

Literary Skills Understand forms of prose: novel.

Reading Skills Make inferences.

Vocabulary Skills Understand academic vocabulary.

VOCABULARY DEVELOPMENT

PREVIEW SELECTION VOCABULARY

Become familiar with the following terms before you begin "María in School."

declarative sentence: a sentence that makes a statement and ends with a period.

Mr. Golden asks the class to write declarative sentences.

imperative sentence: a sentence that gives a command or makes a request. An imperative sentence can end with a period or an exclamation point.

Read this story for tomorrow.

Get out of the way!

exclamatory sentence: a sentence that shows excitement or expresses strong feeling and ends with an exclamation point.

What a surprise it was to win!

UNDERSTANDING ACADEMIC VOCABULARY

Academic vocabulary refers to the terms you use in class to describe what you are studying. Academic vocabulary includes terms for broad subject areas, such as *language arts* or *mathematics,* as well as terms for specific elements of those subjects, such as *plot, characters,* and *style* or *addition, multiplication,* and *division.*

"María in School" includes the academic vocabulary listed above. These words are used in María's language arts class.

María in School

from Call Me María

Judith Ortiz Cofer

© Blend Images/Getty Images

VOCABULARY

declarative sentences: sentences that make a statement.

INFER

How can words be weapons or tools (lines 12–13)?

____

____

____

____

____

____

____

Golden English, Lessons One and Two

Lesson One:

"Everything I will say will be in **declarative sentences,**"
declares Mr. Golden.

There are more than one million words in the English language.
All the poems yet to be written are contained in the dictionary.
A poem is made by choosing the best words and putting them in the best order.
Words are weapons.
Words are tools.

Mr. Golden hands us a list. "Make declarative sentences from these words," Mr. Golden declares.

1. contains a universe
2. sand, concrete, horizon
3. I dream
4. blue, clear

My brain contains a universe.
I dream in Spanish of white sand beaches.
The ground I walk on is hard concrete,
but between the tall buildings, on a clear day,
I can still see the blue horizon.

"María, you are a poet," declares Mr. Golden.

Lesson Two:

Mr. Golden's eyes look tired today. He works as a singer in a band after school. He sang at assembly last week. His voice is like chocolate ice cream, like warm honey, like the golden light of the sun at the end of a winter's day.

"Class, these are **imperative sentences,**" says Mr. Golden.

Sit up straight, Raquel.
I will have to see you after school, Miguel.
Do not use such language in my classroom, Michelle.
Speak up, María.
Look at me, Chanté.
I demand silence in this room!

IDENTIFY

Who is writing these lines in italics (lines 20–24)? Underline the words the writer has used from Mr. Golden's list.

INFER

Underline the **similes**—comparisons between unlike things using the words *like* and *as*—in lines 27–31. How does María feel about Mr. Golden?

VOCABULARY

imperative sentences: sentences that give commands or make requests.

CONNECT

Most teachers use imperative sentences like the ones in lines 33–38. Write an imperative sentence you have heard in your classroom.

VOCABULARY

exclamatory sentence: sentence that shows excitement or expresses strong feeling.

INFER

Use declarative sentences to state the **main idea** of María's exclamatory sentences in lines 45–50.

INFER

María writes the sentences in lines 59–72 to show she knows what the subject of a sentence is. These sentences also tell you something about María. What do they reveal?

Exciting English: I Am a Poet! She Exclaimed

An **exclamatory sentence** is a strong emotion expressed in words. It begins with a capital letter and ends with an exclamation mark.

These are exclamatory sentences:
Mr. Golden is a musician!
Mr. Golden is a singer!
He thinks I am a good writer!
I wrote a poem!
He wrote music for my words!
He wants to sing it at the last assembly!

English Declaration: I Am the Subject of a Sentence

The subject of a sentence (underlined) is the part talked about.
"María, please read some of your poems to our class."
(I do not say this aloud: Oh no, Mr. Golden. I am afraid of what my classmates will think. I will be the subject of their insults.)
They will say:

The girl thinks she is an American.
María thinks she is good in English.
The girl can't write.
María speaks with an accent.
The poems have an accent
just like María's.
The poems are ugly.
She is ugly.
The teacher likes María.
María is the teacher's little pet.
He will say to the class, you are fools.

The class will laugh at María. They will
hate her
and her poem.

Find the subject in these sentences:

> *Their laughter*
> *is what María Alegre*[1] *fears,*
> *also their mockery*
> *of her still-thick accent,*
> *and their teasing*
> *about her poetry.*
> *She will turn into María Triste.*[2]
> *They are silent.*
> *They are waiting*
> *for her to read her poems.*
> *When she finishes reading*
> *she is amazed by what she hears.*
> *Applause!*
> *People are looking at her*
> *in a different way*

"In our society poets are often ignored," Mr. Golden says,
"and almost always poor. Yet they are never unemployed.
They are always at work, on the job,
looking for the truth.
María, you are a poet,"
Mr. Golden declares.

1. **alegre** (ä·lā'gre): Spanish for "happy."
2. **triste** (trēs'te): Spanish for "sad."

Notes

FLUENCY

Read the boxed poem silently, following the punctuation clues. Notice the one-word exclamation in line 86. Think about pauses and the words you will stress. Then, read the poem aloud a few times. How will you use your voice to express María's fear, suspense, surprise, and satisfaction?

IDENTIFY

According to Mr. Golden, what are poets looking for? Circle the answer.

INFER

Whom does María want to get revenge on and why (line 98)?

INTERPRET

The poet William Blake (1757–1827) wrote that he wished he could "see a world in a grain of sand / And a heaven in a wild flower." In your own words, explain what you think this means (line 106).

WORD STUDY

Odes (line 108) are long poems that are usually very serious and written in dignified language. Traditional odes are about lofty subjects, like beauty or truth or death. *Elementary* means "basic or simple."

English: I Am the Simple Subject

"After school, you and I will work together on your poems, María," Mr. Golden tells me after class. "There is an old saying that goes like this: Success is the best revenge."

"But, Mr. Golden, I do not yet have all the words I need to make poems."

"Take words where you find them, María. Do what you have to do to keep writing your stories and poems, María," Mr. Golden said, "just as I must do what I need to do to keep singing my songs.

"You have a gift; it is the gift of metaphor. María, go out and see if you can see the universe in a grain of sand. Here, take this." He hands me a book of poems in both Spanish and English. It is Pablo Neruda's *Elementary Odes, Odas elementales.*

I thank him in words, but answer him only in my thoughts: Mr. Golden *está bien,*[3] I believe you, since you declare that I am a poet, since it is **imperative**[4] that I be a poet, I will be a poet. But how do I become a poet? I live in a small world with few exclamation points and many question marks. Will I have to look for the universe in the cement and the concrete of my street? Will I have to look for metaphors in the plaster of the walls of our home, in the sad notes of my father's guitar late at night, in the sad golden eyes of my friend Uma? Will I have to find poetry in Whoopee's red sneakers and her Tarzan[5] song? Will I have to make poems out of common, ordinary things no one except me cares about? No one will want to read my poems, Mr. Golden.

3. **está bien** (es·tä′ bē′en): Spanish for "it is well," meaning something like "okay."
4. **imperative** (im·per′ə·tiv) *adj.:* absolutely necessary.
5. **Tarzan:** fictional hero who was raised by apes in the African jungle and is famous for his yell.

But later, sitting at my desk by the window where I can see the feet passing by, the shoes and the socks of people whose lives and secret dreams I try to imagine as I do my homework, I open the book and read Pablo Neruda's poem titles . . . and my heart jumps like a small frog inside my chest! Yes, I see that I will have to make poems out of blue socks, red tomatoes, yellow birds, onions, lemons, cats, artichokes, elephants, panthers; about things that work just fine, like a watch in the night (the minutes falling like leaves from a tree, says Pablo Neruda), and also about broken things. And maybe someone in my future, someone who needs to know if her world is too small to write about will hold my book in her hands and read my *poemas elementales,* and say yes, I can be a poet too.

Gracias,[6] Mr. Golden.

MEET THE WRITER

Judith Ortiz Cofer (1952–) draws inspiration for her writing from her childhood. When she was a young girl, her father took a job with the U.S. Navy, and her family moved from Hormigueros, Puerto Rico, to New Jersey. Cofer began her writing career focusing on poetry. She says that writing poems taught her the power of language. Although she calls poetry her obsession, she has written several novels, one of which, *The Line of the Sun,* was nominated for a Pulitzer Prize.

---

6. gracias (grä'sē·äs): Spanish for "thank you."

IDENTIFY

Underline one **simile** in lines 128–129 and two in lines 131–133.

INFER

What does María learn about poetry from reading Pablo Neruda's poem titles?

INTERPRET

What does María want her poems to do (lines 134–137)? Why does she thank Mr. Golden?

SKILLS PRACTICE

María in School

Literary Skills Analyze novel excerpts.

Reading Skills Make inferences.

Inference Chart An **inference** is an educated guess that is based on what you read or observe and on your own life experience. Based on details in "María in School" and on your own experience, make inferences about María in the chart below. Give at least one detail from the text to support each inference.

María's background	María's personality	María's talent
My inference . . .	My inference . . .	My inference . . .
Supporting detail(s):	Supporting detail(s):	Supporting detail(s):

Skills Review

María in School

VOCABULARY AND COMPREHENSION

A. Understand Academic Vocabulary Write an original sentence of your own to illustrate each of the following types of sentences:

1. **Declarative:** ______________________________

____

2. **Imperative:** ______________________________

____

3. **Exclamatory:** ______________________________

____

B. Comprehension Answer the questions below.

1. What does Mr. Golden do besides teach English?

____

____

2. What does Mr. Golden do with one of María's poems?

____

____

3. How does the class react to María's poems?

____

____

4. What does María learn from Pablo Neruda's odes?

____

____

Vocabulary Skills
Understand academic vocabulary.

Collection

6

Our Literary Heritage: World Folk Tales

Werner Forman/Art Resource, NY

Shaman's rattle from the Tlingit Culture, Alaska, c. 1870. Ivory, 19.5 cm. x 28 cm. Denver Art Museum, Denver, Colorado.

Academic Vocabulary for Collection 6

These are the terms you should know
as you read and analyze the selections in this collection.

Folk Tales Stories originally passed on by word of mouth, often over many centuries. In recent times many of these stories have been collected and published in books.

Motifs Common features of folk tales. Magic, fairy godmothers, acts of heroism or escape, tricksters, and explanations of origins are all examples of motifs.

Trickster Tales Stories about a character who outwits other characters. Brer Rabbit is an example of a trickster in African American tales, as is Coyote in Native American stories.

Origin Tales Stories that explain how things came to be. The origins of the earth, or of particular features like mountain ranges or lakes, and even of people, are explained in some folk tales. Other folk tales tell how certain customs or behaviors came about.

Before You Read

The Clever Magistrate *retold by* Linda Fang

LITERARY FOCUS: FOLK TALES

Folk tales are stories that have been passed from generation to generation. Each time the story is told, it takes on a new life, with subtle changes—perhaps some exaggeration here or an added character there. In some folk tales we learn about the lives people lived and the beliefs they held and valued. In other tales we get a glimpse of their humor and learn about their wildest dreams and fantasies.

As you read the folk tale "The Clever Magistrate," notice the customs and values of ancient China it reveals.

READING SKILLS: PREDICTING

Folk tales are a lot of fun to read. Although they have familiar elements, such as people in trouble, rescuers, and heroes, you never know what will happen next. As you read "The Clever Magistrate," make **predictions** about where the story will take you. Here are some tips to help you out.

- Look for clues that hint at, or **foreshadow,** what will happen.
- As the story develops and builds suspense, guess at possible outcomes. Think about where the story might lead.
- Ask yourself questions as you read the story, and revise your predictions as necessary.
- Use your own experiences and knowledge to help you make predictions.

Literary Skills Understand folk tales.

Reading Skills Make predictions.

Vocabulary Skills Clarify word meanings by using contrast.

VOCABULARY DEVELOPMENT

PREVIEW SELECTION VOCABULARY

Preview the following words from the tale before you begin reading "The Clever Magistrate."

relent (ri·lent′) *v.:* become less stern or severe.

The shopkeeper refuses to relent and repeats his stern demand.

commotion (kə·mō′shən) *n.:* noisy disturbance.

The magistrate comes to investigate the commotion.

reluctantly (ri·luk′tənt·lē′) *adv.:* unwillingly.

The farmer reluctantly carries out the unpleasant task.

inevitable (in·ev′i·tə·bəl) *adj.:* unavoidable.

Becoming ill from the cold is inevitable if you don't have a warm coat.

harass (har′əs) *v.:* trouble; torment.

If something bad should happen to the farmer, his family might harass the shopkeeper.

CLARIFYING WORD MEANINGS: CONTRAST

When trying to figure out the meaning of an unfamiliar word, you might look at the context to see if the writer provides a **contrast clue** by telling what the meaning of the word is not. Words such as *not, but, never, unlike, instead,* and *rather* often signal a contrast clue.

In these examples the italicized passages provide contrast clues for the boldface words.

- Maria, *never one to give up,* is **persistent** in her campaign to be elected class president.
- **Vibrant** colors, *not pale pastel* ones, were chosen for the baby's room.
- Many sweets can be *harmful to your health, but* honey is usually **beneficial.**

The Clever Magistrate

retold by **Linda Fang**

Chinese village.

IDENTIFY

Underline the details in lines 1–5 that show when and where this folk tale takes place.

One cold winter day, a farmer was carrying two buckets of spoiled food from a restaurant to his pigsty. As he was passing a coat shop, he accidentally spilled some of the slop on the ground. Sour cabbage, rotten eggs, and fish bones scattered all over the ground. Ugh! Ugh! What a smell!

The shopkeeper, who happened to be standing inside the door, saw this and was furious. He rushed out, grabbed the man, and shouted, "You dirty beggar! Look what you've done in front of my shop! It will be impossible to get rid of the smell! How are you going to pay for the damage?"

"I am so sorry," said the farmer. "I will clean it up right away. As for the damage, all I have is this coin." He took out a coin and handed it to the shopkeeper.

The shopkeeper snatched the coin, put it between his teeth, and bit down on it. The metal was soft, which proved that it contained silver. He thrust it into his pocket and said, "All right, I will take it. But you still need to clean up the mess."

"Let me go and get some rags and a mop," said the farmer. "I will be right back."

"No," said the shopkeeper. "I want you to clean it up right away. It smells so bad that I am going to be sick. Take off your coat and wipe up the mess."

"Please don't ask me to do that!" cried the farmer. "This is the only quilted coat I have, and if I use it to wipe up the mess, it will be ruined. I won't be able to wear it anymore."

"That's your problem, not mine!" said the shopkeeper. "In fact, the coat you are wearing is no better than rags. If you don't do what I say, I am going to take you to court."

The farmer pleaded with him to reconsider, but the shopkeeper would not **relent.** Just then they heard, "Make way for the magistrate![1] Make way for the magistrate!"

The county magistrate was coming down the road in his sedan chair.[2] When he saw the **commotion,** he ordered his guards to put down the chair and bring the two men before him.

"What is the matter?" he asked.

The shopkeeper quickly replied, "*Ta-jen,*[3] this man made a mess in front of my shop. He gave me a coin to pay for the damage, but when I asked him to wipe up the mess, he wouldn't do it."

---

1. **magistrate** (maj′is·trāt′) *n.:* civil official who has the power to enforce the law.
2. **sedan chair:** covered seat for one person that is set on poles and carried by two people.
3. **Ta-jen** (tä·jen′): Chinese for "Your Excellency."

EVALUATE

Pause at line 31. Do you think the shopkeeper is being fair to the farmer? Why or why not?

VOCABULARY

relent (ri·lent′) *v.:* become less stern or severe.

commotion (kə·mō′shən) *n.:* noisy disturbance.

PREDICT

How do you predict the magistrate will settle the argument?

IDENTIFY

Folk tales often repeat information. What is repeated in lines 41–54 that you have already learned?

PREDICT

Pause at line 62. The magistrate seems to be taking the side of the shopkeeper. Do you predict the shopkeeper will win in his conflict with the farmer? Why or why not?

Giraudon / Art Resource, NY

Promenade of Qin Shi Huangdi (221-206 BCE), Tsin dynasty emperor, in a sedan chair. Detail from *The Lives of the Emperors of China.* Qing dynasty, 17th century. Watercolor on silk. Bibliotheque Nationale, Paris, France.

The magistrate stepped down from his chair and went over to look at the mess. Sour cabbage, rotten eggs, and fish bones were scattered all over the place. Ugh! Ugh! What a smell!

"Why don't you clean up the mess?" asked the magistrate.

"He wants me to wipe up the mess with my coat," said the farmer. "It will be ruined if I do so. And this is the only coat I have."

"Is that what you want?" the magistrate asked the shopkeeper.

"Yes, that is exactly what I want."

"And you will not settle for less?"

"No, I will not settle for anything less."

"Well," said the magistrate to the farmer, "if that is what he wants, you'd better do it."

"*Ta-jen*, have mercy! I can't do that!" cried the farmer. "Without the coat I will freeze to death."

"I am sorry," said the magistrate. "But that doesn't change anything. If you don't do it, I will have to put you in jail."

"That is not just!" cried the farmer.

"Hmm . . ." said the magistrate. He looked angry.

"*Ouh! Ouh! Ouh!*" cried the guards. "*Ouh! Ouh! Ouh!*" They looked threatening.

The farmer realized that there was no way out. **Reluctantly,** he used his coat to clean up the mess. Sour cabbage, rotten eggs, and fish bones. Ugh! Ugh! What a smell! He threw the coat into one of his buckets and stood shivering in front of the magistrate.

The shopkeeper laughed. "Ha, ha, ha!"

"Well," said the magistrate to the shopkeeper, "are you satisfied now?"

"Yes, *Ta-jen,* I am completely satisfied."

"No more complaints?"

"No more complaints!" said the shopkeeper.

"Case closed," said the magistrate.

"Case closed."

"But his case against you is now open."

"What!" said the shopkeeper, stunned.

"Well, you see, he is now freezing without a coat. In such weather he could catch a cold. Is that not possible?" asked the magistrate.

"Yes, *Ta-jen.*"

"His cold could develop into pneumonia.[4] Is that not possible?"

"Yes, *Ta-jen.*"

"Then he could die. His family could sue you for murder, and if you are convicted, you would be put to death. Isn't that almost **inevitable**?"

"Yes, *Ta-jen.*"

"Well, I don't think you can afford that, can you?"

"Oh, no, *Ta-jen.* I cannot afford that. What shall I do?"

"Well, it would be better to settle this out of court."

"Yes, yes, we'd better settle this out of court. But how?"

VOCABULARY

reluctantly (ri·luk′tənt·lē) *adv.:* unwillingly.

FLUENCY

Read the boxed passage aloud. Try to use different voices for the shopkeeper and the magistrate. How does the shopkeeper's voice change at the end?

PREDICT

The shopkeeper is shocked that the farmer could have a case against him. What do you think that case will be?

VOCABULARY

inevitable (in·ev′i·tə·bəl) *adj.:* unavoidable.

VISUALIZE

Underline the **simile** in lines 99–100. How do you picture the shopkeeper's face?

ANALYZE

Verbal irony is saying the opposite of what is meant. How might the magistrate's statement in lines 110–111 be ironic?

VOCABULARY

harass (har′əs) *v.:* trouble; torment.

Victoria & Albert Museum, London / Art Resource, NY

Chinese farmer. Plate 26 from a Chinese album of watercolors (c. 1796). Victoria and Albert Museum, London, Great Britain.

"We should get him a coat so he won't catch a cold."

"But where can we get one?"

"Right here, from your coat shop."

The shopkeeper looked as if he had swallowed a fly alive. He yelled at the farmer, "Go get a coat and be gone!"

The farmer went into the shop, picked out a very cheap coat, and came out. The magistrate stopped him.

"You poor thing!" he said. "Look at the coat you've got. It is so thin. You could still catch a cold, isn't that so?"

"Yes, *Ta-jen*."

"You might get pneumonia,[4] isn't that so?"

"Yes, *Ta-jen*."

"You might even die, isn't that so?"

"Yes, *Ta-jen*."

"And then your family could come and **harass** this nice gentleman. I know all your tricks!" The magistrate turned to one of his guards. "Go into the shop and get him the warmest coat you can find."

---

4. **pneumonia** (no͞o·mōn′yə) *n.:* serious infection of the lungs.

So the guard went into the shop and picked out the warmest coat he could find for the farmer. As you might guess, the warmest coat happened to be the most expensive.

When the farmer left, the magistrate smiled at the shopkeeper. "Well, what do you think about the way I settled this case? Didn't I handle it very well?"

"Yes, *Ta-jen*," the shopkeeper said glumly. "There is no question about that."

"I am glad I was able to take care of this case," said the magistrate. "You have to watch out for these troublemakers. Next time, if you have a case like this, don't try to settle it yourself. Be sure to let me handle it for you."

MEET THE WRITER

Linda Fang grew up in China and began storytelling at ten years old. A shy girl, Fang was given a story by a teacher and asked to retell the story in her own words. Since then, Fang has gone on to become an award-winning storyteller who focuses on folk tales from China. Whether she writes stories down or performs them live, Fang is a master at capturing the attention of her audience. During her live performances, she will draw her listeners into a story with costumes and sound effects. Sometimes, she even asks audience members to play characters from the story.

EVALUATE

Pause at line 121. Do you think the shopkeeper is really satisfied with the magistrate's handling of the case? Are you? Explain why or why not.

SKILLS PRACTICE

The Clever Magistrate

Literary Skills Analyze a folk tale.

Folk Tale Chart Folk tales often reveal something about the people who told the tales. We may learn about their customs, beliefs or values, and sense of humor. Fill in the chart below with what you have learned about the people of ancient China who first told "The Clever Magistrate."

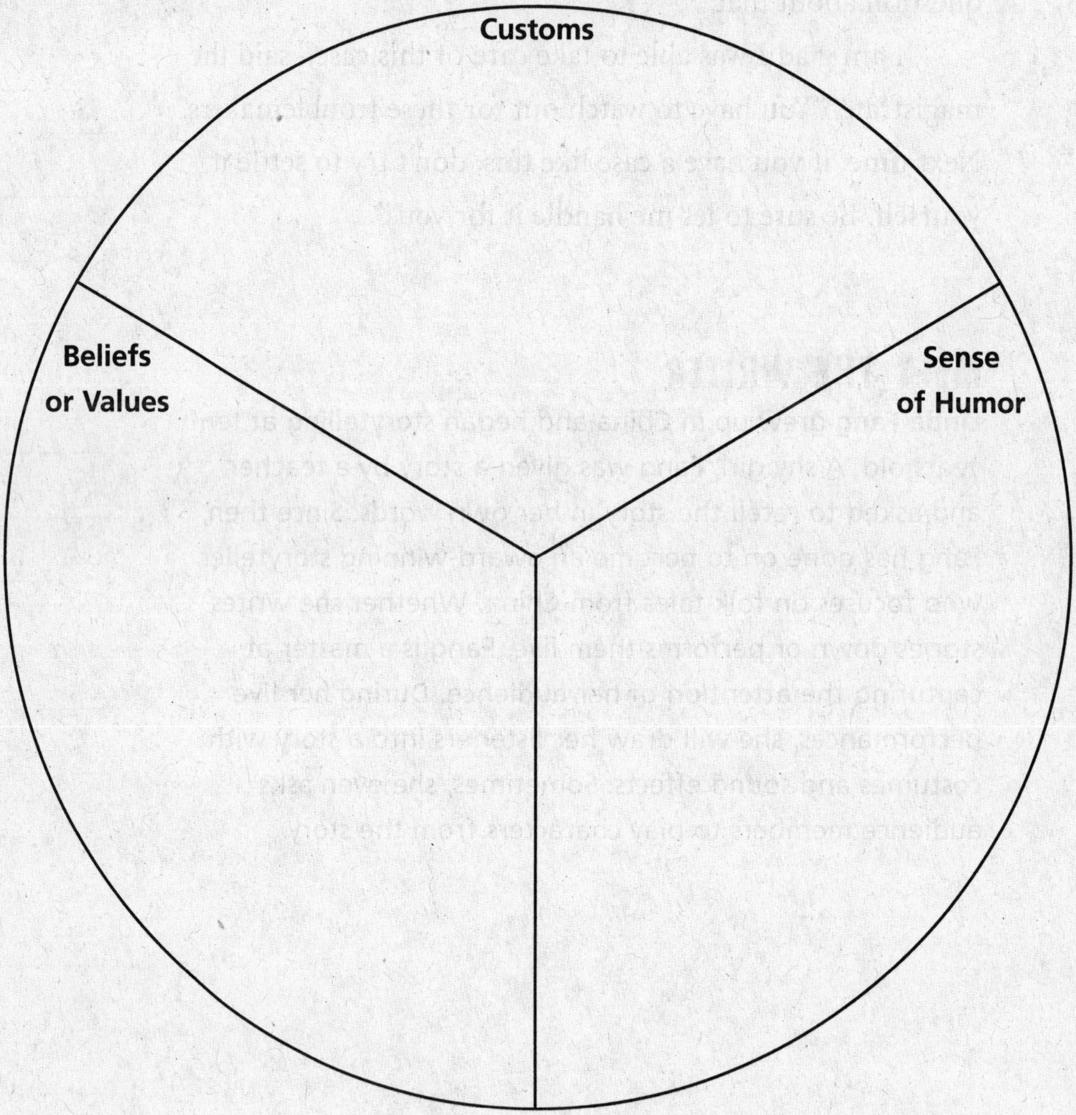

Customs

Beliefs or Values

Sense of Humor

Skills Review

The Clever Magistrate

VOCABULARY AND COMPREHENSION

A. Clarifying Meanings: Contrast Fill in the blanks with the correct Word Bank word. Use contrast clues to help you.

Word Bank

- relent
- commotion
- reluctantly
- inevitable
- harass

1. Instead of the peaceful scene she expects, Mother arrives home to a loud ___________________.

2. Nhu hopes the girls down the block will be friendly today and not ___________________ her on the way to school.

3. Because he does not want to stop playing in the snow, Leroy goes inside ___________________ when his father calls him to dinner.

4. They say that only death and taxes are ___________________. You cannot avoid them.

5. The coach insisted the team do a hundred push-ups at every practice. He would never ___________________.

B. Reading Comprehension Answer each question below.

1. What does the shopkeeper want the farmer to do? Why doesn't the farmer want to do it?

____

____

2. What does the magistrate make the farmer do?

____

____

3. How does the magistrate finally settle the case?

____

____

Vocabulary Skills
Clarify word meanings by using contrast.

How the Animals Kept the Lions Away *retold by* Inea Bushnaq

LITERARY FOCUS: MOTIFS IN FOLK TALES

A **motif** (mō·tēf′) is a feature that is repeated in stories throughout the world. Think for a moment about the stories you heard during your childhood. Chances are that quite a few of those stories involved magic, villains, heroes, and quests to save a kingdom from destruction. Another popular motif that is often found in folk tales is the **trickster**—a character who outwits other characters.

Read on, and meet a group of clever tricksters in the Algerian folk tale "How the Animals Kept the Lions Away."

READING SKILLS: RETELLING

When you see a television show or read a book you like, you may want to tell your friends about it. As you describe what happens in your own words, you **retell** the main events of the story. Retelling is a good way to be sure you understand a story and remember all its key events.

As you read the folk tale that follows, retell the story's key events in the lines provided on each page. When you finish reading, you should be able to retell the whole story.

Literary Skills Understand motifs in folk tales.

Reading Skills Retell a folk tale.

Vocabulary Skills Clarify word meanings by using context clues.

VOCABULARY DEVELOPMENT

PREVIEW SELECTION VOCABULARY

Become familiar with these words before you read "How the Animals Kept the Lions Away."

feigned (fānd) *v.:* pretended.

The rooster feigned ignorance of his improved appearance.

perseverance (pur'sə·vir'əns) *n.:* continued effort; persistence.

The donkey's perseverance finally got him the answer he sought.

conceded (kən·sēd'id) *v.:* admitted as right.

The lion conceded that the donkey had a good argument.

complied (kəm·plīd') *v.:* did what was requested or ordered.

The second lion also complied with the donkey's request.

chided (chīd'id) *v.:* scolded.

The rooster chided the ram for his rude behavior.

USING CONTEXT CLUES

When you come across an unfamiliar word while reading, take a moment to search in the surrounding words or sentences for **context clues** to the word's meaning. Here are some of the types of clues you might find.

Type of Clue	Example
Definition	The rooster found some food that was **wholesome,** or healthful.
Restatement	The food that the rooster found was **wholesome.** It improved his health and well-being.
Example	The rooster found a silo full of barley—very **wholesome** food.
Contrast	The barley the rooster found was **wholesome.** It would not harm his health.

How the Animals Kept the Lions Away

retold by Inea Bushnaq

Frans Lemmens/ zefa/CORBIS

Bedouins with camels in the Sahara desert.

RETELL

Circle the four animals, and then explain what happens to them in the first paragraph. (Why do you think they were left behind by the Bedouins?)

Once when a tribe of Bedouins[1] moved their camp to a new site, they left behind them a lame rooster, a broken-backed donkey, a sick ram, and a desert greyhound suffering from mange.[2] The animals swore brotherhood and determined to live together. They wandered until they came to an unfrequented oasis,[3] where they decided to settle.

One day when the rooster was flying to the top of a tree, he noticed something important: the opening to a grain silo

1. **Bedouins** (bed′o͞o·inz′) *n.:* Arabic-speaking people who move from place to place in the deserts of the Middle East.
2. **mange** (mānj) *n.:* skin disease of animals.
3. **unfrequented** (un·frē′kwent′id) *adj.:* seldom visited. **oasis** (ō·ā′sis) *n.:* place in the desert made fertile by the presence of water.

full of barley. The food was wholesome, and he began to visit the place daily. Soon his feathers became glossy as polished silk, and his comb began to glow like the fire inside a ruby. The donkey, observing the improvements, asked his friend, "How is it that your cap has grown so bright?" The rooster **feigned** surprise and tried to change the subject. But with the **perseverance** of his race, the donkey continued to pester the fowl until at last he said, "Very well, I shall show you the reason why my cap has grown so bright, but it must remain a secret between us." The donkey promised to be discreet and the rooster led him to the grain silo.

VISUALIZE

Underline the **similes** in lines 10–11 that help you picture the rooster's new appearance.

VOCABULARY

feigned (fānd) *v.:* pretended.

perseverance (pur'sə·vir'əns) *n.:* continued effort; persistence.

WORD STUDY

Circle the nearby context clue that helps reveal that *discreet* (line 19) means "keeping silent."

RETELL

What are the key events in lines 7–19?

At the sight of the barley the donkey flung himself into the grain and fed until he could eat no more. Brimming with well-being, he danced back to the others and said, "I feel the urge to sing come upon me. With your permission I shall bray awhile!" The animals objected. "What if a lion should hear you?" they said. "He will surely come and devour us all!" But despite his friends, the donkey could not contain his high spirits. He cantered off by himself and began to bray long and noisily.

Now, a lion did hear the sound and came streaking across the wilderness on his silent feet until he was within one spring of the donkey. Almost too late the donkey became aware of the danger. "Sire," he said. "I see that my fate has been written, but I beg you to do me the favor not to devour me without my friends. It would be more honorable, considering that the animals of this oasis have sworn an oath of brotherhood to live together and die together, if you made an end of us all without exception." The lion **conceded** the merit of this plea and allowed the donkey to guide him to his friends.

When the other animals saw the donkey leading a lion toward them, they put their heads together and said, "How can we defend ourselves against a lion!" And they made their plans. When the lion came near they all said with one voice, "Greetings and welcome, uncle lion!" Then the ram butted him in his side and knocked the breath out of his lungs, the rooster flew up and pecked at his eyes, and the dog buried his teeth in the lion's throat. The lion died, of course. His flesh was given to the dog to eat, but the animals kept his skin and tanned it.

After that the four friends were able to live in peace for a time. However, soon the donkey was announcing, "I sense

PREDICT

Underline the **foreshadowing** clue in lines 25–26, and pause at line 28. What do you predict will happen when the donkey makes a loud noise?

VOCABULARY

conceded (kən·sēd′id) *v.:* admitted as right.

RETELL

How do the animals defeat the lion (lines 40–49)?

INFER

Why does only the greyhound eat the lion's flesh (line 48)?

© B. von Hoffmann/Robertstock.com

that I must bray again!" "Be still, O ill-omened animal!" said the others. But the donkey could not suppress his feelings, and his unmelodious call rang repeatedly in the air.

A second lion prowling that quarter of the desert was attracted to the braying. With water running in his mouth, he hurried to the oasis. Again the donkey invited the lion to kill all the animals of the oasis together, and the lion gladly **complied.** This time too the rooster, the ram, and the dog

Notes

WORD STUDY

One way to figure out the meaning of unfamiliar words is to look for a familiar word part. If you know what *omen* and *melody* mean, you can probably figure out the meanings of *ill-omened* (line 52) and *unmelodious* (line 54). What do you think the words mean?

VOCABULARY

complied (kəm·plīd′) *v.:* did what was requested or ordered.

put their heads together when they saw the lion approaching and made a plan.

But what they said to the visitor was, "Welcome, may you be a thousand times welcome!" Then the rooster hinted to the ram, "Our guest should be made comfortable and have a carpet to sit on!" The ram trotted into their dwelling and brought out the tanned lion skin. "Be ashamed, O ram!" **chided** the rooster when he saw him. "Our guest is of a noble tribe. Do you want to disgrace us by offering him that old, worn-out mat?" Meekly the ram carried the lion skin back into the house and brought it out a second time. This time the dog expressed impatience. "Surely we have a softer carpet than that, O ram! Besides, this one is quite faded." Obediently the ram took the lion skin inside and returned with it a third time. Now the donkey chimed in, "For one of such eminence as the lion, nothing but the finest can serve the occasion! Choose more carefully from among our store!" The ram withdrew into the house, but the lion did not linger further. He jumped to his feet and without bidding his hosts a formal farewell, ran away as fast as he was able.

Although the donkey continued to bray from time to time, no lion was seen near the animals' oasis again.

VOCABULARY

chided (chīd′id) *v.:* scolded.

WORD STUDY

Circle clues to the meaning of *eminence* (line 74). What do you think the word means? (If you cannot guess, look it up in a dictionary.)

FLUENCY

Read the boxed passage silently until you are sure you understand it. Look up any words whose meanings you cannot figure out. Then, read the passage aloud. Try to use a different voice for each animal.

RETELL

Tricksters are a **motif,** or repeated feature, in many folk tales. How do the animals trick the second lion?

MEET THE WRITER

Inea Bushnaq knows the power and importance of stories. Born in Jerusalem to a Palestinian family, Bushnaq remembers being entranced by the tales she was told by her father and his family. As an adult, Bushnaq decided to compile a book of Arab folk tales. She spent five years going from door to door in small Palestinian villages and recording the tales she heard. She published these stories and her translations of folk tales she found in compilations by other collectors in her book *Arab Folktales*. During the Gulf War in 1991, Bushnaq was invited to tell some of these stories to students in New York City schools. Bushnaq now lives in New York City, teaches in its public schools, and continues to write.

Notes

How the Animals Kept the Lions Away

Reading Skills
Retell a folk tale.

Retelling Chart Retelling a story is not only fun, it is also a good way to be sure you understand the story and remember its key events. Look back at the Retell questions you answered as you read "How the Animals Kept the Lions Away." Then, fill in the left-hand column below with the key events. (You may find more or fewer than six events.) Finally, in the right-hand column, retell the whole story in your own words.

Key Events in the Story	My Retelling
1.	
2.	
3.	
4.	
5.	
6.	

Skills Review

How the Animals Kept the Lions Away

VOCABULARY AND COMPREHENSION

A. Using Context Clues Write the appropriate word from the Word Bank in each blank in the paragraph below. Use context clues to help you choose the right words.

Word Bank

feigned
perseverance
conceded
complied
chided

Alicia was tired of having to take care of her baby sister in the mornings, so she (1) ____________________ sleep, pretending to be still in dreamland. The (2) ____________________ of the crying baby, however, woke their mother. Mama picked up the baby and gently (3) ____________________ Alicia. "Don't you know, honeybunch, that I work late and need to get some sleep? I count on you to take care of little Maya for me." Alicia didn't want to admit it, but she finally (4) ____________________ that Mama was right. After that day, she didn't resist anymore. She (5) ____________________ with her mother's request and took care of her baby sister each morning.

B. Reading Comprehension Answer each question below.

1. What do the four animals swear to do after the Bedouins leave them behind? ____

    ____

2. How do the animals defeat the first lion? ____________________

    ____

3. How do the animals defeat the second lion? ____________________

    ____

    ____

Vocabulary Skills
Clarify word meanings by using context clues.

The Old Woman Who Lived with the Wolves by Chief Luther Standing Bear

LITERARY FOCUS: FOLK TALES

There are many reasons that **folk tales** remain popular and continue to be handed down from generation to generation. They are usually lively or amusing tales. They have appealing—or funny or scary—characters. They have surprising events or endings. And they teach important lessons about life.

As you read "The Old Woman Who Lived with the Wolves," think about the lessons this tale teaches and the reasons it has been handed down through generations of Sioux families.

READING SKILLS: CAUSE AND EFFECT

Many folk tales tell you how something came about. Like most explanations, such tales present a series of causes and effects. Here's an example of a typical cause-and-effect sequence.

Cause →	Effect →	Cause →	Effect
The miller brags about his daughter's spinning.	The king hears and demands that she spin straw into gold.	She requests help from a funny little man.	Rumpelstiltskin spins the straw into gold.

As you read "The Old Woman Who Lived with the Wolves," look for cause-and-effect relationships.

Literary Skills Understand folk tales.

Reading Skills Understand cause and effect.

Vocabulary Skills Clarify word meanings by identifying synonyms.

VOCABULARY DEVELOPMENT

PREVIEW SELECTION VOCABULARY

Get to know these words before you read "The Old Woman Who Lived with the Wolves."

enticed (en·tīsd′) *v.:* attracted; tempted; lured.

Sometimes wild wolves enticed pet dogs to join their packs.

traversed (trə·vʉrsd′) *v.:* crossed.

The Sioux traversed many valleys and streams on their way to a new camp.

mystified (mis′tə·fīd′) *v.:* puzzled.

Marpiyawin had been gone so long that the smell of people mystified her.

offensive (ə·fen′siv) *adj.:* unpleasant; disgusting.

The smell of human beings is often offensive to wild animals.

CLARIFYING WORD MEANINGS: SYNONYMS

Synonyms are words that have the same or similar meanings. When you look up a word you don't know in a dictionary, you will often find a synonym that you do know. Each sentence below contains an italicized word that is a synonym for one of the vocabulary words. The vocabulary word appears in parentheses following its synonym.

- Sarah was *tempted* (enticed) into the bakery by the wonderful smell.
- Juan and his scout troop *crossed* (traversed) ridges and peaks on their hike.
- The community thought the smell coming from the dump was *disgusting* (offensive).
- The driver was *puzzled* (mystified) by the strange sounds coming from the engine.

The Old Woman Who Lived with the Wolves

Chief Luther Standing Bear

© Joseph Sohm; ChromoSohm Inc./CORBIS

Native American tepees.

SUMMARIZE

In reading **folk tales,** you often learn something about the people who have told the tale. Summarize what you have learned about the Sioux in the first paragraph.

The Sioux[1] were a people who traveled about from place to place a great deal within the borders of their own country. They did not trespass upon the territory of their neighbor Indians, but liked to make their home first here and then there upon their own ground, just as they pleased. It was not like moving from one strange town to another, but wherever they settled it was home. Taking down and putting up the tipis[2] was not hard for them to do.

1. **Sioux** (so͞o) *n.:* Native American people of the Great Plains. The Sioux are divided into three main groups, the Dakota, Nakota, and Lakota. Known for their bravery and fighting abilities, the Sioux fiercely resisted the white man's expansion into their land.
2. **tipis** (tē′pēz) *n.:* often spelled "tepees"; Sioux word for tent dwellings shaped like cones and made from animal skins and wooden poles.

The reasons for their moving were many. Perhaps the grass for their ponies ran short, or the water in the creek became low. Maybe the game had gone elsewhere, and maybe the people just moved the camp to a fresh green spot, for the Sioux loved pure water, pure air, and a clean place on which to put their tipis.

One day, long ago, a Sioux village was on the march. There were many people in the party, and many children. A great number of horses carried the tipis, and herds of racing and war horses were being taken care of by the young men. In this crowd was a young woman who carried with her a pet dog. The dog was young and playful, just past the puppy age. The young woman was very fond of her pet, as she had cared for it since it was a wee little thing with eyes still closed. She romped along with the pup, and the way seemed short because she played with it and with the young folks when not busy helping her mother with the packing and unpacking.

One evening Marpiyawin[3] missed her dog. She looked and she called, but he was not to be found. Perhaps someone liked her playful pet and was keeping him concealed, but after a search she became satisfied that no one in camp was hiding him. Then she thought that perhaps he had lain down to sleep somewhere along the way and had been left behind. Then, lastly, she thought that the wolves had **enticed** him to join their pack. For oftentimes the Sioux dogs were coaxed away and ran with the wolf-pack, always returning, however, in a few days or weeks to the village.

So Marpiyawin, thinking the matter over, decided that she would go back over the way her people had journeyed and that somewhere she would find her dog. She would then bring him back to camp with her. Without a word to

3. **Marpiyawin** (mär·pē·yäh′win).

INFER

What **inferences** can you make about the Sioux based on the information in lines 9–19?

IDENTIFY CAUSE & EFFECT

What does Marpiyawin think may be the **cause** of her dog's absence? What **effect** does the dog's absence have on Marpiyawin?

VOCABULARY

enticed (en·tīsd′) *v.:* attracted; tempted; lured.

Circle a word in the following sentence that is a **synonym** for *enticed.*

PREDICT

Marpiyawin thinks nothing can happen to her in the mountains. Do you think she will be safe there alone? Why or why not?

anyone, she turned back, for she had no fear of becoming lost. Nothing could befall her, so why should she fear? As she walked back, she came to the foothills at the base of the mountains where her village people had spent the summer. As she slept that night, the first snowfall of the autumn came so silently that it did not awaken her. In the morning everything was white with snow, but it was not far to the place where the village had been in camp and so determined was she to find her dog that she decided to keep going. Marpiyawin now felt that her pet had gone back to the old camping-ground, as dogs often do, and was now there howling and crying to be found.

That afternoon the snow fell thicker and faster and Marpiyawin was forced to seek shelter in a cave, which was rather dark, but warm and comfortable. She was not hungry, for in her little rawhide bag was still some *wasna*.[4] She was tired, however, so it was not long till she fell asleep, and while she slept she had a most wonderful vision. In her dream the wolves talked to her and she understood

4. **wasna** (wäsh·nä′) *n.:* traditional Sioux food made of dried cornmeal, dried berries, and fat.

them, and when she talked to them they understood her too. They told her that she had lost her way, but that she should trust them and they would not see her suffer from cold or hunger. She replied that she would not worry, and when she awoke it was without fear, even though in the cave with her were the wolves sitting about in a friendly manner.

The blizzard raged outside for many days; still she was contented, for she was neither cold nor hungry. For meat the wolves supplied her with tender rabbits and at night they kept her body warm with their shaggy coats of fur. As the days wore on, she and the wolves became fast friends.

But clear days finally came and the wolves offered to lead her back to her people, so they set out. They **traversed** many little valleys and crossed many creeks and streams; they walked up hills and down hills, and at last came to one from which she could look down upon the camp of her people. Here she must say "Good-bye" to her friends and companions—the wolves. This made her feel very sad, though she wanted to see her people again. Marpiyawin thanked all the wolves for their kindness to her and asked what she might do for them. All they asked was that, when the long winter months came and food was scarce, she bring to the top of the hill some nice fat meat for them to eat. This she gladly promised to do and went down the hill toward the camp of her people.

As Marpiyawin neared the village, she smelled a very unpleasant odor. At first it **mystified** her; then she realized it was the smell of human beings. At once the knowledge came to her that the smell of humans was very different from the smell of animals. This was why she now knew that animals so readily track human beings and why the odor of

IDENTIFY CAUSE & EFFECT

What **effect** does her dream have on Marpiyawin when she awakes?

CLARIFY

Explain how Marpiyawin survives the blizzard.

PREDICT

Underline the wolves' request in lines 82–85. Do you think Marpiyawin will be able to honor this request? Why or why not?

VOCABULARY

traversed (trə·vursd') *v.:* crossed.

Circle a word in the sentence that is a **synonym** for *traversed*.

mystified (mis'tə·fīd') *v.:* puzzled.

man is sometimes so **offensive** to them. She had been with the wolves so long that she had lost the odor of her people and now was able to see that, while man often considers the animal offensive, so do animals find man offensive.

Marpiyawin came to the camp of her people and they were happy to see her, for they had considered her lost and thought she had been taken by an enemy tribe. But she pointed to the top of the hill in the distance, and there sat her friends, their forms black against the sky. In great surprise her people looked, not knowing what to say. They thought she must have just escaped a great danger. So she explained to them that she had been lost and would have perished had not the wolves saved her life. She asked them to give her some of their fat meat that she might carry it to the top of the hill. Her people were so grateful and happy that a young man was sent about the camp telling of the

© Tim Davis/CORBIS

VOCABULARY

offensive (ə·fen′siv) *adj.:* unpleasant; disgusting.

Re-read lines 87–96, and circle a word that is a **synonym** for *offensive*.

ANALYZE

Folk tales often include lessons about life. What lesson about life might lines 87–96 reveal?

safe return of Marpiyawin and collecting meat from each tipi. Marpiyawin took the meat, placed the bundle on her back, and went up the hill, while the village people looked on in wonder. When she reached the hilltop she spread the meat on the ground and the wolves ate it.

Ever after that, when the long winter months came and food was scarce and hard to find, Marpiyawin took meat to her friends the wolves. She never forgot their language and oftentimes in the winter their voices calling to her would be heard throughout the village. Then the people would ask the old woman what the wolves were saying. Their calls would be warnings that a blizzard was coming, or that the enemy was passing close and to send out a scout, or to let the old woman know that they were watching her with care.

And so Marpiyawin came to be known to the tribe as "The Old Woman Who Lived with the Wolves," or, in the Sioux language, as "Win yan wan si k'ma nitu ompi ti."

MEET THE WRITER

Chief Luther Standing Bear (1868–1939) was born on the Pine Ridge Reservation in South Dakota to a Sioux chief. Raised in the traditional Sioux way, Standing Bear was later sent to the Carlisle Indian School, a boarding school in Pennsylvania that aimed to assimilate Native Americans into American culture by teaching them English and job skills. After graduating, Standing Bear returned to South Dakota, where he became a community leader and campaigned for Native American rights. When he was around sixty years old, Standing Bear published his first book. Hoping to preserve the Sioux way of life for future generations, he went on to write books about Sioux customs and traditions, as well as *Stories of the Sioux,* a collection of Sioux folk tales.

FLUENCY

Practice reading the boxed passage aloud until you can read all the long sentences smoothly and without hesitation.

ANALYZE

How does Marpiyawin continue to help the wolves? How do the wolves help her and her people? What overall lesson about life have you learned from this **folk tale**?

The Old Woman Who Lived with the Wolves

Literary Skills Analyze a folk tale.

Reading Skills Analyze cause and effect.

Cause-and-Effect Chart **Folk tales** often use a series of **causes and effects** to describe how something came to be. Fill in the chart below with causes and effects from "The Old Woman Who Lived with the Wolves." Add more boxes if you need them.

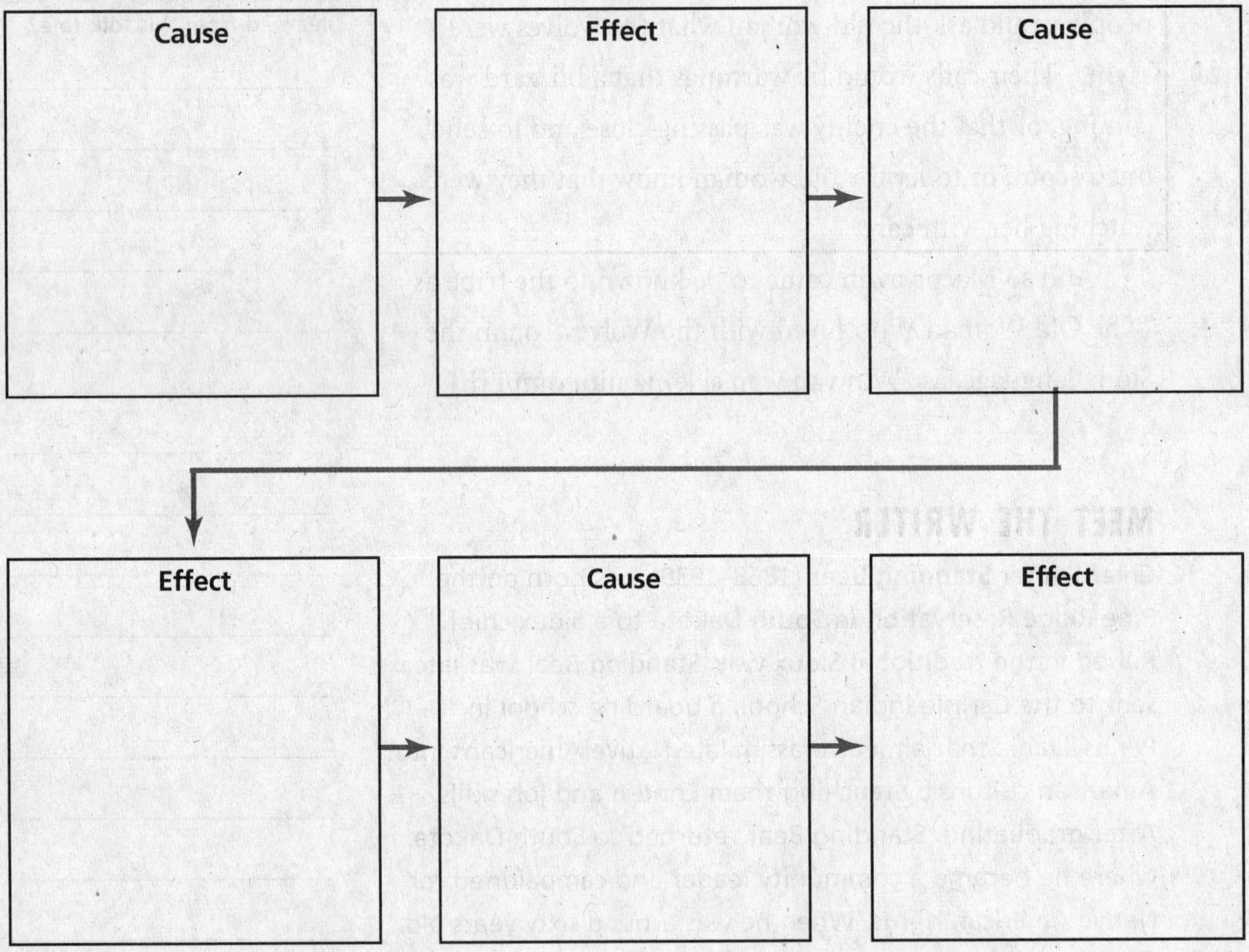

Cause	→	Effect	→	Cause

↓

Effect	→	Cause	→	Effect

Skills Review

The Old Woman Who Lived with the Wolves

VOCABULARY AND COMPREHENSION

A. Clarifying Word Meanings: Synonyms Choose the word or phrase that is the best synonym for each Word Bank word. Write the letter of the synonym in the correct blank.

Word Bank

enticed
traversed
mystified
offensive

_____ **1.** enticed **a.** puzzled

_____ **2.** traversed **b.** unpleasant

_____ **3.** mystified **c.** tempted

_____ **4.** offensive **d.** crossed

B. Reading Comprehension Answer each question below.

1. Why did Marpiyawin leave her people and travel alone in the mountains?

____

____

2. How do the wolves help Marpiyawin survive a blizzard?

____

____

3. How does Marpiyawin manage to return to her people?

____

____

4. Why does Marpiyawin come to be called "The Old Woman Who Lived with the Wolves"?

____

____

SKILLS FOCUS

Vocabulary Skills
Clarify word meanings by identifying synonyms.

Collection 7

Literary Criticism: Where I Stand

© Dennis Wilson/CORBIS

Academic Vocabulary for Collection 7

These are the terms you should know
as you read and analyze the selections in this collection.

Plot The series of related events that make up a short story, novel, play, or narrative poem. Plot is what happens in a story. Plot is usually based on a conflict that exists between opposing forces.

Characters The people who take part in a short story, novel, play, or narrative poem. A character can also be animal.

• • •

Biography The story of a person's life told by another person. Biographies are based on historical facts. Most biographers also include their own impressions and opinions of their subjects.

Primary Sources Firsthand sources often used for doing research. Primary sources include such documents as letters, journals, interviews, wills, contracts, and bills of sale.

• • •

Literary Criticism The process of analyzing a literary work and evaluating or judging its quality.

Biographical Approach A form of literary criticism in which a text is analyzed to show how it reflects the writer's own life experiences.

Dear Benjamin Banneker

by Andrea Davis Pinkney

LITERARY FOCUS: BIOGRAPHY

A **biography** is the factual story of a person's life written by another person. Biography is one of the most popular forms of literature. Biographies can help us learn more about real people and events from history. Biographies can also help us imagine what it was like to live in another time and place. The best biographers are careful researchers; they study the lives and times of their subjects by using such **primary sources** as letters, journals, diaries, interviews, and even wills, contracts, and bills of sale.

In the biography you are about to read, Andrea Pinkney tells the story of Benjamin Banneker, an African American man who lived in the 1700s. Although slavery was still legal in the United States at this time, Banneker was a free man. Despite the limitations set upon him because of his race, Banneker became an astronomer, authored a popular almanac, and helped survey Washington, D.C., when the nation's capital was being built. Like many other Americans of the eighteenth century, Banneker was an expert in many fields. He also was an eloquent and brave spokesperson for his people.

READING SKILLS: EVALUATING THE BIOGRAPHY

Biographies are based on facts that can be verified. They also contain details that the writers have inferred from research as well as the writers' opinions about their subjects. As you read and evaluate a biography, ask yourself these questions.

- Has the writer used reliable primary sources to support this picture of a person and the time during which he or she lived?
- Which details in the biography are taken from the writer's imagination?
- What opinions about the subject does the writer present?

Literary Skills Understand biography.

Reading Skills Evaluate biography.

Vocabulary Skills Use affixes to clarify meaning.

VOCABULARY DEVELOPMENT

PREVIEW SELECTION VOCABULARY

Take a few minutes to review these words before you begin to read "Dear Benjamin Banneker."

calculations (kal′kyoo·lā′shənz) *n.:* mathematical figurings.

Banneker's almanac was based on calculations involving the movements of the stars and the cycles of the moon.

impartial (im·pär′shəl) *adj:* treating all sides in the same way; fair; not partial.

Banneker wished that his achievements could be viewed with impartial eyes.

conferred (kən·furd′) *v.:* gave something to someone else; granted; talked with.

Banneker reminded Jefferson that God conferred certain rights on all people.

degraded (dē·grād′id) *adj.:* disgraced; brought down; stripped of dignity.

Jefferson regretted the degraded condition of enslaved people.

commenced (kə·menst′) *v.:* begun.

Jefferson wished to see some system commenced to help the African Americans.

USING AFFIXES

An **affix** is a word part added to the beginning or end of a word to change its meaning. An affix added to the front of a word is a **prefix.** An affix added to the back of a word is a **suffix.** Often, if you know the meaning of a word's affix, you can make a good guess at the word's meaning. Here are affixes used in some of the words listed above.

Affix	Meaning
–tion	"the action of"
im–	"no; not"
con–	"with"
de–	"down"
com–	"with; together"

As you read, notice words that use one of these affixes. Does knowing the meaning of the affix help make the meaning of the word clear?

Dear Benjamin Banneker

Andrea Davis Pinkney

BACKGROUND: Literature and Social Studies

During Benjamin Banneker's time, most Africans living in the Americas were enslaved. Free blacks, like Banneker, were in the minority. In 1790, for example, free blacks made up nine percent of the total recorded black population of 757,000. Many free blacks had ancestors who were indentured servants—servants who worked for an employer for a certain period of time in exchange for passage to America. Others had been freed by the people who had owned them. Some people held in slavery, when hired out by their owners, were allowed to save part of their wages. This allowed some of them eventually to buy their freedom.

IDENTIFY

Re-read lines 1–12. Underline details that indicate where this biography is set. Circle details that indicate when it takes place.

INFER

Pause at line 12. List at least three facts you have learned about Banneker.

No slave master ever ruled over Benjamin Banneker as he was growing up in Maryland along the Patapsco River. He was as free as the sky was wide, free to count the slugs that made their home on his parents' tobacco farm, free to read, and to wonder: *Why do the stars change their place in the sky from night to night? What makes the moon shine full, then, weeks later, disappear? How does the sun know to rise just before the day?*

Benjamin's mother, Mary, grew up a free woman. His daddy, Robert, a former slave, gained his freedom long before 1731 when Benjamin was born. Benjamin Banneker had official papers that spelled out his freedom.

But even as a free person, Benjamin had to work hard. When Benjamin grew to be a man, he discovered that to

Photo by MPI/Getty Images

Benjamin Banneker, 1791.

earn a decent living he had little choice but to tend to the tobacco farm his parents left him, a grassy hundred acres he called Stout.

Benjamin worked long hours to make sure his farm would yield healthy crops. After each harvest, Benjamin hauled hogshead[1] bundles of tobacco to sell in town. The work was grueling[2] and didn't leave him much time for finding the answers to his questions about the mysterious movements of the stars and cycles of the moon.

But over the course of many years, Benjamin managed to teach himself astronomy at night while everyone else slept.

There were many white scientists in Benjamin's day who taught themselves astronomy and published their own almanacs. But it didn't occur to them that a black man—free or slave—could be smart enough to calculate the movements of the stars the way Benjamin did.

1. **hogshead** (hôgz'hed') *n.* used as *adj.:* barrel holding from 63 to 140 gallons.
2. **grueling** (gro͞o'liŋ) *adj.:* exhausting; very difficult.

Notes

WORD STUDY

Astronomy (line 25) comes from the Greek words *astron,* meaning "star," and *nomos,* meaning "law." What laws do you think astronomy is concerned with?

INFER

Think about lines 26–30. Write down at least one conclusion you can draw about the time period in which Banneker lived.

INFER

Re-read lines 36–43. Why was an almanac so important in Banneker's time?

ANALYZE

Underline the historical facts in lines 47–58 that the author probably learned through her research. Circle details that probably come from the writer's imagination.

VOCABULARY

calculations (kal'kyoo·lā'shənz) *n.:* mathematical figurings.

Benjamin wanted to prove folks wrong. He knew that he could make an almanac as good as any white scientist's. Even if it meant he would have to stay awake most nights to do it, Benjamin was determined to create an almanac that would be the first of its kind.

In colonial times, most families in America owned an almanac. To some, it was as important as the Bible. Folks read almanacs to find out when the sun and moon would rise and set, when eclipses would occur, and how the weather would change from season to season. Farmers read their almanacs so they would know when to seed their soil, when to plow, and when they could expect rain to water their crops.

Beginning in 1789, Benjamin spent close to a year observing the sky every night, unraveling its mysteries. He plotted the cycles of the moon and made careful notes.

The winter of 1790 was coming. In order to get his almanac printed in time for the new year, Benjamin needed to find a publisher quickly. He sent his **calculations** off to William Goddard, one of the most well-known printers in Baltimore. William Goddard sent word that he wasn't interested in publishing Benjamin's manuscript. Benjamin received the same reply from John Hayes, a newspaper publisher.

Benjamin couldn't find a publisher who was willing to take a chance on him. None seemed to trust his abilities. Peering through his cabin window at the bleak wintry sky, Benjamin's own faith in his almanac began to shrivel, like the logs burning in his fireplace.

Finally, in late 1790, James Pemberton learned of Benjamin Banneker and his almanac. Pemberton was the president of the Pennsylvania Society for the Abolition of Slavery, a group of men and women who fought for the rights of black people. Pemberton said Benjamin's almanac

Benjamin Banneker's
PENNSYLVANIA, DELAWARE, MARY-
LAND, AND VIRGINIA
ALMANAC,
FOR THE
YEAR of our LORD 1795;
Being the Third after Leap-Year.

BANNAKER.

PHILADELPHIA:
Printed for WILLIAM GIBBONS, Cherry Street

Title page to *Benjamin Banneker's Almanac,* 1795.

was proof that black people were as smart as white people. He set out to help Benjamin get his almanac published for the year 1791.

With Pemberton's help, news about Benjamin and his almanac spread across the Maryland countryside and up through the channels of the Chesapeake Bay. Members of the abolitionist societies of Pennsylvania and Maryland rallied to get Benjamin's almanac published.

But as the gray days of December grew shorter and colder, Benjamin and his supporters realized it was too late in the year 1790 to publish Benjamin's astronomy tables for 1791. Benjamin would have to create a new set of calculations for an almanac to be published in 1792.

IDENTIFY

What historical facts do you learn from studying this cover of Banneker's 1795 almanac?

WORD STUDY

An *abolitionist* (line 70) was someone who worked to abolish, or wipe out, slavery in the United States. Why would the abolitionists want to help Banneker publish his almanac?

EVALUATE

Pause at line 91. Underline the details on this page so far that describe what Banneker was thinking. How do you suppose the writer knew this?

INTERPRET

What does Banneker mean by saying that he is taking "a liberty which Seemed to me Scarcely allowable" (lines 96–97)?

Benjamin knew many people would use and learn from his almanac. He also realized that as the first black man to complete such a work, he'd receive praise for his accomplishment. Yet, Benjamin wondered, what good would his almanac be to black people who were enslaved? There were so many black people who wouldn't be able to read his almanac. Some couldn't read and were forbidden to learn. Others, who could read, had masters who refused to let them have books. These thoughts were never far from Benjamin's mind as he worked on his 1792 almanac.

Once his almanac was written, Benjamin realized he had another task to begin. On the evening of August 19, 1791, Benjamin lit a candle and sat down to write an important letter to Secretary of State Thomas Jefferson. The letter began:

Maryland, Baltimore County,
Near Ellicott's Lower Mills August 19th. 1791.
Thomas Jefferson Secretary of State.

Sir, I am fully sensible of the greatness of that freedom which I take with you on the present occasion; a liberty which Seemed to me Scarcely allowable, when I reflected on the distinguished, and dignifyed station in which you Stand; and the almost general prejudice and prepossession[3] *which is so previlent*[4] *in the world against those of my complexion.*

Years before, in 1776, Thomas Jefferson wrote the Declaration of Independence, a document that said "all men are created equal." But Thomas Jefferson owned slaves. How, Benjamin wondered, could Thomas Jefferson sign his

3. **prepossession** (prē′pə·zes′shun) *n.:* opinion formed beforehand; bias.
4. **previlent,** now spelled "prevalent" (prev′ə·lənt) *adj.:* widespread. In the 1700s, English spellings had not yet been standardized.

name to the declaration, which guaranteed "life, liberty and the pursuit of happiness" for all? The words Thomas Jefferson wrote didn't match the way he lived his life. To Benjamin, that didn't seem right.

Benjamin knew that all black people could study and learn as he had—if only they were free to do so. Written on the finest paper he could find, Benjamin's letter to Thomas Jefferson said just that. His letter reminded Thomas Jefferson that, at the time of the American Revolution when he was struggling against British tyranny, he had clearly seen the right all men have to freedom:

> *Sir how pitiable is it to reflect, that altho you were so fully convinced of the benevolence[5] of the Father of mankind, and of his equal and* ***impartial*** *distribution of those rights and privileges which he had* ***conferred*** *upon them, that you should at the Same time counteract[6] his mercies, in detaining by fraud and violence so numerous a part of my bretheren[7] under groaning captivity and cruel oppression, that you should at the Same time be found guilty of that most criminal act, which you professedly detested in others, with respect to yourselves.*

Along with his letter, Benjamin enclosed a copy of his almanac.

Eleven days later, Benjamin received a reply from Thomas Jefferson. In his letter, Jefferson wrote that he was glad to get the almanac and that he agreed with Benjamin, black people had abilities that they couldn't discover because they were enslaved. He wrote:

---

5. **benevolence** (bə·nev′ə·ləns) *n.:* good will; kindliness.
6. **counteract** (kount′·ər·act′) *v.:* act against; offset one action by an opposing action.
7. **bretheren,** now spelled "brethren" (bre*th*′ren) *n.:* brothers; fellow members of a group.

INFER

Pause at line 116. Describe how the writer is presenting Banneker's character, based on the thoughts, opinions, and actions described in lines 107–116.

VOCABULARY

impartial (im·pär′shəl) *adj.:* treating all sides the same; fair; not partial.

conferred (kən·furd′) *v.:* gave something to someone else; granted; talked with.

FLUENCY

Read the boxed passage aloud. Pause briefly at the commas so that the meaning of each group of words is clear.

IDENTIFY

State in your own words the main idea Banneker is expressing to Jefferson.

VOCABULARY

degraded (dē·grād′id) *adj.:* disgraced; brought down; stripped of dignity.

commenced (kə·menst′) *v.:* begun.

SUMMARIZE

Re-read lines 135–141. In your own words, summarize Jefferson's response to Banneker.

IDENTIFY

What **main idea** is Jefferson expressing in lines 145–149?

Philadelphia, Aug. 30. 1791.

> *Sir, I Thank you sincerely for your letter of the 19th instant and for the Almanac it contained. No body wishes more than I do to see such proofs as you exhibit, that nature has given to our black brethren, talents equal to those of the other colors of men, and that the appearance of a want of them is owing merely to the **degraded** condition of their existence. . . .*

Jefferson wrote Benjamin that he wanted things to change. He hoped, in time, that black people would be treated better. He said:

> *I can add with truth, that no body wishes more ardently*[8] *to see a good system **commenced** for raising the condition both of their body & mind to what it ought to be, as fast as the imbecility*[9] *of their present existence, and other circumstances which cannot be neglected, will admit.*

Benjamin reread the secretary of state's letter several times. Then he folded it carefully and tucked it in one of his astronomy books for safekeeping. Benjamin had spoken his mind in the hope that all people would someday be free.

In December 1791, store owners started selling Benjamin Banneker's Pennsylvania, Maryland, Delaware, and Virginia almanac for the year 1792. Townsfolk from near and far purchased the book. The first edition sold out right away.

Benjamin's almanac contained answers to some of the questions he had asked himself when he was a boy watching the sky. It included cycles of full moons and new moons, times of sunrise and sunset, tide tables for the Chesapeake Bay, and news about festivals and horse habits.

8. **ardently** (är′dənt·lē) *adv.:* passionately.
9. **imbecility** (im′bə·sil′ə·tē) *n.:* foolishness; stupidity.

Portable reflecting telescope from about 1767.

The success of Benjamin's almanac meant that he was free to leave tobacco farming behind. Benjamin sold most of his land but kept his cabin so that he could spend the rest of his days studying astronomy, asking more questions, and finding the answers.

Benjamin published an almanac every year until 1797. His 1793 almanac included the letter he had written to Thomas Jefferson, along with the secretary of state's reply.

Benjamin didn't live to see the day when black people were given their freedom. But his almanacs and the letter he wrote to Thomas Jefferson showed everybody that all men are indeed created equal.

AUTHOR'S NOTE

Benjamin Banneker was a self-taught mathematician and astronomer. Some folks say he was America's first black man of science. But perhaps his most remarkable accomplishment was that he spoke out against racism long before civil rights became a large movement in America.

Notes

IDENTIFY

Two valuable primary sources—letters—are quoted in this biography. Underline the sentence that cites the source of these letters.

IDENTIFY

Pause at line 180. Underline what the writer says is Banneker's "most remarkable accomplishment."

EVALUATE

Pause at line 183. What details in the letter (lines 95–101 and 117–126) justify the author's statement that Banneker called Jefferson a hypocrite?

In his letter written to Secretary of State Thomas Jefferson in August 1791, Benjamin attacked the institution of slavery and dared to call Jefferson a hypocrite.[10] This correspondence helped establish Benjamin Banneker as a vital character on the stage of American history.

When Benjamin was a boy, his grandma Molly taught him to read and write. She used the Bible—the only book she owned—as a text. But Benjamin was most drawn to mathematics. While helping his parents work their tobacco farm, he practiced arithmetic by counting the steps needed to plant and harvest tobacco.

Along with mathematics, Benjamin was fascinated by machinery and how it worked. At the age of twenty-one, Benjamin built a wooden clock by duplicating the gears from a borrowed pocket watch. His handcrafted timepiece was rare in eighteenth century America. Most people back then told time by watching the position of the sun in the sky. Benjamin's clock kept perfect time for more than fifty years.

For much of his adulthood Benjamin lived a quiet, humble life as a tobacco farmer. But in 1788, when Benjamin was fifty-seven years old, he began to teach himself astronomy.

Through his studies of astronomy, Benjamin learned to predict the weather. He even predicted an eclipse of the sun. An accomplished scientist, Benjamin used his skills to create an almanac—something no black man had ever done before.

In January 1791, President George Washington and Secretary of State Thomas Jefferson hired Benjamin to help survey a new nation's capital, which was later named Washington, D.C. Benjamin worked alongside Major

IDENTIFY

Circle Banneker's age when he began to teach himself astronomy (line 201).

---

10. **hypocrite** (hip′ə·krit′) *n.:* person who pretends to be more honorable than he or she really is.

Andrew Ellicott IV, one of the finest surveyors in the United States. Using the stars as his guide, Benjamin helped Ellicott lay the city's boundaries.

Like many trailblazers, Benjamin stood up for what he thought was right, and spoke out against what he believed to be wrong. It took almost 100 years for slaves to be granted their freedom from the time Benjamin wrote to Thomas Jefferson, voicing his views on the injustices of slavery.

Yet Benjamin Banneker, one of the first black men in American history to correspond with a government official, was brave enough to challenge the secretary of state to live up to the ideal Jefferson promised when he wrote the Declaration of Independence in 1776: "life, liberty and the pursuit of happiness" for everyone.

EVALUATE

Biographers combine historical facts about their subject with their own impressions and opinions. Circle the biographer's opinion on Banneker's historical importance in lines 215–217. Do you agree with it? Why or why not?

MEET THE WRITER

Andrea Davis Pinkney (1963–) is a writer and editor of books for young people that celebrate the history and heritage of African Americans. Pinkney spent part of her childhood living in a Connecticut suburb, where she was one of only a few African Americans—an experience she later used as the basis for her young adult novel *Hold Fast to Dreams.* (The title is an allusion to the poem by Langston Hughes on page 174.) Pinkney graduated from Syracuse University with a journalism degree. In 2002, she was named vice president and publisher of Houghton Mifflin's Children's Division. In addition to her biography of Benjamin Banneker, Pinkney has published biographies of the dancer and choreographer Alvin Ailey, the musician Duke Ellington, and the singer Ella Fitzgerald. She is married to the illustrator Brian Pinkney, with whom she has collaborated to create many award-winning children's books.

EVALUATE

Write down any questions you would like to ask this biographer about Banneker.

Dear Benjamin Banneker

Literary Skills Analyze a biography.

Reading Skills Evaluate a biography.

Fact/Imagination and Opinion Chart A **biography** examines the life of an actual person. Most details in a biography are based on fact, but some details come from the author's imagination. Some details will even reflect the writer's opinion of the person. Fill in the first column of the chart below with three details from "Dear Benjamin Banneker" that are examples of fact. Fill in the second column with three details that the writer has imagined or that reflect the writer's opinion.

Details Based on Fact	Details Reflecting Writer's Imagination and Opinion
1.	1.
2.	2.
3.	3.

Skills Review

Dear Benjamin Banneker

VOCABULARY AND COMPREHENSION

A. Using Affixes **Affixes** are word parts that can be added to a word to change its meaning. A **prefix** is an affix added to the beginning of a word. A **suffix** is an affix added to the end of a word. Answer the following questions about affixes and the way they affect word meaning.

Word Bank

calculations
impartial
conferred
degraded
commenced

1. The suffix *–tion* can turn a verb into a noun. What verb is found in the word *calculation*? ______________________

2. The prefix *im–* means "not." What does *impartial* mean? ______________________

3. The prefix *con–* means "with." When teachers *confer* with parents, what are they doing? Use the word *with* in your answer. ______________________

4. The prefix *de–* means "down." How is the idea of "down" used in the word *degraded*? ______________________

B. Reading Comprehension Answer each question below.

1. What kinds of calculations were in Banneker's almanacs? ______________________

2. How did Banneker eventually get his first almanac published? ______________________

3. Why did Banneker write to Thomas Jefferson? ______________________

Vocabulary Skills
Use affixes to clarify meaning.

Before You Read

The Whistle by Anne Estevis

LITERARY FOCUS: BIOGRAPHICAL APPROACH

Writers often use their own life experiences to create fiction. The **setting** may be based on memories of a special place. The **characters** may be based on people they know. The **plot** may include events from their own lives. The **theme** might involve issues that have been important to them. When you consider how the writer's life experiences are reflected in a work, you are using a **biographical approach** to literary criticism.

The setting of "The Whistle" is a small Mexican American community in southern Texas in the 1940s and 1950s, an area of the country that the author Anne Estevis is very familiar with. Estevis was born and raised in south Texas, in Corpus Christi. In writing "The Whistle," Estevis recalls the time and place of her childhood and evokes the culture of this region.

As you read "The Whistle," note how the writer's firsthand experiences are used to make this story seem very real.

READING SKILLS: SUMMARIZING

Summarizing is a useful tool. When you **summarize,** you retell the most important points in a text. When you summarize a story, you identify the series of causes and effects that make up the plot. You identify the story's setting (if it is important), and you describe the main characters and their conflicts.

The side notes in the story that follows will give you practice with summarizing.

Literary Skills Understand a biographical approach to literary criticism.

Reading Skills Summarize.

Vocabulary Skills Clarify word meanings by using restatement.

VOCABULARY DEVELOPMENT

PREVIEW SELECTION VOCABULARY

Review the following words before you begin "The Whistle."

savory (sā′vər·ē) *adj.:* pleasing to the smell or taste; appetizing.

The pleasant smell of the savory goat stew made Chatita hungry.

discerned (di·sʉrnd′) *v.:* detected; recognized.

Chatita had trouble understanding her grandmother, but she discerned enough words to catch the older woman's meaning.

infuriated (in·fyoor′ē·āt′id) *adj.:* angry; enraged.

The children's infuriated grandmother glared at them in anger.

raspy (ras′pē) *adj.:* making a rough, scraping sound.

After yelling for help for so long, the grandmother's voice was hoarse and raspy.

penalize (pē′nə·līz′) *v.:* impose a penalty on; punish.

The grandmother resolved to penalize Chatita by giving her the silent treatment, a punishment her granddaughter hated.

permeated (pʉr′mē·āt′id) *v.:* spread through.

With Chatita and her grandmother not speaking, a new tension permeated the household.

CLARIFYING WORD MEANINGS: RESTATEMENT

You're probably familiar with the phrase "in other words . . ." People use that phrase to signal that they are going to restate something in simpler words. Writers use restatement for emphasis, for clarity, or even to avoid repetition. In the passage below, for example, the meaning of *villa* is clarified in a sentence following the term.

> Nestled high in the mountains was the **villa** of the Fontaine family. If you squinted, you could just make out the red-tiled roof of the country house among the trees.

Words or phrases that provide restatements often appear near the difficult word.

The Whistle

Anne Estevis

My paternal grandmother Carmen was a tiny woman, not even five feet tall. She came to live with us because she said she needed to help my mother with the heavy load of raising a family. Having my grandmother around was usually pleasant; however I remember a time when I wished she would find another family to care for. It was during the late autumn when I was fourteen years old. My parents had gone to San Antonio because my mother's father was very ill.

Before leaving, Mamá said to my abuela,[1] "Please take care of Chatita and the boys while I am gone."

Then Mamá turned around and quietly said to my brothers and me, "Children, please take care of your grandmother."

For several days we all took good care of one another. Then, on Saturday, the third day of my parents' absence, a cool front blew in a short while after we had eaten our noon meal. It wasn't terribly cold, just a little nippy.

My grandmother took note of the pleasant weather and remarked, "What a nice day it is! I think I will clean the storage shed." She retied her sagging apron, put on her sweater, and marched directly out to the shed.

WORD STUDY

Paternal in line 1 means "related through the father." The narrator's paternal grandmother is her father's mother.

IDENTIFY

Pause at line 9. Circle details that describe the grandmother's appearance. Underline phrases that tell how the narrator feels about her grandmother.

INFER

Pause at line 22. Why might a cool front bring weather that is considered pleasant? (Remember that this story takes place in south Texas.)

---

1. abuela (ä·bwe'lə): Spanish for "grandmother."

While my grandmother toiled in the shed, I went about my Saturday chores as usual: washing the bedding, cleaning out the ice box, feeding the chickens, cleaning the lantern chimneys,[2] and polishing my only pair of shoes. My brothers Keno and Chuy had been instructed by our father to prepare the fields for winter vegetable planting, so I was alone in the house. I liked it this way because I could do my work without interruption and get finished sooner.

In the late afternoon I took some vegetable peelings out to the chickens and noticed that the sky was cloudy and the wind was blowing harder than it had earlier. The day was turning cold. I glanced toward the storage shed and wondered how much longer my abuela would be working. I faintly heard what sounded like a goat bleating, so I looked around. Seeing nothing, I hurried back into the house to finish my chores. I especially wanted to get the lanterns put back together before dark.

Later I went out to get some firewood and while picking up small pieces of kindling from near the woodpile I heard again what I thought was a bleating goat. Still, I couldn't see the animal. Perhaps Keno or Chuy had brought home a kid to slaughter. They did that occasionally. We all enjoyed the **savory** meat of *cabrito;*[3] I was beginning to feel hungry just thinking about it. I thought I should look for the animal, but decided to get the fire in the stove going first because I could see Chuy coming toward the house on the tractor. Keno was already at the tractor shed, and the boys usually wanted coffee as soon as they got to the house.

The house quickly warmed from the fire in the cook-stove. I was just putting on the pot for coffee when my brothers stomped into the kitchen.

---

2. **lantern chimneys** *n.:* glass tubes that surround the flames of candles or oil lamps.
3. **cabrito** (kä·brē'tô): Spanish for "young goat."

INFER

Re-read lines 23–30. Circle each of the narrator's chores. Write one or two inferences you can make about the narrator, her family, or their lifestyle based on the details in this paragraph.

SUMMARIZE

Pause at line 39. Summarize the main events of the story so far, and identify the main characters.

VOCABULARY

savory (sā'vər·ē) *adj.:* pleasing to the smell or taste; appetizing.

PREDICT

Pause at line 75. What do you think Chatita is so upset about?

PREDICT

Why do you think Chatita mentions that the latch hook is in place (lines 76–77)?

WORD STUDY

Circle the words in line 86 that tell you the meaning of *Huercos desgraciados.*

SUMMARIZE

Pause at line 86. Think about what has happened since Keno and Chuy came back into the house. What is the problem?

VOCABULARY

discerned (di·surnd′) *v.:* detected; recognized.

© Darrell Lecorre/ Masterfile

"It's really getting cold out there!" said Chuy as he hovered over the big stove.

"Is the coffee ready, Chatita?" Keno asked.

I shook my head.

"What about the goat? Are you going to butcher it?"

Neither answered. Chuy stopped warming his hands and turned away from the stove to look at me. Keno continued washing up in the enamel wash pan.

"I said, are you going to butcher the goat?"

"What goat are you talking about?" responded Keno.

"We don't have any goats," said Chuy.

I gasped and said, "Oh, my goodness! Come with me! Hurry!" I bounded out the kitchen door with my brothers behind me.

As we approached the storage shed I could see that the outside latch hook on the door was in place. I flipped the hook up and flung open the door. There, sitting on the floor, wrapped up in burlap bags like a mummy, was a cold and shivering grandmother. She tried to talk, but her voice was almost gone.

My brother helped the tiny woman to her feet and Keno carried her into the house as quickly as he could. All the way she was croaking like a frog, but I'm sure I **discerned** the words "*¡Huercos desgraciados!*" repeated over and over. This meant that we were wretched brats, or maybe worse.

My brothers placed her in the chair nearest the kitchen stove while I fetched a soft woolen blanket to wrap her in. Chuy poured a cup of coffee and set it before her. Then we all sat down around the table staring at our obviously **infuriated** grandmother.

"What unfortunate children you are. You have no brains!" she said in a **raspy** voice. Her entire body was shivering. "You left me to die out there!" She shook her fist at each one of us and then looked squarely at me. "You, Telésfora. You must be deaf!" She shook a crooked index finger at me.

I knew she was very angry with me because she used my real name.

"I called and called for you. The wind blew the door shut and it locked. All afternoon I yelled, but you didn't come. I nearly froze to death!" She scowled and slowly turned her head away from me.

"But I didn't hear you," I answered. "I'm sorry. Please, Abuelita. I'm truly sorry!"

How could I have confused my grandmother's voice with that of a bleating goat? I felt terribly guilty and ashamed. I knew that the shed door was prone to latch by itself if it was slammed. That's why a wooden stake for propping the door open was usually kept nearby. But this time the stake had not been used, and now my grandmother was shaking and shivering and glaring at me.

"Just you wait, Telésfora. Just you wait until your father gets home. I'll have him punish you," she said and her bottom lip quivered and her nostrils flared.

My parents came home in a few days and of course the first thing that occurred was that Abuelita told her story to my father.

VOCABULARY

infuriated (in·fyoor′ē·āt′id) *adj.:* angry; enraged.

raspy (ras′pē) *adj.:* making a rough, scraping sound.

FLUENCY

Read the boxed passage aloud several times. Use punctuation clues to guide your reading. As you read this dialogue, let the pitch and tone of your voice convey the grandmother's fury. How would Chatita's voice sound? Use your imagination and clues from the text to bring this scene to life.

SUMMARIZE

Pause at line 115. Sum up how the grandmother got locked in the shed.

"Son, Telésfora left me locked in the storage shed all afternoon on Saturday. I called and called for her, but she declares she didn't hear me. She says she heard a goat bleating. Can you imagine that I could possibly sound like a goat?" my grandmother said.

My father was very concerned, of course. I admitted to him that, indeed, I had mistakenly thought I heard a goat and that I was terribly sorry that I hadn't checked on Abuelita as I should have. He scolded me severely. But this wasn't enough punishment, according to my grandmother, so she decided to **penalize** me herself by refusing to speak to me. This made me very sad, and it seemed to affect all of us. A sense of sorrow and discomfort **permeated** our family.

Two weeks later I asked to go with my father to the big yellow store in town. While Papá made his purchases, I bought a silver whistle and a long piece of blue satin ribbon. I threaded the ribbon through the ring on the whistle and tied the ends of the ribbon together.

That evening, I placed the whistle in a little box and wrapped it in some colored paper. After supper, I approached my grandmother.

"This is for you, Abuelita. I'm terribly sorry about what happened to you in the shed. I hope you can forgive me."

My grandmother looked at me and said nothing. Then she took the box and opened it. She pulled the whistle out by its ribbon.

"Well, Telésfora, whatever is this for?" she asked, keeping her eyes on the whistle.

"It's to wear around your neck when you are outside. If you need me, just blow the whistle and I'll come to you," I said.

IDENTIFY CAUSE & EFFECT

Re-read lines 124–131. Underline the details that tell you how the grandmother decides to punish Chatita. Circle details that describe the **effect** of this punishment.

VOCABULARY

penalize (pē′nə·līz′) *v.:* impose a penalty on; punish.

permeated (pur′mē·āt′id) *v.:* spread through.

PREDICT

Pause at line 141. How do you think Chatita's grandmother will respond to the whistle?

"And how can I be sure you'll hear this little whistle? You couldn't even hear me yelling at you!" But Abuela put it around her neck anyway.

The next evening, while I was feeding the chickens, I heard a faint whistle. I stopped what I was doing and stood very still. Then I heard the whistle more distinctly. Yes! It was definitely coming from inside the storage shed. I rushed to the shed and found the door latched. That surprised me because the wind wasn't blowing at all. There was no way that the door could have slammed shut by itself. Something seemed really strange about this, and I was suspicious. I unlatched the door and opened it. There stood my grandmother with the whistle in her mouth. She quickly removed it and said, "I think your papá needs to do something about that crazy door latch. Don't you think so, Chatita?"

She hurried out of the shed and we started toward the house. I could see that she was smiling, and I think I even heard her chuckling.

MEET THE WRITER

Anne Estevis (1936–) is a teacher, scholar, and writer. In *Down Garrapata Road,* a collection of short stories that includes "The Whistle," Estevis brings to life her experience of growing up Mexican American in the American Southwest during the 1940s and 1950s. Estevis was born in Corpus Christi, Texas, and later moved with her family to a ranch near Santa Rosa, New Mexico. Her mother, originally from New Mexico, taught Estevis to value the traditions, customs, and stories of the American Southwest and of the Mexican Americans who live there. In Estevis's long career, she taught students of many ages—from the elementary through the graduate level.

INFER

Re-read lines 153–164. How do you think Chatita's grandmother came to be locked in the shed this time? Underline the details that support your answer.

SUMMARIZE

Summarize what happens after Chatita gives the whistle to her grandmother. How is their **conflict** resolved?

SKILLS PRACTICE

The Whistle

Literary Skills Use a biographical approach to literary criticism.

Biographical Approach Chart When you take a **biographical approach** to literary criticism, you explore the way a writer's life experiences may be reflected in a text. Review the biography of Anne Estevis on page 249. Then, fill out the chart below to show how Estevis's background, experiences, and interests may be seen in "The Whistle." In the first column, list key details about the story's setting and characters, as well as any other details you would like to include. In the second column, explain how these details relate to Estevis's background.

Story Elements and Details	Writer's Background
Setting:	
Characters:	
Details in Story:	

Skills Review

The Whistle

VOCABULARY AND COMPREHENSION

A. Clarifying Word Meanings: Restatement Each numbered item below contains a word in boldface. Underline the details in each passage that contain a restatement of each boldface word.

Word Bank
savory
discerned
infuriated
raspy
penalize
permeated

1. When Chatita imagined a **savory** goat stew, she grew hungry for this flavorful dish.
2. The children could barely **discern** what the grandmother was saying. It was upsetting not to be able to make out her words.
3. Even after she warmed up, the grandmother's **raspy** voice did not change. It remained scratchy and hoarse.
4. The grandmother felt that Chatita should be **penalized** for her mistake. She decided to punish the girl severely.

B. Reading Comprehension Answer each question below.

1. Who are the characters in this story? ______________________

____

2. Why does Chatita's grandmother get angry with Chatita? __________

____

____

3. What does Chatita do to end her conflict with her grandmother?

____

____

4. What does Chatita's grandmother do to show she forgives her?

____

____

Vocabulary Skills
Clarify word meanings by using restatement.

Collection 8

Reading for Life

Yellow Dog Productions/Getty Images

Academic Vocabulary for Collection 8

These are the terms you should know
as you read and analyze the selections in this collection.

Public Documents Informational documents that inform the public. Voter-registration packets, swimming regulations at a public pool, and weather bulletins are examples of public documents.

Consumer Documents Informational documents used in the buying and selling of products. Instruction manuals, warranties, and contracts are examples of consumer documents.

Workplace Documents Informational documents used in offices, factories, and other work sites. Memos, schedules, and project guidelines are examples of workplace documents.

Technical Directions Documents used to explain or establish procedures for using technology. How-to instructions and installation manuals provide technical directions.

Museum Announcement / Press Release / Metro Map

READING FOCUS: ANALYZING PUBLIC DOCUMENTS

We, the public, get a lot of information from public documents. Any document (printed or electronic) that gives information to us is called a **public document.** Public documents may be issued by schools, places of worship, government agencies, courts, libraries, and fire and police departments, for example. The following are some examples of public documents:

Type of Document	Purpose
Elevator certificate	To inform public when and by whom elevator inspection was last performed
Calendar of local events	To inform townspeople of community events and services
Evacuation booklet	To inform public of emergency procedures in the event of a disaster

IDENTIFYING TEXT STRUCTURES

Unlike novels, stories, and poems, which are often read for enjoyment, public documents are read for one reason: to get information. It's your job as a reader to locate the information you need and to clarify its meaning. Use text-structure clues to find and make sense of the information in public documents.

Reading Skills Analyze information in public documents; identify text structures.

Common Text Structures

- headings (capture main point of text that follows)
- bulleted lists (give information in logical order)
- numbered lists (give information in a specific sequence)
- charts, graphs, and illustrations (capture information visually)
- captions (describe visuals)
- boldface and italics (give emphasis to text; highlight important ideas)

READING AN ANNOUNCEMENT

Let's follow one person's experience in finding information in public documents. Meet Maria Sanchez. Maria has two great passions: music and anything Cuban. Her grandparents had been musicians in Cuba before they immigrated to the United States. Imagine her excitement when she came across the following announcement in *The Washington Post.*

THE SMITHSONIAN'S NATIONAL MUSEUM OF AMERICAN HISTORY

presents

"¡*Azúcar!* The Life and Music of Celia Cruz." May 18.

- **Place:** 14th Street and Constitution Avenue NW
- **Time:** open daily 10:00 A.M.–5:30 P.M.
- **Phone Number:** For more information, call (202) 633-1000.

TEXT STRUCTURE

Circle the boldface text in lines 5–6. What important information does the boldface type convey?

TEXT STRUCTURE

Why is the information in lines 7–11 organized in a bulleted list?

IDENTIFY

Circle the part of the announcement that tells you what to do if you need more information.

Cuban singer Celia Cruz,

READING A PRESS RELEASE

Celia Cruz, the legendary Cuban singer, is one of Maria's heroes, so she can't wait to get to the exhibit. First, though, she wants more information. An Internet search using the key words "Smithsonian" and "Celia Cruz" yields the following press release from the museum:

IDENTIFY

Circle the date the press release was made public. Underline the date the exhibit opens.

EVALUATE

Pause at line 11. Keep in mind that one of the purposes of this press release is to persuade people to attend the exhibit. Underline the reasons the Smithsonian is presenting the exhibit. Would you be interested in going to see it? Why or why not?

SUMMARIZE

Re-read lines 19–21. Summarize the important information provided about Celia Cruz's career.

Smithsonian *Press Release*

April 1, 2005

The Smithsonian Celebrates Life and Legacy of Queen of Salsa Celia Cruz

The Smithsonian's National Museum of American History will explore the life of legendary Cuban-born singer Celia Cruz (1925–2003) and her impressive career with "*¡Azúcar!* The Life and Music of Celia Cruz," a new exhibition opening May 18, 2005.

"Celia Cruz embodied the American Dream and the story of her life and career will allow our visitors to explore the themes of American identity and the many contributions Latinos have made to American culture and popular music," said museum director Brent D. Glass.

Over the course of a career that spanned six decades and took her from humble beginnings in Havana, Cuba, to a world-renowned artist, Celia Cruz became the undisputed Queen of Latin Music. Combining a piercing and powerful voice with a larger-than-life personality and stage costumes, she was one of the few women to succeed in the male dominated world of Salsa music. Upon her death, she was celebrated around the world as the "Queen of Latin Music" and the "Queen of Salsa." Salsa is music born in New York City of Cuban and other Afro-Caribbean mixed musical genres. In her personification of Salsa, Cruz came to represent all Latinos.

"¡Azúcar!" will highlight important moments in Cruz' life and career through photographs, personal documents, costumes, rare footage, music videos and music. The show will begin with her childhood and early appearances with the band, "La Sonora Matancera," in Cuba. Among the dozen featured costumes will be a dress from a 1950s performance in Cuba and the dress she wore at her last public appearance, designed by Narciso Rodríguez. The

exhibition title, *"¡Azúcar!"*—meaning sugar—is taken from her famous rallying cry.

To view the exhibition and for updates on the traveling version of *"¡Azúcar!* The Life and Music of Celia Cruz" visit <u>http://americanhistory.si.edu/celiacruz</u>

The National Museum of American History traces American heritage through exhibitions of social, cultural, scientific and technological history. Collections are displayed in exhibitions that interpret the American experience from Colonial times to the present.

IDENTIFY

Why is line 33 underlined?

CLARIFY

Pause at line 38. In your own words, explain the National Museum of American History's purpose.

Locating Information: A Map

Now Maria has all the information she needs—except how to get to the museum. She again looks online, this time for a map of the Metro, the underground rail system in Washington, D.C. Study the map below to find out what route Maria should take to travel from her home near Dupont Circle to the Smithsonian.

IDENTIFY

Suppose a friend wants to come from Friendship Heights to go see the exhibit. How would you tell her to get there?

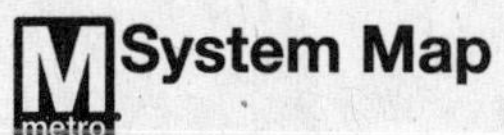

Legend

- Red Line • Glenmont to Shady Grove
- Orange Line • New Carrollton to Vienna/Fairfax-GMU
- Blue Line • Franconia-Springfield to Largo Town Center
- Green Line • Branch Avenue to Greenbelt
- Yellow Line • Huntington to Mt Vernon Sq/7th St-Convention Center

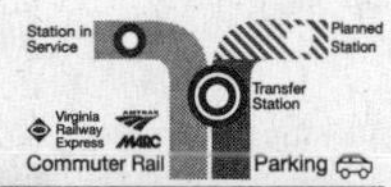

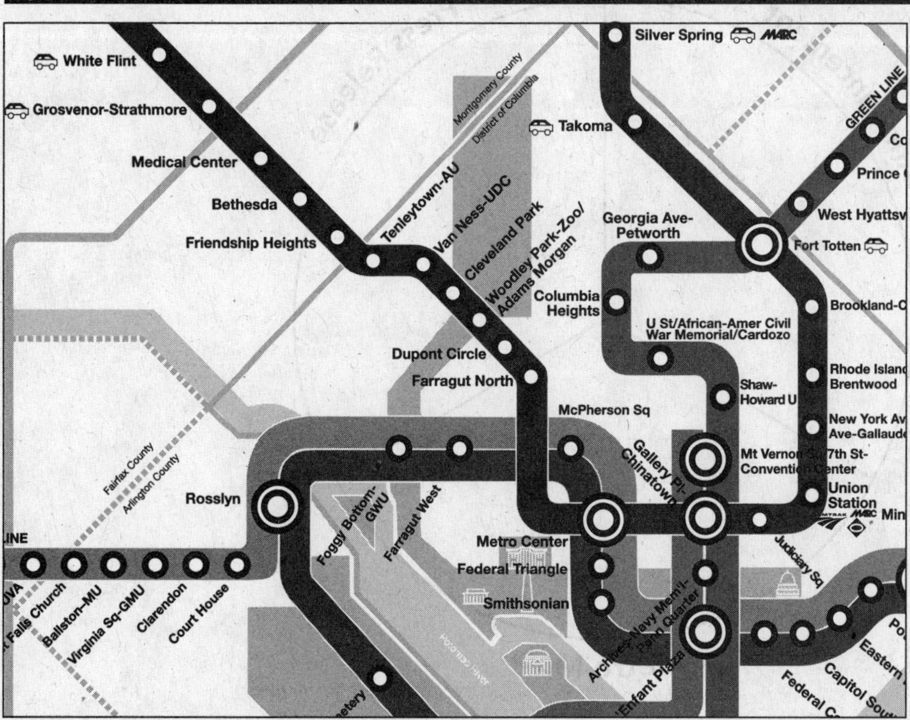

Washington, D.C. Metro System Map from *Washington Metropolitan Area Transit Authority* Web site, accessed March 6, 2006 at http://wmta.com/metrorail/systemmap.cfm.

IDENTIFY

After visiting the Smithsonian, Maria decides to go to the African American Civil War Memorial. Circle both locations on the map. Then, explain how Maria should get from point to point.

SKILLS PRACTICE

Museum Announcement / Press Release / Metro Map

Information-Locator Wheel The documents you just read contain a lot of information. Write the number of each item from the Information Bank in the area of the wheel that shows where each piece of information can be found.

1. the way to the Smithsonian from Fairfax County
2. the way Celia Cruz embodied the American dream
3. the cross streets of the Smithsonian
4. the Metro lines that lead to the Smithsonian
5. Celia Cruz's birth and death dates
6. the Web site address to find updates on the exhibit
7. the Smithsonian's phone number
8. Celia Cruz's nicknames
9. the meaning of *azúcar*
10. the hours the Smithsonian is open

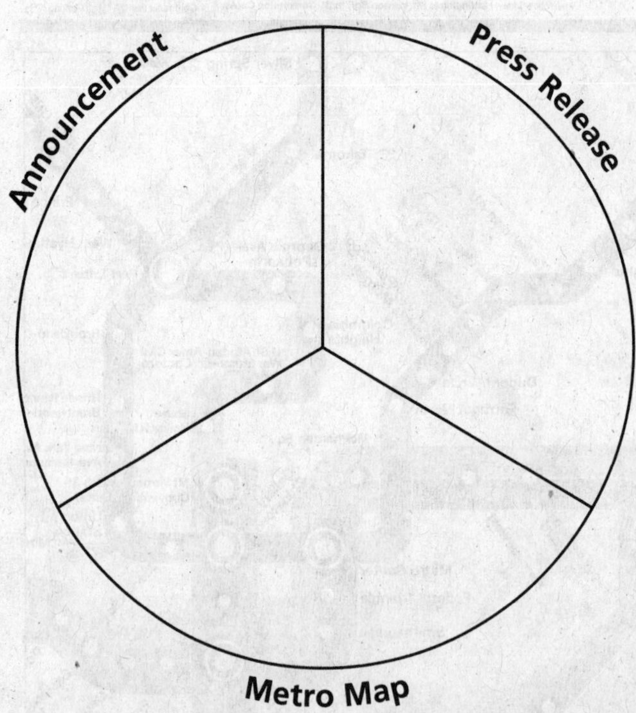

Museum Announcement / Press Release / Metro Map

COMPREHENSION

Reading Comprehension Answer the questions that follow

1. Why was Maria excited when she came across the announcement in *The Washington Post*? ______

______

______

2. Where and when is the exhibit being held? ______

______

______

3. What is exceptional about Cruz's success in the world of salsa music?

______

______

4. How can you find out more information about the traveling exhibit on Celia Cruz? ______

______

______

5. Why are the subway lines on the map presented in different shades of gray? ______

______

______

VividPlayer Download Instructions

READING FOCUS: ANALYZING TECHNICAL DIRECTIONS

The purpose of **technical directions** is to guide the reader through a series of steps in order to achieve a goal (assembling a piece of furniture, building a model airplane, and so on). Although directions may not be the most exciting things to read, they can be real timesavers—and even lifesavers—when written effectively and followed correctly.

Effective directions, regardless of their subject matter, contain the same basic features:

- a complete list of supplies, tools, or ingredients needed
- a series of steps, numbered or lettered to indicate sequence
- diagrams or charts to illustrate complex steps
- clearly labeled warnings

IDENTIFYING TEXT STRUCTURES

Many informational texts, especially those containing technical directions, are formatted in certain ways to make information stand out more clearly. The more familiar you are with these features, the better you'll be able to locate and digest the information within these texts.

Common Text Structures

- headings (capture main point of text that follows)
- bulleted lists (give information in logical order)
- numbered lists (give information in a specific sequence)
- charts, graphs, and illustrations (capture information visually)
- captions (describe visuals)
- boldface and italics (give emphasis to text; highlight important ideas)

Reading Skills Analyze technical directions; identify text structures.

Following Technical Directions

Maria is so inspired by what she sees at the Smithsonian that she decides to check out the online exhibit. In order to access everything the exhibit has to offer, however, she needs to download VividPlayer software. She does this by following the directions on the company's Web site.

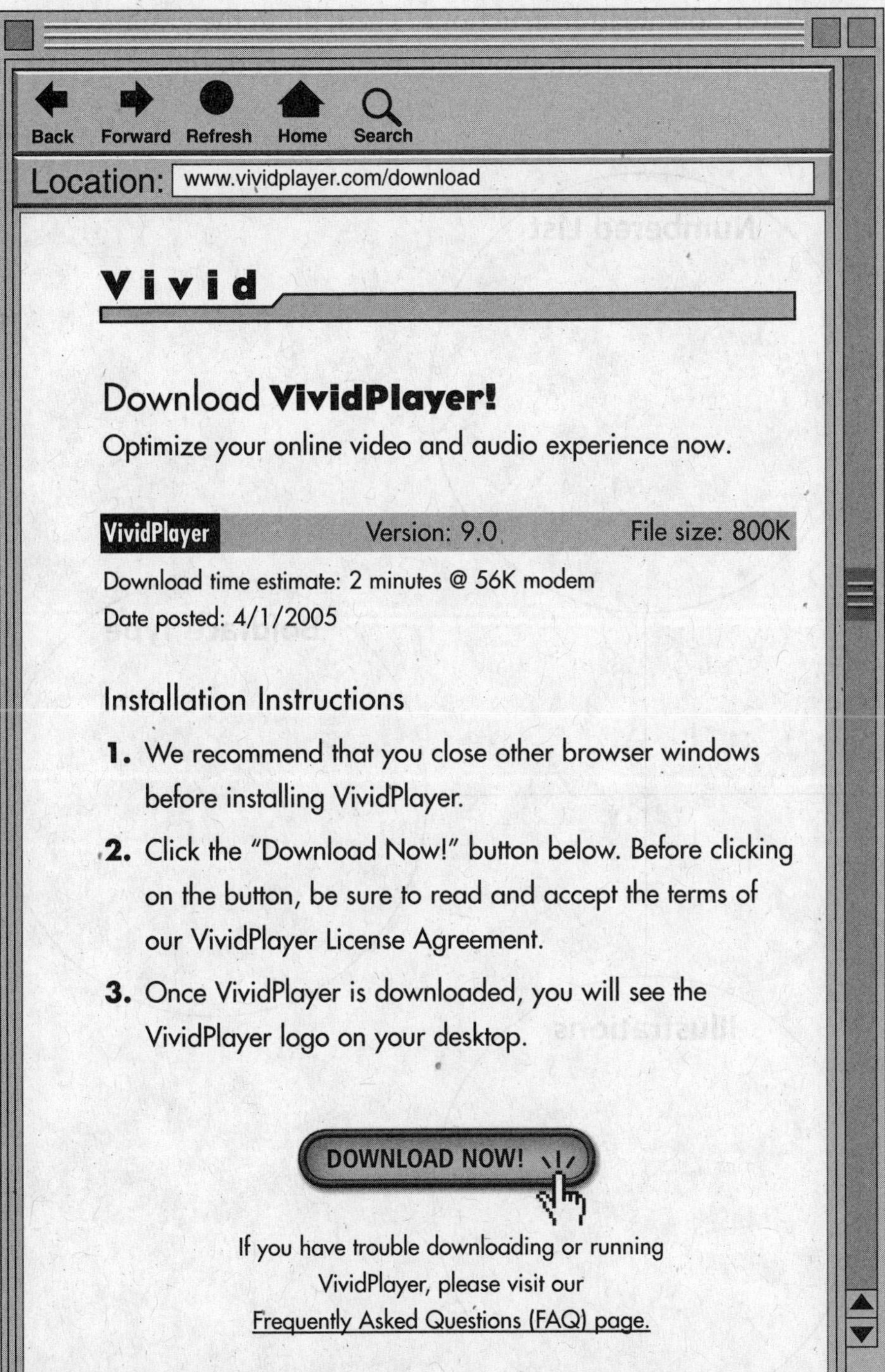

INFER

Why do you think the company provides an estimated time for downloading the software?

TEXT STRUCTURE

Why are the installation instructions set in a **numbered list?**

TEXT STRUCTURE

Why is there an illustration of a hand pointing to the words "Download Now"?

VividPlayer Download Instructions

Technical Directions Organizer Technical directions may focus on any number of topics, from fixing a hard disk to building a hang glider. Most technical directions, however, contain common features and text structures to make accessing the information predictable and easy. Read through the VividPlayer download instructions. Then, fill in the graphic organizer below with the information provided in each part of the instructions.

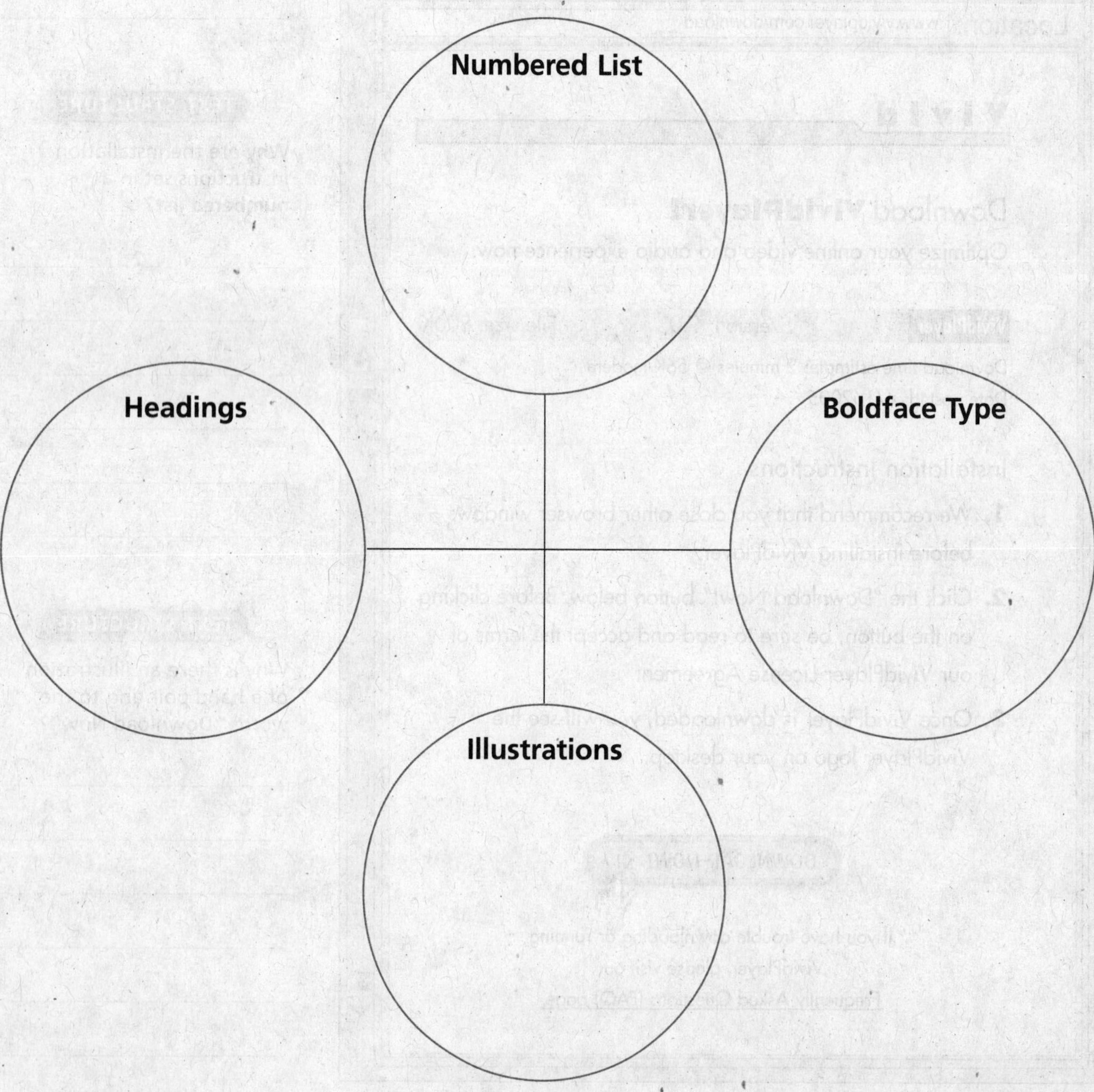

Skills Review

VividPlayer Download Instructions

COMPREHENSION

Reading Comprehension Answer the questions that follow.

1. Why does Maria decide to download VividPlayer? ________________

____

____

____

2. What do the instructions recommend one do before starting to install VividPlayer? ________________________________

____

____

3. What should Maria read before downloading VividPlayer?

____

____

____

4. How will Maria know if she has successfully downloaded VividPlayer? ________________________________

____

____

5. Why is "Frequently Asked Questions (FAQ) page" underlined?

____

____

____

Part Two

Reading Informational Texts

Academic Vocabulary for Part 2

These are the terms you should know as you read and analyze the informational selections in this section.

Comparison Description of how two or more things are alike.

Contrast Description of how two or more things are different.

Cause An event that makes something happen.

Effect What happens as a result of a cause.

Argument A position supported by evidence.

Evidence Details a writer uses to support his or her position.

Main Idea The most important point in a text or section of text.

Summary A brief restatement of the main events or ideas in a text.

• • •

Text Features Special type, such as boldface, italics, capitals, and bullets, that calls attention to important information.

Headings Titles at the tops of pages or sections.

Illustrations Drawings, photos, art, graphs, maps, or other visuals.

Captions Descriptions of art, illustrations, charts, or maps. A caption usually appears beneath or next to the visual it describes.

Sidebars Short articles set off from the main text that focus on a topic related to the text.

Footnotes Definitions and/or examples of difficult terms within the text. Footnotes are numbered and usually appear at the bottom of the text page.

Before You Read

MAGAZINE ARTICLE

Hard at Work by Ritu Upadhyay

READING SKILLS: UNDERSTANDING TEXT STRUCTURES

Text structures help us locate and understand information we read in articles and books. As you read "Hard at Work," look at how the following structures are used:

- **Main headings and subheads** Words or short phrases that hint at the main idea of the text that follows. A main heading may be followed by one or more subheads.
- **Illustrations** Art, photographs, charts, or maps that accompany a text.
- **Captions** Descriptions of art, photographs, charts, or maps. A caption usually appears beneath the visual it describes.
- **Sidebars** Short articles set off from the main text that focus on a topic related to the text.
- **Footnotes** Definitions and/or examples of difficult or unfamiliar terms within the text. Footnotes usually appear at the bottom of the page.

VOCABULARY DEVELOPMENT: PREVIEW SELECTION VOCABULARY

Preview these vocabulary words before you begin to read.

estimated (es′tə·māt′id) *v.* used as *adj.:* approximate; almost correct or exact.

The estimated number of child workers in many countries would shock most Americans.

exposed (ek·spōzd′) *v.:* put in a situation that can be harmful.

Children in Ecuador are often exposed to unsafe conditions that could harm them in the long term.

mistreatment (mis·trēt′mənt) *n.:* harmful treatment.

We should consider not buying bananas to take a stand against the mistreatment of child workers.

hazardous (haz′ər·dəs) *adj.:* dangerous.

Workers are exposed to hazardous conditions, including dangerous machinery and chemicals.

Reading Skills
Understand text structures.

Hard at Work

Ritu Upadhyay

AP Photo/Kent Gilbert

A child worker hauls bananas in Ecuador.

Ten-year-old Wilbur Carreno is less than four feet tall and weighs only 50 pounds. He is small for his age. That's exactly what makes him good at his job.

Wilbur spends his afternoons climbing banana trees four times his height. He expertly ties the heavy stalks of bananas so the trees won't droop from the weight of the fruit. "I've been working since I was 8," he told *Time for Kids*. "I finish school at noon and then go to the field."

In Wilbur's poor country of Ecuador,[1] one in every four children is working. An **estimated** 69,000 kids toil away on the vast banana plantations along the country's coast. Ecuador is the world's largest banana exporter. Kids working in the industry are **exposed** to harmful chemicals, pull loads twice their weight and use sharp, heavy knives.

1. **Ecuador** (ek′wə·dôr′): Located in northeastern South America, Ecuador is one of the smallest countries on the continent.

TEXT STRUCTURE

Look at the photograph before you begin reading. What do you think this article will be about?

VOCABULARY

estimated (es′tə·māt′id) *v.* used as *adj.*: approximate; almost correct or exact.

exposed (ek·spōzd′) *v.:* put in a situation that can be harmful.

TEXT STRUCTURE

Underline the subhead in line 15. Explain what you think the topic of this section will be.

INTERPRET

Re-read the quotations in lines 29–32. How do they shed light on the topic of the article?

TEXT STRUCTURE

How much do banana exporters in Ecuador get paid for a 43-pound crate of bananas? How much do consumers in the U.S. pay for a crate of the same size?

Do Kids Belong on the Job?

Child labor is certainly not limited to Ecuador. The United Nations estimates that 250 million kids around the world are forced to work. Many countries don't have laws limiting kids' work.

A concerned group called Human Rights Watch conducted a study of Ecuador's banana plantations. They found that most children begin working on plantations around age 10. Their average workday lasts 12 hours! By age 14, 6 out of 10 no longer attend school. Many families face the difficult choice of either putting food on their tables or sending their kids to school.

The family of Alejandro, 12, struggles with that choice. Alejandro has had to work beside his father, Eduardo Sinchi, on a plantation. "I don't want my kids to work," says Sinchi. "I want them in school, but we have few options." Sinchi has nine children and earns as little as $27 a week. "It isn't even enough for food, let alone school, clothes, transportation."

Slim Pickings

Ecuador supplies a quarter of the bananas sold in the U.S. Most of the money from sales goes to U.S. grocery stores. Workers in Ecuador get little money. Here's about how much a 43-pound crate costs as it goes from the plantation to you.

- $2.40 Amount per crate a U.S. distributor pays banana exporters in Ecuador. Of this, about $1.54 goes to plantation workers.
- $7.50 What supermarkets pay a distributor for a crate
- $22 What you would pay for 43 pounds of bananas at the grocery store

Hard Work for Little Pay

Sinchi's pay is typical in Ecuador. The average banana worker earns just $6 a day. One reason pay is so low is that Ecuadorians are not allowed to form work groups called unions. In countries like Costa Rica, where laws allow unions, some banana workers earn $11 a day. Such countries have fewer child workers because better pay means parents can afford to keep their kids in school.

Ecuador's big banana companies have begun to do something about child labor. Last year, they signed an agreement not to hire kids younger than 15 and to protect young workers from chemicals. "We need to eliminate child labor," says Jorge Illingworth, of Ecuador's Banana Exporters Association. But small plantations did not sign the agreement, and, he says, they employ 70% of the kids.

Banning child labor is a start, but it doesn't really help families like the Sinchis. Now that Alejandro can't work, his family suffers more. The answer, most believe, is better pay for Ecuador's adult workers. For that to happen, U.S. shoppers would have to put up with higher banana prices or stop buying Ecuador's bananas to make their point. Guillermo Touma fights to help Ecuador's workers. "If we could raise awareness," he says, "we could raise wages and invest in education for our children."

Child Labor in the U.S.A.

The **mistreatment** of child workers is not just a foreign problem. Throughout its history, the United States has counted on kids to lend a hand in fields and factories. In the 1800s, children as young as 7 worked in textile mills for 12 hours a day. By the end of the 19th century, almost 2 million kids performed **hazardous** jobs in mills, mines and factories.

IDENTIFY CAUSE & EFFECT

Pause at line 56. Underline the reason that pay is so low for banana workers in Ecuador.

IDENTIFY

Pause at line 67. What needs to happen before families like the Sinchis receive the help they need?

VOCABULARY

mistreatment (mis·trēt′mənt) *n.:* harmful treatment.

Lines 69–75 give examples of the mistreatment of young workers to help clue you in to the word's meaning. Underline these examples.

hazardous (haz′ər·dəs) *adj.:* dangerous.

TEXT STRUCTURE

How does the photograph help you understand the child labor issue?

A yarn mill in Mississippi (1911).

Many concerned citizens worked to change this. Photographer Lewis Hine, who took this photo of young cotton mill workers, was one of them. In 1938, a U.S. law was passed that limits work hours for kids and requires safe conditions. The law still exists, but it is not always enforced. An estimated 800,000 children work illegally in the U.S. today, mostly in farming and related industries. Some work with heavy machinery, poisonous chemicals or under other conditions that could harm them.

SKILLS PRACTICE

Hard at Work

Text Structures Chart You can use the text structures in informational pieces to help you find different kinds of information. Read through "Hard at Work," and fill in the chart below with examples of the types of text structures it contains.

Reading Skills
Analyze text structures.

Title of Text:	Photographs and Captions (What Are They About?):
Headings (What Are They?):	**Main Idea:**

Hard at Work

VOCABULARY AND COMPREHENSION

Word Bank

estimated
exposed
mistreatment
hazardous

A. Selection Vocabulary Write the Word Bank words on the blanks to complete this paragraph. Use each word only once.

After gathering information about child labor, I was disgusted by the (1)____________________ of these children. They are (2)____________________ to numerous dangers during the day, including heavy knives and (3)____________________ materials. I don't know the (4)____________________ number of child workers, but it's obvious even one is too many.

B. Reading Comprehension Answer each question below.

1. What product is Ecuador known for exporting?

____

____

2. List two facts uncovered by Human Rights Watch during their study in Ecuador.

____

____

3. What steps has Ecuador taken to put an end to child labor?

____

____

4. What U.S. law was passed in 1938?

____

____

Before You Read

I Am a Native of North America

by Chief Dan George

READING SKILLS: ANALYZING COMPARISON AND CONTRAST

When you **compare** two things, you look for ways in which they are similar. When you **contrast** two things, you look for ways in which they are different. Look at the examples in the chart below.

Cantaloupe and Honeydew

Comparison	Contrast
• both fruits • both melons • both roundish • both have rinds • both taste sweet	• Cantaloupe has a rough green-gray rind; honeydew has a smooth green rind. • Cantaloupe has bright orange flesh; honeydew has light green flesh.

Read "I Am a Native of North America," and then compare and contrast the information you find in it.

VOCABULARY DEVELOPMENT: PREVIEW SELECTION VOCABULARY

Preview these vocabulary words before you begin to read.

distinct (di·stiŋkt′) *adj.:* separate; different.

Chief Dan George views the Native American and white cultures as distinct.

justifies (jus′tə·fīz′) *v.:* proves or shows to be right or valid.

Chief Dan George finds nothing that justifies the mistreatment of nature.

indifferent (in·dif′ər·ənt) *adj.:* unfeeling or uninterested.

According to Chief Dan George, white people tend to be indifferent to Native American values.

integration (in′tə·grā′shən) *n.:* joining of different racial or ethnic groups in a society.

Cultures can benefit from integration.

Reading Skills
Understand comparison-and-contrast texts.

I Am a Native of North America

Chief Dan George

© Bettmann/CORBIS

Chief Dan George

Notes

VOCABULARY

distinct (di·stiŋkt′) *adj.:* separate; different.

In the course of my lifetime I have lived in two **distinct** cultures. I was born into a culture that lived in communal houses. My grandfather's house was eighty feet long. It was called a smoke house, and it stood down by the beach along the inlet.[1] All my grandfather's sons and their families lived in this large dwelling. Their sleeping apartments were separated by blankets made of bull rush reeds,[2] but one

1. **inlet** *n.:* narrow strip of water that flows from the sea to the land.
2. **bull rush reeds** *n.:* tall, thin grass from marsh plants.

open fire in the middle served the cooking needs of all. In houses like these, throughout the tribe, people learned to live with one another; learned to serve one another; learned to respect the rights of one another. And children shared the thoughts of the adult world and found themselves surrounded by aunts and uncles and cousins who loved them and did not threaten them. My father was born in such a house and learned from infancy how to love people and be at home with them.

And beyond this acceptance of one another there was a deep respect for everything in nature that surrounded them. My father loved the earth and all its creatures. The earth was his second mother. The earth and everything it contained was a gift from See-see-am[3] . . . and the way to thank this great spirit was to use his gifts with respect.

I remember, as a little boy, fishing with him up Indian River and I can still see him as the sun rose above the mountain top in the early morning . . . I can see him standing by the water's edge with his arms raised above his head while he softly moaned . . . "Thank you, thank you." It left a deep impression on my young mind.

And I shall never forget his disappointment when once he caught me gaffing[4] for fish "just for the fun of it." "My Son," he said, "the Great Spirit gave you those fish to be your brothers, to feed you when you are hungry. You must respect them. You must not kill them just for the fun of it."

This then was the culture I was born into and for some years the only one I really knew or tasted. This is why I find it hard to accept many of the things I see around me.

I see people living in smoke houses hundreds of times bigger than the one I knew. But the people in one apartment

3. **See-see-am:** name of the Mighty Spirit, or "The Chief Above," in the language of the Salish people.

4. **gaffing** *v.* used as *adj.:* catching fish with a barbed spear.

INTERPRET

Pause at line 16. Underline three key details in the first paragraph about the culture Chief Dan George was born into. What do these details tell you about the culture?

FLUENCY

Read the boxed passage aloud. Before you begin, make sure you can pronounce all of the words in the passage. Try to capture the disappointment of Chief Dan George's father when you read his dialogue.

do not even know the people in the next and care less about them.

It is also difficult for me to understand the deep hate that exists among people. It is hard to understand a culture that **justifies** the killing of millions in past wars, and is at this very moment preparing bombs to kill even greater numbers. It is hard for me to understand a culture that spends more on wars and weapons to kill, than it does on education and welfare to help and develop.

It is hard for me to understand a culture that not only hates and fights its brothers but even attacks nature and abuses her. I see my white brother going about blotting out nature from his cities. I see him strip the hills bare, leaving ugly wounds on the face of mountains. I see him tearing things from the bosom of mother earth as though she were a monster, who refused to share her treasures with him. I see him throw poison in the waters, **indifferent** to the life he kills there; and he chokes the air with deadly fumes.

My white brother does many things well for he is more clever than my people but I wonder if he knows how to love well. I wonder if he has ever really learned to love at all. Perhaps he only loves the things that are his own but never learned to love the things that are outside and beyond him. And this is, of course, not love at all, for man must love all creation or he will love none of it. Man must love fully or he will become the lowest of the animals. It is the power to love that makes him the greatest of them all . . . for he alone of all animals is capable of love.

Love is something you and I must have. We must have it because our spirit feeds upon it. We must have it because without it we become weak and faint. Without love our self-esteem weakens. Without it our courage fails. Without love we can no longer look out confidently at the world.

COMPARE & CONTRAST

Pause at line 41. What difference between the two cultures has Chief Dan George identified?

VOCABULARY

justifies (jus′tə·fīz′) *v.:* proves or shows to be right or valid.

indifferent (in·dif′ər·ənt) *adj.:* unfeeling or uninterested.

COMPARE & CONTRAST

According to Chief Dan George, how did the white culture and the Native American culture treat nature differently? Back up your statement with details from lines 49–57.

EVALUATE

Do you agree with the point the writer makes in lines 58–67? Why or why not?

Instead we turn inwardly and begin to feed upon our own personalities and little by little we destroy ourselves.

You and I need the strength and joy that comes from knowing that we are loved. With it we are creative. With it we march tirelessly. With it, and with it alone, we are able to sacrifice for others.

There have been times when we all wanted so desperately to feel a reassuring hand upon us . . . there have been lonely times when we so wanted a strong arm around us . . . I cannot tell you how deeply I miss my wife's presence when I return from a trip. Her love was my greatest joy, my strength, my greatest blessing.

I am afraid my culture has little to offer yours. But my culture did prize friendship and companionship. It did not look on privacy as a thing to be clung to, for privacy builds up walls and walls promote distrust. My culture lived in big family communities, and from infancy people learned to live with others.

My culture did not prize the hoarding of private possessions; in fact, to hoard was a shameful thing to do among my people. The Indian looked on all things in nature as belonging to him and he expected to share them with others and to take only what he needed.

Everyone likes to give as well as receive. No one wishes only to receive all the time. We have taken much from your culture . . . I wish you had taken something from our culture . . . for there were some beautiful and good things in it.

Soon it will be too late to know my culture, for **integration** is upon us and soon we will have no values but yours. Already many of our young people have forgotten the old ways. And many have been shamed of their Indian ways by scorn and ridicule. My culture is like a wounded deer that has crawled away into the forest to bleed and die alone.

IDENTIFY CAUSE & EFFECT

Pause at line 74. Underline the effects of the disappearance of love from a culture.

INTERPRET

Pause at line 85. Do you think the writer is sincere when he says "my culture has little to offer yours"? Explain.

COMPARE & CONTRAST

What does Chief Dan George imply is the difference between the Native American view of private possessions and the white culture's view? Explain.

VOCABULARY

integration (in′tə·grā′shən) *n.:* joining of different racial or ethnic groups in a society.

INTERPRET

Circle the word that Chief Dan George frequently repeats in lines 106–113. Why do you think he repeats this word toward the close of the piece? Explain.

The only thing that can truly help us is genuine love. You must truly love us, be patient with us and share with us. And we must love you—with a genuine love that forgives and forgets . . . a love that forgives the terrible sufferings your culture brought ours when it swept over us like a wave crashing along a beach . . . with a love that forgets and lifts up its head and sees in your eyes an answering love of trust and acceptance.

This is brotherhood . . . anything less is not worthy of the name.

I have spoken.

I Am a Native of North America

Comparison-and-Contrast Chart Compare and contrast Chief Dan George's view of Native American culture and white culture by completing the Venn diagram below.

Reading Skills
Analyze comparison-and-contrast texts.

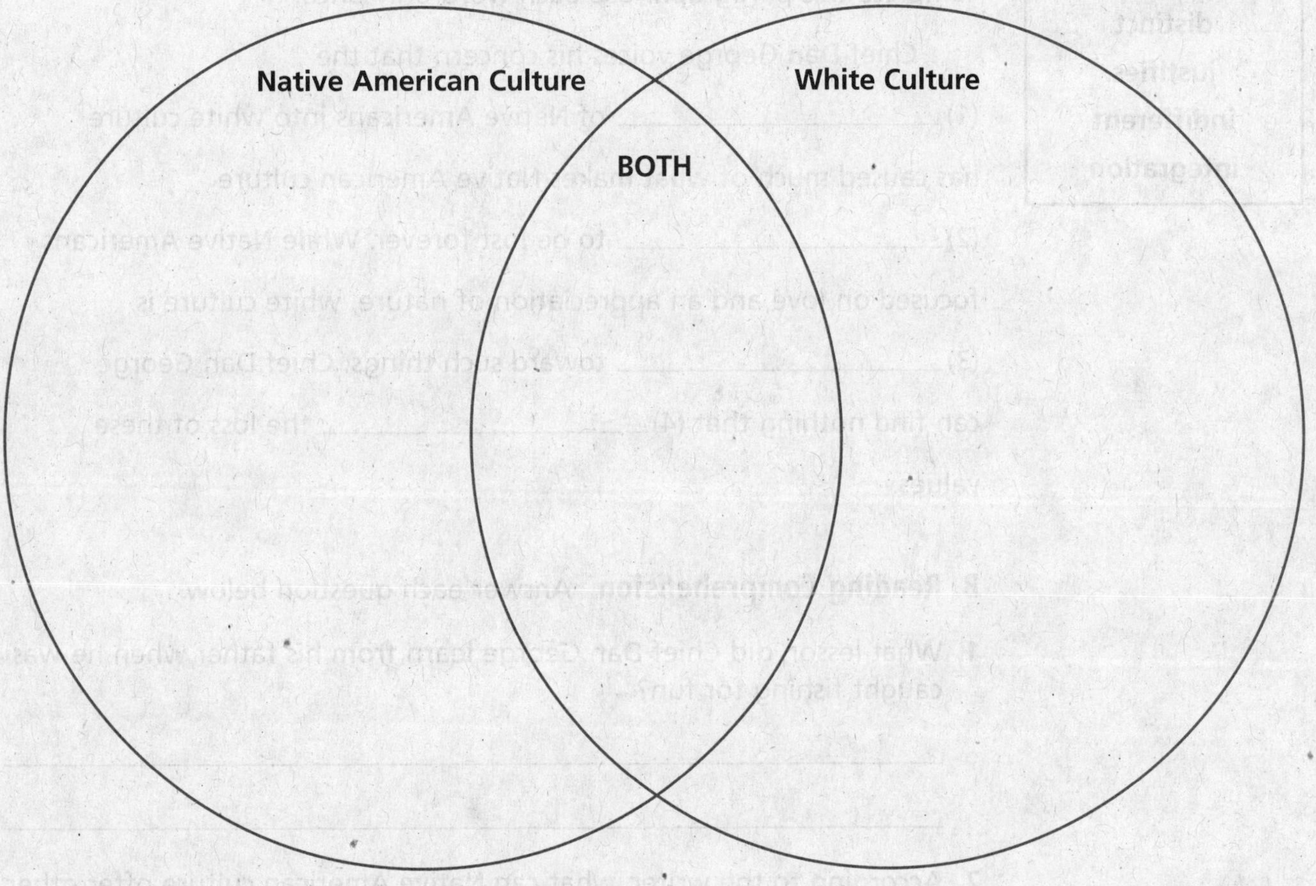

Native American Culture

BOTH

White Culture

I Am a Native of North America

VOCABULARY AND COMPREHENSION

Word Bank
distinct
justifies
indifferent
integration

A. Selection Vocabulary Write the Word Bank words on the blanks to complete this paragraph. Use each word only once.

Chief Dan George voices his concern that the (1)____________________ of Native Americans into white culture has caused much of what makes Native American culture (2)____________________ to be lost forever. While Native Americans focused on love and an appreciation of nature, white culture is (3)____________________ toward such things. Chief Dan George can find nothing that (4)____________________ the loss of these values.

B. Reading Comprehension Answer each question below.

1. What lesson did Chief Dan George learn from his father when he was caught fishing for fun?

____

____

2. According to the writer, what can Native American culture offer other cultures?

____

____

3. According to Chief Dan George, what is the attitude of many young Native Americans toward their culture?

____

____

Before You Read

Feng Shui Your Room by E. Renee Heiss

READING SKILLS: ANALYZING CAUSE AND EFFECT

You know from experience that one thing leads to another. If you sleep through your alarm, you'll miss your Spanish class. Sleeping through your alarm is a **cause**—it makes something happen. An **effect** is what happens as a result of an event—you've missed your Spanish class.

As you read "Feng Shui Your Room," look for such transition words as *because* and *when*. These words are clues that tell you the writer is going to describe a cause and effect.

VOCABULARY DEVELOPMENT: PREVIEW SELECTION VOCABULARY

Preview these vocabulary words before you begin to read.

principles (prin′sə·pəlz) *n.:* ideas on which a plan or system is based.

The principles of feng shui can benefit children and adults in their everyday lives.

prosperity (präs·per′ə·tē) *n.:* success.

I decided to rearrange my room so that I might attract prosperity.

clutter (klut′ər) *n.:* things scattered in a messy way.

My mother saw that my room was filled with clutter and insisted that I clean it up right away.

delicate (del′i·kit) *adj.:* pleasing in its lightness; fine.

The delicate music playing in the background helped me concentrate on my studies.

circulate (sur′kyoo·lāt′) *v.:* to move about freely.

If you allow your ch'i to circulate around your room, you will feel more energetic.

Reading Skills
Analyze cause and effect.

Feng Shui Your Room

E. Renee Heiss

VOCABULARY

principles (prin′sə·pəlz) *n.:* ideas on which a plan or system is based.

IDENTIFY CAUSE & EFFECT

What is the **effect** of ch'i flowing "like a summer breeze" (line 5)?

Feng shui (pronounced fung shway) originated in China over 4,000 years ago. The **principles** of this ancient Chinese decorating philosophy[1] tell us that everything has a ch'i (chee), or positive energy force. When ch'i flows around like a summer breeze, you can feel better about yourself. To find out how feng shui works in your bedroom, follow these simple rules:

ARRANGEMENT—Your bed is the center of your room. Don't line up your bed directly with your door but make sure you can still see it. If you have a really weird-shaped room, hang a mirror so you can see your door from your bed. You should be able to get in and out of your bed from both sides. Use sheets and covers in soft, earth tones.

As you come through your door, the right, rear corner of your room is your relationships corner. Here is where

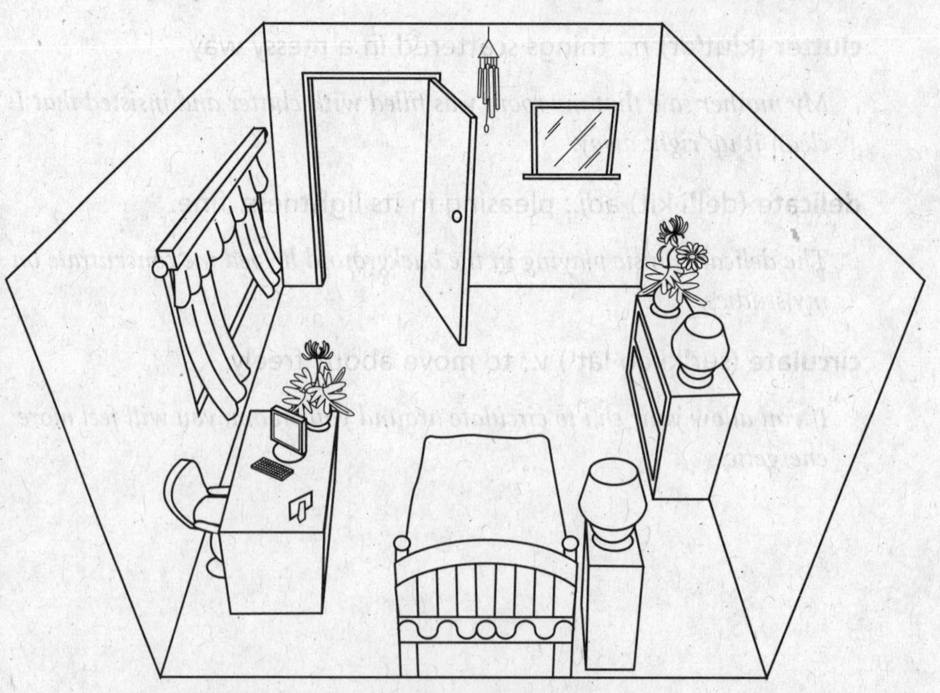

1. **philosophy** *n.:* set of beliefs on how to live.

you should place pictures of your family and friends. Add some living plants to keep your relationships alive. Make sure there is light for your plants.

Your desk is another important part of your room. It should be positioned so that when you sit at your desk, you face the door, and you have your back to a wall. If you have an alcove[2] in your room, face your desk so you look out from the alcove.

Decorate in twos: two lamps, two pictures, etc. but never have four of anything because four things create a box that traps ch'i. If you have only one of something, use the mirror again to create the illusion of two things.

A fish tank attracts **prosperity** and good times for two reasons. The fish is the Chinese symbol for plenty. Also, the moving water from the filter will help move the ch'i around your room. Never use stagnant or still water for betta fish[3] because this stops the ch'i. An alternative to a fish tank might be one of the flowing-water sculptures.

Finally, eliminate **clutter.** Organize your room so you can find things easily. Ch'i gets trapped in piles of stuff sitting around your room. When you have a neat room, you'll feel better and so will your parents!

COLOR AND LIGHT—Bright colors attract ch'i, but dark colors trap ch'i. Blues and violets reduce stress and confusion. Yellow is good for your mental outlook and grades in school. Green brings luck, growth, and peace. Use red accents in a few places like on a pillow; too much red can make you angry.

Light pulls a powerful force on the ch'i. When considering light in your room, remember how the yin-yang[4] is

---

2. **alcove** *n.:* recessed part of a room.
3. **betta fish** *n.:* These beautiful fish are common in many aquariums. Two male betta fish cannot inhabit the same tank, however, because they will fight each other.
4. **yin-yang** *n.:* Chinese symbol representing two opposite but complementary forces that combine to form a whole.

IDENTIFY CAUSE & EFFECT

Pause at line 27. What can cause ch'i to be trapped?

VOCABULARY

prosperity (präs·per′ətē) *n.:* success.

IDENTIFY CAUSE & EFFECT

Pause at line 33. Circle the transition word that lets you know that you will be reading about a **cause-and-effect relationship.** Then, place a c next to the cause and an e next to the effect.

VOCABULARY

clutter (klut′ər) *n.:* things scattered in a messy way.

INFER

Pause at line 43. Why might the color red make people angry? Explain.

Photo by Daisuke Morita

Wind chimes.

shaped; half is light and half is dark. You should be able to see half of your room in shadows and half in light. Two lamps are a good number to have in your room—perhaps one on your desk and one by your bed.

SOUND—Just like light and color, certain sounds attract the positive ch'i, and other sounds send the ch'i packing for another room. Wind chimes are an excellent choice for **delicate** sounds in your room; they attract the positive ch'i. Hang the wind chimes near your door to keep the positive ch'i flowing around and around.

Your room's feng shui is very complex and combines arrangement, color, light, and sound in a delicate balance that allows your ch'i to **circulate** freely. When this happens, you begin to experience a calm you never thought possible. As you become more relaxed, it is only natural that you'll have more energy, and your grades might even go up. Arranging your room this way may seem a little strange at first, but you'll get used to it. Use feng shui principles and watch the good things come into your life!

IDENTIFY CAUSE & EFFECT

Pause at line 55. Underline the **effect** of hanging wind chimes by a door.

IDENTIFY CAUSE & EFFECT

Underline the phrase "As you become more relaxed" (line 60). According to the article, what will **cause** one to become more relaxed? What are the possible **effects** of becoming more relaxed?

VOCABULARY

delicate (del′i·kit) *adj.:* pleasing in its lightness; fine.

circulate (sur′kyoo·lāt′) *v.:* to move about freely.

Feng Shui Your Room

Cause-and-Effect Chart Fill in the chart below with information from "Feng Shui Your Room" to complete each cause-and-effect relationship.

Reading Skills
Analyze cause and effect.

Cause	Effect
	You feel better about yourself.
You have a fish tank with moving water in your room.	
You include blues and violets when decorating your room.	
	You have more energy and your grades improve.

Feng Shui Your Room

VOCABULARY AND COMPREHENSION

Word Bank

principles
prosperity
clutter
delicate
circulate

A. Selection Vocabulary Write the Word Bank words on the blanks to complete this paragraph. Use each word only once.

If you've been in my room, you've probably noticed that it is filled with (1)____________________. However, this year that's going to change, thanks to the (2)____________________ of feng shui. I'm hoping that adding light colors and (3)____________________ music will help me become more relaxed. I'm also hoping to be more energetic after I allow the ch'i to (4)____________________ around my room. By taking these steps, I have no doubt (5)____________________ will come to me this year.

B. Reading Comprehension Answer each question below.

1. What is ch'i?

____

____

2. What four factors are important in feng shui?

____

____

3. Why does a fish tank attract good fortune?

____

____

4. Why should you reorganize your room?

____

____

Before You Read

All Together Now by Barbara Jordan

READING SKILLS: TRACING AN AUTHOR'S ARGUMENT

You may think of an argument as an angry discussion with someone, but the word can also mean "debate." When a writer presents an **argument** in an informational text, he or she is simply trying to persuade you to agree with a certain point of view. The writer will probably use evidence in the form of reasons, facts, statistics, examples, or quotations from experts to support the argument.

As you trace the **author's argument** in the speech "All Together Now," keep these questions in mind:

- What is the subject of this text?
- What is the writer's point of view on the subject?
- What evidence does the writer use to support her argument?

VOCABULARY DEVELOPMENT: PREVIEW SELECTION VOCABULARY

Preview these vocabulary words before you begin to read.

tolerant (täl′ər·ənt) *adj.:* having respect for views or traits different from your own.

Parents can teach their children to be tolerant of people from different backgrounds.

culminated (kul′mə·nāt′id) *v.:* reached its highest point.

The U.S. civil rights movement culminated in the mid-1960s.

fatigue (fə·tēg′) *n.:* physical or mental exhaustion.

Protestors may have felt fatigue, but they continued to work toward their goals.

momentum (mō·men′təm) *n.:* increasing strength.

The struggle for civil rights lost momentum before race relations fully improved.

indispensable (in′di·spen′sə·bəl) *adj.:* necessary; required.

If we are to get along, respect for others is an indispensable value.

Reading Skills
Understand an author's argument.

All Together Now

Barbara Jordan

BACKGROUND: Informational Text and Social Studies

Barbara Jordan's life was marked by landmark achievements. She was the first African American student to attend Boston University Law School and became the first African American to be the keynote speaker at the Democratic National Convention. She was praised for her speaking ability after speaking at the impeachment hearings against President Richard M. Nixon in 1974. In this speech, she discusses the importance of people working together to improve relations between white people and African Americans.

© AP Photo

Barbara Jordan

VOCABULARY

tolerant (täl′ər·ənt) *adj.:* having respect for views or traits different from your own.

IDENTIFY

Re-read lines 1–9. What is the subject of Jordan's speech? What is her point of view on the subject?

When I look at race relations today I can see that some positive changes have come about. But much remains to be done, and the answer does not lie in more legislation.[1] We *have* the legislation we need; we have the laws. Frankly, I don't believe that the task of bringing us all together can be accomplished by government. What we need now is soul force—the efforts of people working on a small scale to build a truly **tolerant,** harmonious society. And parents can do a great deal to create that tolerant society.

We all know that race relations in America have had a very rocky history. Think about the 1960s when Dr. Martin Luther King, Jr., was in his heyday[2] and there were marches and protests against segregation[3] and discrimination. The

1. **legislation** (lej′is·lā′shən) *n.:* act of making laws; laws.
2. **heyday** (hā′dā′) *n.:* period of greatest success or strength.
3. **segregation** (seg′rə·gā′shən) *n.:* separation of people by race or ethnicity.

Dr. Martin Luther King, Jr.

movement **culminated** in 1963 with the March on Washington.

Following that event, race relations reached an all-time peak. President Lyndon B. Johnson pushed through the Civil Rights Act of 1964, which remains the fundamental piece of civil rights legislation in this century. The Voting Rights Act of 1965 ensured that everyone in our country could vote. At last, black people and white people seemed ready to live together in peace.

But that is not what happened. By the 1990's the good feelings had diminished. Today the nation seems to be suffering from compassion **fatigue,** and issues such as race relations and civil rights have never regained **momentum.**

Those issues, however, remain crucial. As our society becomes more diverse, people of all races and backgrounds will have to learn to live together. If we don't think this is important, all we have to do is look at the situation in Bosnia[4] today.

How do we create a harmonious society out of so many kinds of people? The key is tolerance—the one value that is **indispensable** in creating community.

If we are concerned about community, if it is important to us that people not feel excluded, then we have to do something. Each of us can decide to have one friend of a different race or background in our mix of friends. If we do this, we'll be working together to push things forward.

4. **Bosnia** (bäz'nē·ə): country in southeastern Europe. During the 1990s, Bosnia experienced a bloody civil war between different racial and religious groups.

VOCABULARY

culminated (kul'mə·nāt'id) *v.:* reached its highest point.

fatigue (fə·tēg') *n.:* physical or mental exhaustion.

momentum (mō·men'təm) *n.:* increasing strength.

indispensable (in'di·spen'sə·bəl) *adj.:* necessary; required.

INFER

Re-read lines 33–37. What does Jordan imply can happen when people of different races and backgrounds fail to get along?

EVALUATE

Underline Jordan's advice about what we can do to keep people from feeling excluded in lines 43–44. What is your opinion of this advice? Do you think Jordan is providing an effective solution to the problem? Explain.

EVALUATE

Pause at line 58. Underline Jordan's belief about the way children become prejudiced. Do you agree with her belief? Why or why not?

One thing is clear to me: We, as human beings, must be willing to accept people who are different from ourselves. I must be willing to accept people who don't look as I do and don't talk as I do. It is crucial that I am open to their feelings, their inner reality.

What can parents do? We can put our faith in young people as a positive force. I have yet to find a racist baby. Babies come into the world as blank as slates and, with their beautiful innocence, see others not as different but as enjoyable companions. Children learn ideas and attitudes from the adults who nurture them. I absolutely believe that children do not adopt prejudices unless they absorb them from their parents or teachers.

The best way to get this country faithful to the American dream of tolerance and equality is to start small. Parents can actively encourage their children to be in the company of people who are of other racial and ethnic backgrounds. If a child thinks, "Well, that person's color is not the same as mine, but she must be okay because she likes to play with the same things I like to play with," that child will grow up with a broader view of humanity.

I'm an incurable optimist.[5] For the rest of the time that I have left on this planet I want to bring people together. You might think of this as a labor of love. Now, I know that love means different things to different people. But what I mean is this: I care about you because you are a fellow human being and I find it okay in my mind, in my heart, to simply say to you, I love you. And maybe that would encourage you to love me in return.

It is possible for all of us to work on this—at home, in our schools, at our jobs. It is possible to work on human relationships in every area of our lives.

FLUENCY

Read the boxed passage aloud. What attitude will you convey? Circle or underline words that you stumbled over. Then, read the passage again, paying careful attention to those challenging words.

5. **optimist** (äp′tə·mist′) *n.:* person who believes good things will happen.

All Together Now

Argument Chart In "All Together Now," the author presents an argument for how to bring Americans together to create a more tolerant society. Fill in the chart below to trace the author's argument.

Reading Skills
Analyze and trace an author's argument.

Argument or Point of View
Detail That Supports Argument
Detail That Supports Argument
Detail That Supports Argument

All Together Now

VOCABULARY AND COMPREHENSION

Word Bank

tolerant
culminated
fatigue
momentum
indispensable

A. Selection Vocabulary Write the Word Bank words on the blanks to complete this paragraph. Use each word only once.

The work of activists in the 1960s was (1)__________________ in bringing about the passage of civil rights legislation. However, efforts to improve race relations have lost (2)__________________, and people still cling to their prejudices. You can help make your community more (3)__________________ simply by making friends with classmates from diverse backgrounds. Once your efforts have (4)__________________ in a diverse group of friends, you will be surprised by the things you can learn from one another. So get started reaching out to others right away—and don't let homework and (5)__________________ slow you down!

B. Reading Comprehension Answer each question below.

1. What piece of legislation guaranteed U.S. citizens' right to vote?

2. What value does Jordan argue is the most important in creating a sense of community?

3. According to Jordan, what can parents do to help society overcome prejudice?

Before You Read

Bernie Williams: Yankee Doodle Dandy by Joel Poiley

READING SKILLS: IDENTIFYING THE MAIN IDEA

When you tell someone the most important point in an informational text, you're describing its main idea. The **main idea** is the reason *why* the writer wrote the material. As you read "Bernie Williams: Yankee Doodle Dandy," keep the following questions about the main idea in mind:

- Does the title of the text tell you the main idea directly, or does it hint at it?
- Is there a sentence near the beginning or end of the selection that states its main idea?
- What main idea is suggested by the details in the text?

VOCABULARY DEVELOPMENT: PREVIEW SELECTION VOCABULARY

Preview these vocabulary words before you begin to read.

enrolled (en·rōld′) *v.:* joined officially.

Before deciding to pursue baseball, Bernie Williams enrolled in other sports while he was growing up.

extracurricular (eks′trə·kə·rik′yo͞o·lər) *adj.:* not part of a school's course of study or one's regular routine.

He enjoyed taking part in extracurricular activities after the school day was over.

envisioned (en·vizh′ənd) *v.:* imagined as a future possibility.

Bernie's parents envisioned a successful baseball career for their son.

devote (di·vōt′) *v.:* give something, such as time or effort, to a cause; apply oneself fully.

Bernie Williams knew he had to devote a great amount of time to baseball if he wanted to be a professional player.

pursuit (pər·so͞ot′) *n.:* attempt to achieve something.

One must sometimes confront many obstacles in the pursuit of a dream.

Reading Skills
Identify the main idea.

Bernie Williams: Yankee Doodle Dandy

Joel Poiley

© AP Photo/Roberto Borea

Bernie Williams

VOCABULARY

enrolled (en·rōld′) *v.:* joined officially.

extracurricular (eks′trə·kə·rik′yo͞o·lər) *adj.:* not part of a school's course of study or one's regular routine.

IDENTIFY

Pause at line 10. Underline the important facts you've learned about Bernie Williams so far.

New York Yankees center fielder[1] Bernie Williams understands the importance of being well-rounded.

By age 8, Williams could play Puerto Rican folk songs on the guitar. Later he was trained in classical guitar. At 17, he had excelled in baseball and was signed by the Yankees. He also **enrolled** in college and considered becoming a doctor. "Probably all of it came from my parents' influence," Williams says. "My dad and my mom wanted me to stay off the streets and they enrolled me in a whole bunch of **extracurricular** activities.

1. **center fielder:** baseball player who covers the area of the field past second base.

"The good thing about it is that I developed a whole bunch of interests other than baseball."

Running for Fun

Williams won four gold medals at age 15 at an international track meet. He was one of the world's top 400-meter runners in his age group. "I could always run fast," Williams says. "When I was 8 or 9, I was better in track than baseball. All I could do was run. So my parents put me into a track club, which was great, because it gave me a great base for my physical conditioning."

But Williams was determined to play baseball, and he practiced every day after school with his dad. Baseball ability ran in the family. One uncle played professional ball in the minor leagues in the 1950s, and another was a well-known amateur player in Puerto Rico.

Since Williams's high school specialized in music, it had no baseball team. He continued to learn about the game by playing in youth leagues and recreation ball. Williams played against future big-league all-stars Juan Gonzalez and Ivan Rodriguez in youth-league ball.

Hard to Leave Home

It wasn't easy for Williams to leave home and play pro ball. His mother, a teacher, encouraged him to continue his education.

"My dad was a merchant marine,[2] a more aggressive-type person who encouraged me to play," Williams says. "The odds of making it aren't good. And back then, considering the type of player I was, I would have never **envisioned** this type of career."

Williams took college classes in biology during the off-seasons, but it reached a point where he had to make a decision between college and baseball.

---

2. merchant marine: person who helps operate commercial ships.

IDENTIFY MAIN IDEA

Pause at line 25. What main idea does Bernie Williams's willingness to practice baseball every day hint at?

IDENTIFY

Pause at line 30. Underline the sentence that explains how Bernie Williams was able to practice baseball even though his school didn't have a baseball team.

VOCABULARY

envisioned (en·vizh′ənd) *v.:* imagined as a future possibility.

FLUENCY

Look over the boxed passage for any words you might have difficulty pronouncing. Then, read the passage aloud until you can do so without stumbling.

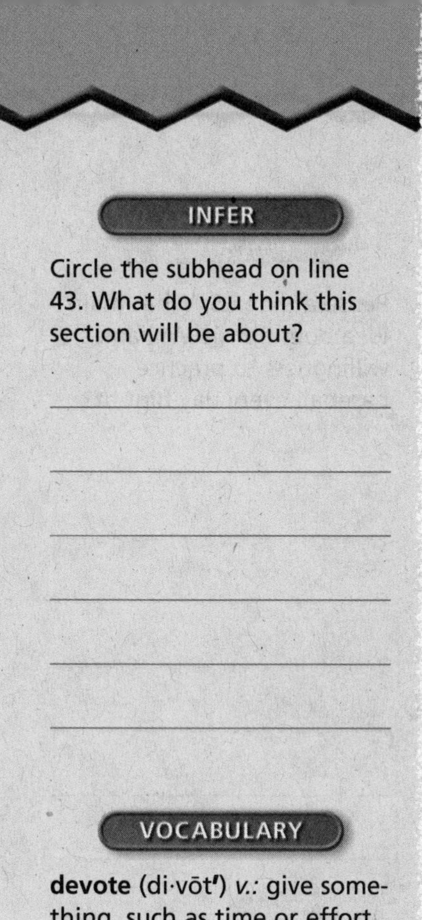

The Long Climb

Williams showed the Yankees he had skills. But he was in high school and still learning the game when he signed. It took parts of seven years in the minor leagues before he made the majors for good in 1993.

He almost packed his bags and went home in 1990 after being sent back to the minors. His mother surprised him by encouraging him to keep at it.

"She said I had worked too hard to quit," Williams says. "I was not doing well in school because I didn't have the time to devote to it, and I wasn't developing as a player because my mind was on other stuff. So I made the decision to **devote** myself 100 percent to baseball."

By 1996, Bernie was a solid everyday player smashing home runs from either side of the plate. But his big national splash occurred in the playoffs, when he helped the Yankees win their first world championship in 18 years.

No Hype Needed

With Williams getting stronger and more confident each season, the Yankees won three more world championships from 1998 to 2000. A five-time All-Star, Williams became known as a clutch player who delivered key hits with the game on the line.

Not bad for a guy who is so quiet in the locker room his teammates rarely know when he comes and goes.

"There's not too much flash to Bernie," former Yankees pitcher Andy Pettitte says. "The joke in the clubhouse is that we never know where Bernie is because he's so quiet."

Williams does his talking on the field with his bat and glove, which teammates and opponents respect.

"He's very laid back, but he's a very good player," says former Yankees right fielder Paul O'Neill, who retired in

INFER

Circle the subhead on line 43. What do you think this section will be about?

VOCABULARY

devote (di·vōt′) *v.:* give something, such as time or effort, to a cause; apply oneself fully.

WORD STUDY

Underline the words in lines 64–65 that help you figure out the meaning of the phrase *clutch player.*

IDENTIFY MAIN IDEA

Writers often use quotations from other people to support their main ideas. What main idea might the quotations in lines 68–70 and 73–79 support?

2001 after playing next to Williams for eight years. "A lot of players can hit or they can throw or they can run, but Bernie can do a lot of things.

"The hype is unimportant to him. Some players need that to thrive, but Bernie doesn't."

A Relaxing Tune

Bernie unwinds by playing and listening to all types of music. He often entertains teammates with free concerts on his Fender Stratocaster electric guitar. He and O'Neill, who plays drums, have jammed together.

"He's very good," O'Neill says. "We've had a lot of fun playing together."

Opponents such as the Kansas City Royals' Roberto Hernandez enjoy playing against Williams because he doesn't show off or display emotion on the field.

EVALUATE

Pause at line 89. Underline the reason opponents respect Williams. Is this a good reason to respect someone? Why or why not?

INTERPRET

Pause at line 100. What is the difference between a music fan and a music student? Explain.

VOCABULARY

pursuit (pər·so͞ot′) *n.:* attempt to achieve something.

WORD STUDY

Use context clues to help you guess at the meaning of the word *deviate* in line 109. What do you think the word means?

ANALYZE

What does Bernie Williams's interest in music tell you about him as a person?

"I'm happy to know him from our years in winter ball because he's a class individual," Hernandez says. "And he has not changed as he's become a star. He's the same person I knew when he started out.

"In Puerto Rico, everyone knows about players like Roberto Alomar and Juan Gonzalez. Bernie is definitely the quiet superstar because you never hear about him until the season starts. He just does his job."

Bernie Williams isn't only a fan of music, he's a student. His schooling in Puerto Rico taught him to read, play and understand what makes rap different from rock and roll.

"In school they taught me a general appreciation of well-made music," Williams says. "It can be classical, rock, heavy metal; if it's well made, you notice.

"I like the blues. I like the freedom that jazz gives, as far as the improvisation (making it up as you go). I like classical because it's the **pursuit** of perfection. It can be a masterpiece that somebody wrote, and it's timed and specifically written for you to play it in a certain way and you can't deviate from that."

Williams once played on stage at The Bottom Line, a famous club in New York City. He also had his Fender Stratocaster electric guitar signed by "The Boss," rocker Bruce Springsteen.

"That was awesome," Williams says, smiling.

And what does he listen to before a game?

"It depends who's pitching," Williams says. "If it's a flame-thrower I might listen to heavy metal to pump me up. Sometimes even new age. I like listening to jazz because it's challenging to figure out the harmonies and how the instruments come together."

SKILLS PRACTICE

Bernie Williams: Yankee Doodle Dandy

Reading Skills
Analyze the main idea.

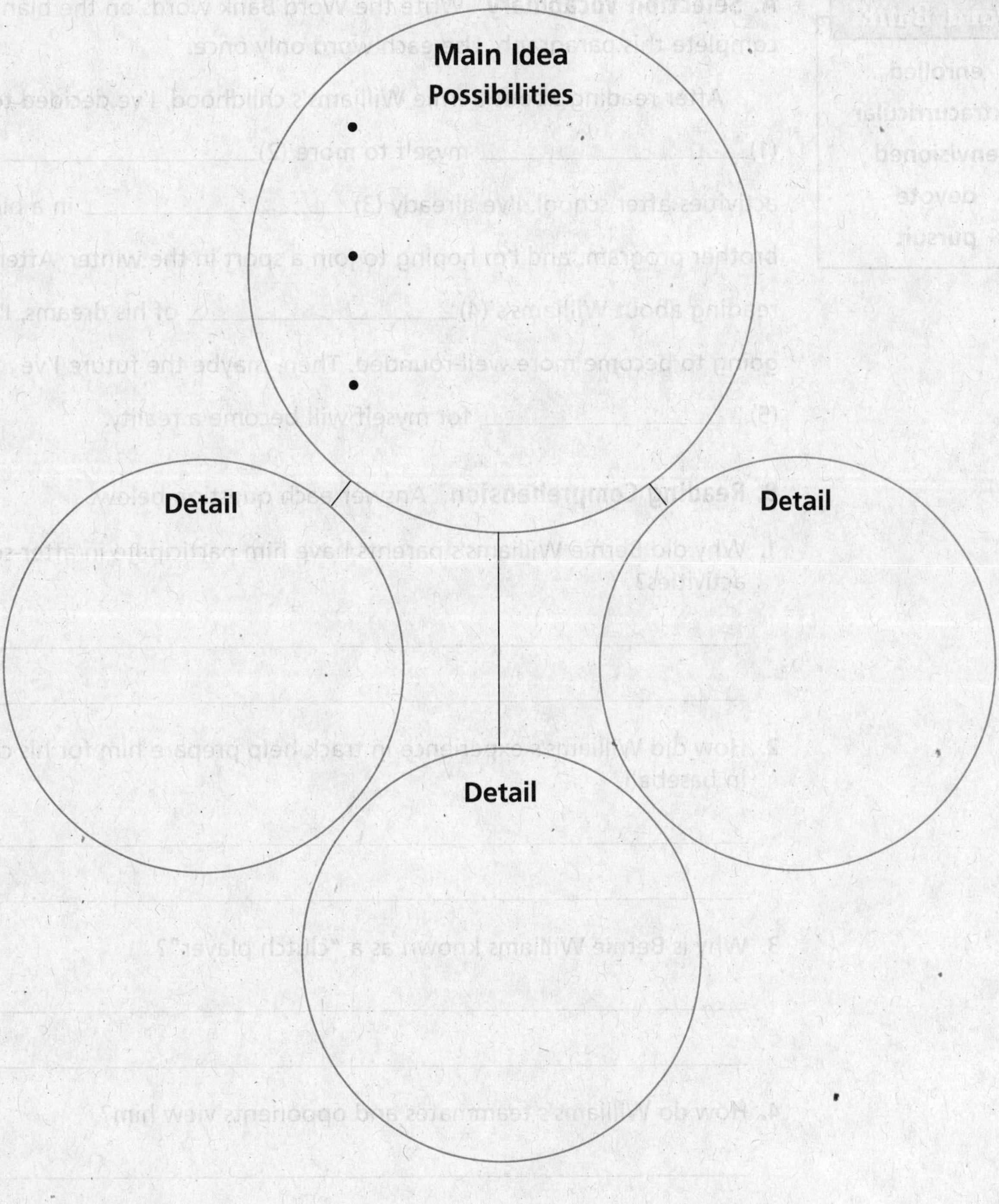

Main Idea Chart The main idea of a text is its most important idea. Read through the article again, and jot down important details in the diagram below. Then, record possibilities for what you think the main idea of the article might be. Finally, circle the statement that you think best expresses the main idea.

Main Idea Possibilities

-
-
-

Detail

Detail

Detail

Bernie Williams: Yankee Doodle Dandy

VOCABULARY AND COMPREHENSION

Word Bank

enrolled
extracurricular
envisioned
devote
pursuit

A. Selection Vocabulary Write the Word Bank words on the blanks to complete this paragraph. Use each word only once.

After reading about Bernie Williams's childhood, I've decided to (1)________________ myself to more (2)________________ activities after school. I've already (3)________________ in a big brother program, and I'm hoping to join a sport in the winter. After reading about Williams's (4)________________ of his dreams, I'm going to become more well-rounded. Then, maybe the future I've (5)________________ for myself will become a reality.

B. Reading Comprehension Answer each question below.

1. Why did Bernie Williams's parents have him participate in after-school activities?

____

____

2. How did Williams's experience in track help prepare him for his career in baseball?

____

____

3. Why is Bernie Williams known as a "clutch player"?

____

____

4. How do Williams's teammates and opponents view him?

____

____

Coming to Amreeka: The First Wave of Arab Immigrants (1880–1924)

by Aida Hasan Damuni

READING SKILLS: SUMMARIZING

If you were to tell some friends about a trip you took, you probably wouldn't tell them every little detail. If you did, your friends would quickly become bored by your description. Instead, you would summarize your trip, telling your friends about the main events or high points of the journey. **Summarizing**—restating the key details of a text in a much shorter form than the original—is a great way to review the main ideas of a text. As you read "Coming to Amreeka: The First Wave of Arab Immigrants (1880–1924)," pause every so often to summarize what you've read.

VOCABULARY DEVELOPMENT: PREVIEW SELECTION VOCABULARY

Preview these vocabulary words before you begin to read.

resides (ri·zīdz′) *v.:* lives in a place.

Today, a large population of Arab Americans resides in the United States.

census (sen′səs) *n.* used as *adj.:* official count of population and record of economic status, age, gender, ethnicity, and so on.

Census records provide valuable information for people studying immigration.

peddling (ped′liŋ) *v.* used as *n.:* traveling from place to place selling products.

Selling products such as tablecloths, rugs, and handkerchiefs, Arab immigrants often made money by peddling.

isolation (ī′sə·lā′shən) *n.:* separation from other people.

Some immigrants, living in large cities, experienced isolation in their new country.

Reading Skills
Summarize a text.

Coming to Amreeka:

The First Wave of Arab Immigrants (1880–1924)

Aida Hasan Damuni

SUMMARIZE

Pause at line 16. In your own words, explain which idea from this paragraph you would include in a summary.

SUMMARIZE

Pause at line 21. If you were writing a **summary,** do you think you would include the list of modern-day countries that made up Greater Syria? Explain.

VOCABULARY

resides (ri·zīdz′) *v.:* lives in a place.

census (sen′səs) *n.* used as *adj.:* official count of population and record of economic status, age, gender, ethnicity, and so on.

When my Muslim grandfather, Hasan Mansour, first arrived in America in 1912, he was a lone Arab traveler in his mid-teens. His voyage by ship from his Palestinian village to the shores of America lasted nearly a month. It took him to Chicago, Illinois, where he lived most of his life.

Grandfather may have been the youngest of his village to immigrate to America at that time. But he was not the first Palestinian immigrant in Chicago, and he certainly was not the first Arab. In fact, by the end of the nineteenth century, a number of American cities and towns—such as Boston and Worcester, Massachusetts; Fort Wayne, Indiana; and Cedar Rapids, Iowa—already were populated with Arab communities. New York's Manhattan and Brooklyn had reached a population of more than 10,000 Syrians. (The largest community of Arab Americans in the United States today **resides** in Dearborn, Michigan.)

Hasan came to America during what is characterized as the first wave of immigration—the period roughly between 1880 and 1924. The majority of these Arabs were Christians from Greater Syria. (This included today's Lebanon, Jordan, Syria, Palestine, and Israel.) However, all Arabs at the time mistakenly were called "Turks." U.S. immigration records until 1899 and **census** records until 1920 grouped Arabs together with Turks, Armenians,[1] and others under the general category "Turkey in Asia."

---

1. **Armenians:** citizens of Armenia, a country east of Turkey, in southwestern Asia.

Arabs came to America for various reasons. For some, like my grandfather, it was an escape from being drafted into the Turkish military under the ruling Ottoman Empire.[2] Unlike other immigrant groups, however, most Arabs did not have something pushing them away. They simply felt that America offered the promise of new opportunities and freedoms. "Chain migration" usually resulted when fellow Arabs sent home descriptions of the opportunities in "Amreeka." As new immigrants arrived in America, they were helped by those who had come before them. A small group from his Palestinian village greeted Hasan in Chicago. They provided him with a place to stay and an honest but exhausting means of making money—**peddling.**

Peddling was hard work, but it proved appropriate for the independent nature of Arabs. New immigrants would make their way to one of the many growing Arab settlements.[3] With the help of family and friends, newcomers would be outfitted with some wares and given instructions on how to talk to customers and show their products. With suitcases full of goods such as linen tablecloths, small rugs, and handkerchiefs, Arab peddlers traveled all over the United States and sometimes into Mexico and Canada.

At first, peddlers used sign language to communicate with their customers. Then, they learned basic English from their customers and the families with whom they roomed during their travels. Every few weeks, peddlers would return to their supply settlement, where small communities of Arabs lived together in tiny, crowded rooms. Here, they had the support of fellow Arabs. It also allowed them to avoid the slums and cultural **isolation** that other immigrants were going through in the bigger cities. Peddlers generally

2. **Ottoman Empire:** powerful Muslim empire that, in its height in the sixteenth and seventeenth centuries, controlled lands from Asia to northern Africa.
3. **settlements** (set′'l·mənts) *n.:* small communities.

IDENTIFY CAUSE & EFFECT

According to the information in lines 26–34, why did most Arab immigrants come to America? Underline the answer.

VOCABULARY

peddling (ped′liŋ) *v.* used as *n.:* traveling from place to place selling products.

FLUENCY

Practice reading the boxed passage aloud. Pay attention to the punctuation to help you determine what to emphasize and where to pause or stop.

WORD STUDY

Wares, in line 43, is another word for "goods" or "products." It is usually plural, but its singular form is found in compound words. What compound words can you think of that use the singular form of *wares*?

______

______

______

______

VOCABULARY

isolation (ī′sə·lā′shən) *n.:* separation from other people.

SUMMARIZE

What information from lines 48–58 would you include in a **summary**? Underline it.

SUMMARIZE

Would you include any information from lines 59–63 in a summary? Why or why not?

IDENTIFY

Circle the **main idea** in lines 64–71.

© Ed Kashi/CORBIS

preferred to save their hard-earned money for their intended return to their homelands.

But many Arab peddlers went on to own small businesses in America. Some even started multimillion-dollar businesses. One example of such success is Arab American Joseph M. Haggar, who first manufactured work pants and then became famous for men's dress slacks.

With the building of the first Arab churches in the late 1890s and then mosques[4] in 1919, many Arab communities began to make the transition from temporary to permanent residents. It is these individuals, the first wave of Arab immigrants, who laid the foundation for the nearly three-million-strong Arab Americans in the United States today. Arab Americans throughout the United States can claim an identity and existence centuries in the making.

4. **mosques** (mäsks) *n.:* buildings in which people of the Muslim faith hold religious services.

Coming to Amreeka: The First Wave of Arab Immigrants (1880–1924)

Reading Skills
Summarize a text.

Summary Chart Summarizing a text can help you remember its key details and determine its main idea. In a summary you use your own words to restate the key information in the text. A summary is always much shorter than the text itself.

Fill out the chart that follows with details from "Coming to Amreeka: The First Wave of Arab Immigrants (1880–1924)." Then, write a summary of the article and its main idea in the boxes at the right.

Key Details

Summary

Main Idea

Coming to Amreeka: The First Wave of Arab Immigrants (1880–1924)

Word Bank

resides
census
peddling
isolation

VOCABULARY AND COMPREHENSION

A. Selection Vocabulary Write the Word Bank words on the blanks to complete this paragraph. Use each word only once.

Can you imagine leaving the country in which your family (1)__________________? Those immigrants who made a living by (2)__________________ goods had to work hard and travel far from the towns in which they settled. Returning to Arab communities, however, helped them avoid a feeling of (3)__________________ in their new country. Not all Arabs stayed in the United States permanently, but many did. According to data from (4)__________________ records, the Arab American population continues to grow today.

B. Reading Comprehension Answer each question below.

1. Before they learned English, how did Arab peddlers communicate with their customers?

____

____

2. What is "chain migration"?

____

____

3. Why does the author mention Joseph M. Haggar?

____

____

Before You Read

The First Mexican Americans

by Stephen Currie

READING SKILLS: EVALUATING EVIDENCE

If someone told you that a magic potion would enable you to fly, would you believe it? You'd probably want evidence that the potion works before you'd try it out. In the same way, when you read an informational text, you need to evaluate its **evidence,** the details that a writer uses to support a position.

As you read "The First Mexican Americans," ask yourself these questions:

- **Is the evidence adequate?** Is there enough evidence to support the writer's position?
- **Is the evidence accurate?** Are there mistakes or errors in the evidence that is presented? Does the evidence come from a source you can trust?
- **Is the evidence appropriate?** Does the evidence relate directly to the writer's conclusion?

VOCABULARY DEVELOPMENT: PREVIEW SELECTION VOCABULARY

Preview these vocabulary words before you begin to read.

vibrant (vī′brənt) *adj.:* lively; exciting.

Parts of the vibrant culture of Spain are evident in Mexico.

descended (dē·send′id) *v.* used as *adj.:* came from a source.

The citizens of northern Mexico were originally descended from Spanish settlers.

hostile (häs′təl) *adj.:* very unfriendly.

At first the Spanish were hostile toward the Indians, but eventually the two peoples intermarried.

extensive (ek·sten′siv) *adj.:* great in size, scope, or amount.

Extensive changes occurred after the United States took over northern Mexico.

negotiation (ni·gō′shē·ā′shən) *n.:* a discussion with the purpose of reaching an agreement.

Northern Mexico became part of the United States after conflict and negotiation.

Reading Skills
Evaluate evidence.

The First Mexican Americans

Stephen Currie

© Bob Daemmrich/The Image Works

IDENTIFY

In what way were the first Mexican Americans different from most other groups of immigrants?

Most immigrant groups traditionally have journeyed to the United States by land, by sea, or by air. But that was not the case with the first Mexican Americans who came to this country. They never left their homeland to get here. When borders shifted, the United States came to them.

These early Mexican Americans mostly lived in what is now the southwestern United States, especially the present-day states of California, Arizona, New Mexico, and Texas. (Some also lived in Louisiana, Florida, and Colorado.) Prior to the 1500s, only American Indians resided in this region. This changed in the early part of the sixteenth century when Spanish explorers from Mexico and Cuba began to travel through the Southwest.

At first, the explorers were interested mainly in finding gold. But as Spanish leaders learned more about the area, they realized it made sense to build forts, missions,[1] and villages there. In 1598, Spanish settlers founded the town of San Juan de los Caballeros in present-day New Mexico. Soon, this community was home to more than one hundred families. Spain's colonization[2] had begun.

The Spanish influence quickly spread elsewhere in the Southwest. By the 1800s, the Spanish had built cities such as Santa Fe (New Mexico), San Antonio (Texas), and Los Angeles (California). This region was the northernmost part of the Spanish colony known as New Spain. But the geographic distance between Spain and the Americas was great. The Spanish became distracted by wars and quarrels in Spain. As a result, Spain's power in the New World started to fade and Mexico began to take more control of its own affairs. When Mexico won its independence from Spain in 1821, the Southwest came under Mexican authority.

By that time, the people of the Southwest, or northern Mexico, had established a rich and **vibrant** culture. In some ways, this culture originated in Spain. After all, Spanish was the official language. And the dominant religion, Roman Catholicism, also came from Spain. The Spanish influence made sense: Many northern Mexicans were **descended** from the original settlers of San Juan de los Caballeros and other early Spanish communities.

But in other ways, the people of northern Mexico were not Spanish at all. Years of living in the area's deserts and mountains had changed their lifestyles. The people of the Southwest ate corn, peppers, and other foods not widely

1. **missions** *n.:* here, the headquarters of a religious institution.
2. **colonization** (kälʹə·ni·zāʹshən) *n.:* forming of a community in a distant land that remains under the control of the founding nation.

IDENTIFY

Underline the **evidence** in lines 21–24 that supports the claim that Spanish influence spread throughout the Southwest.

EVALUATE

Re-read lines 32–39. Does the writer provide adequate **evidence** for his claim that the people of northern Mexico established a rich and vibrant culture? Why or why not?

VOCABULARY

vibrant (vīʹbrənt) *adj.:* lively; exciting.

descended (dē·sendʹid) *v.* used as *adj.:* came from a source.

known in Spain. They told stories about North American animals that Europeans had never heard of, much less seen. After a while, the Mexicans of the Far North even pronounced certain words differently from the Spanish pronunciations.

The American Indians of the region played an important role in this change. While at times **hostile** toward the Indians, the Spanish nonetheless recognized the tribes' **extensive** hands-on experience with the land. So instead of relying on European methods, the Spanish adopted Indian ways of watering crops and hunting animals. These new routines kept them alive while changing their culture.

As time went on, it became increasingly difficult to tell the difference between the Spanish and the American Indians. The Spanish recognized marriages between Europeans and Indians. As a result, the people of northern Mexico began to reflect various ethnic groups. By the time Mexico won its independence, combined Spanish and Indian traditions made for one uniquely Mexican culture.

The people of northern Mexico thought of themselves as Mexican. In the 1830s and 1840s, though, the U.S. government decided that it wanted northern Mexico. By 1850, through a combination of war (U.S.-Mexican War, 1846–1848) and **negotiation** (Treaty of Guadalupe Hidalgo,[3] signed in 1848), nearly all of Mexico's Far North was under U.S. jurisdiction.[4] Without moving, the people of northern Mexico became immigrants. Culturally, they still were Mexican; politically, however, they had become the first Mexican Americans.

---

3. **Treaty of Guadalupe Hidalgo:** agreement, signed after the Mexican-American War, in which Mexico gave up its northern lands to the United States.
4. **jurisdiction** (jo͝or′is·dik′shən) *n.:* authority; control.

IDENTIFY

What **evidence** in lines 40–48 supports the claim that "in other ways, the people of northern Mexico were not Spanish at all"?

INTERPRET

Pause at line 55. Does the writer provide adequate evidence for his claim that the Spanish and the Native Americans were unfriendly to each other? Explain.

FLUENCY

Read lines 63–72 aloud. Be sure to read slowly enough so that the information is clear to the listener.

IDENTIFY

Underline the writer's conclusion in lines 69–72.

VOCABULARY

hostile (häs′təl) *adj.:* very unfriendly.

extensive (ek·sten′siv) *adj.:* great in size, scope, or amount.

negotiation (ni·gō′shē·ā′shən) *n.:* a discussion with the purpose of reaching an agreement.

The First Mexican Americans

Reading Skills Evaluate evidence.

Evidence Chart Use the chart below to evaluate the adequacy and appropriateness of the **evidence** in the article "The First Mexican Americans." Go through the text, and in the first two columns of the chart, list the writer's ideas and opinions and the evidence he uses to support them. Then, in the third and fourth columns, state whether the evidence is appropriate and adequate. Finally, in the box at the bottom of the chart, write a few sentences summing up your evaluation of the writer's use of the evidence in the article.

Writer's Idea/Opinion	Evidence	Appropriate?	Accurate?
1.			
2.			
3.			
Your Evaluation			

The First Mexican Americans

VOCABULARY AND COMPREHENSION

Word Bank

vibrant
descended
hostile
extensive
negotiation

A. Selection Vocabulary Write the Word Bank words on the blanks to complete this paragraph. Not every word will be used.

The earliest Mexican Americans were (1)____________________ from the Spanish and American Indians. When groups of different people live in the same area, they might initially be (2)____________________ toward one another. However, through (3)____________________, the people get to accept one another. Oftentimes, a (4)____________________ culture can emerge from this blending.

B. Reading Comprehension Answer each question below.

1. What were early Spanish explorers interested in finding in Mexico?

____

____

2. Name two things the people of northern Mexico had in common with the people of Spain.

____

____

3. How did Native Americans influence the culture of Mexico?

____

____

4. How did northern Mexico come under U.S. control?

____

____

Before You Read

So You Want to Start a Club . . .

Tips from the Association of School Clubs

READING SKILLS: ANALYZING INFORMATION IN PUBLIC DOCUMENTS

What time does the city library open? When do lifeguards go on duty at the town pool? You can usually find answers to such questions in **public documents.** Although public documents may be issued by almost anyone (church officials, politicians, schools, parks committees, and so on), all these documents have one thing in common: They exist to inform us, the public. As you read "So You Want to Start a Club . . . ," use these tips to help you understand information and locate it quickly and easily.

- Look for a title or subtitle to identify the purpose of the document.
- Scan the text for heads, subheads, and such special features as bulleted or numbered lists and boldface text, which highlight important information.
- Study diagrams and illustrations, which can provide additional information.
- Carefully re-read any information that seems confusing.

As you read "So You Want to Start a Club . . . ," keep track of where you find the information in the document.

Reading Skills
Analyze information in public documents.

ANALYZE INFORMATION

Underline the title and subtitle of the article (lines 1–2). What do they tell you about the purpose of this document?

INFER

Why is the word *commitment* set in boldface type?

ANALYZE INFORMATION

Circle the subhead in line 16. What does the subhead tell you about the information that will be provided in lines 17–23?

Association of School Clubs

newsletter

Volume 1 *Spring*

So You Want to Start a Club . . .

Tips from the Association of School Clubs

Have you ever considered starting a school club? Perhaps you've thought about starting a club that celebrates your culture or that is devoted to a hobby you and your friends share. Clubs can be a lot of fun, but they can be a lot of work as well. That's why it's important to consider a number of things before you launch your club.

1. Do you have what it takes?

Starting and running a club take **commitment.** You often need to devote a lot of time and effort to attracting interest in and support for the club and making sure it runs smoothly. You'll need to maintain a positive attitude and listen carefully to others' views. Think about what it will take to see the project through, and ask others for their help.

2. Will people want to join your club?

As you develop your ideas for your club, you'll want to make sure there will be enough student interest in it. Be sure your club isn't similar to ones that already exist. If your club offers something **unique,** students will be more likely to join it. Talk to other students about your ideas. They can offer useful suggestions that will help you refine your ideas to make your club more appealing.

3. Do you have a plan?

In order to persuade your school to approve your club and to attract members, you need a **detailed plan.** Creating a

1

Spanish-speakers' club, for example, is a good idea to start with, but you need to consider the following issues:

- The club's purpose
- A time and place to meet
- How often you plan to meet
- How people will find out about the club

A well-thought-out plan inspires confidence. If your plan is vague, people won't support it.

Plan for the Spanish-Speakers' Club

Purpose:

The club will be open to all students—

1. to give fluent speakers the chance to speak Spanish with their classmates on a regular basis

2. to give other students the chance to improve their Spanish

3. to encourage an appreciation for the language

When: Lunch, every Wednesday at 12:00 PM

Where: The cafeteria (Permission will be requested to reserve a table and post a sign.)

Getting Members: Post fliers. Make announcements in Spanish classes.

With commitment and careful planning, you can make your new club a **success.**

2

ANALYZE INFORMATION

Why is the information in lines 29–32 set in a bulleted list?

INFER

Why do you think the illustration of a plan for the Spanish-Speakers' Club is included in the document?

So You Want to Start a Club . . .

Reading Skills Analyze information in public documents.

Key Information Chart We can find almost any type of information in public documents, from how and where to vote to how we can cure a disease in a developing nation. Fill out the chart below with five pieces of key information you found in "So You Want to Start a Club . . ." Then, describe where in the document you found that information; for example, is it under a subhead, in a graphic, or in a list?

Key Information	Where Information Is Located

Skills Review

So You Want to Start a Club . . .

COMPREHENSION

Reading Comprehension Answer each question below.

1. According to the document, why does it take commitment to start and run a club?

2. Why is it important to make your club unique?

3. Why is it beneficial to talk to other students before launching your club?

4. What issues should you consider when developing a plan for your club?

5. According to the information presented in the plan for the Spanish-Speakers' Club, what are two ways to build membership in the club?

Index of Authors and Titles

All Together Now 288
Alvarez, Julia 156, *161*

Bambara, Toni Cade 52, *63*
Bernie Williams: Yankee Doddle Dandy 294
Bushnaq, Inea 208, *213*

Chief Dan George 274
Chief Luther Standing Bear 218, *223*
Clever Magistrate, The 198
Clifton, Lucille 107, *108*, 135
Cofer, Judith Ortiz 186, *191*
Coming to Amreeka: The First Wave of Arab Immigrants (1880–1924) 302
Currie, Stephen *308*

Damuni, Aida Hasan 302
Dear Benjamin Banneker 230
Dive, The 6
Dreams 174
Dream Variations 175

Estevis, Anne 244, *249*

Fang, Linda 198, *203*
Feng Shui Your Room 282
Figueredo, D. H. 120, *129*
First Mexican Americans, The 308

Giovanni, Nikki 180, *181*

Hard at Work 267
Haskins, Jim 140, *149*
Heiss, E. Renee 282
How the Alvarez Girl Found Her Magic 156
How the Animals Kept the Lions Away 208
Hughes, Langston 174, 175, *176*
Hum 82

I Am a Native of North America 274
Identity 133
in the inner city 107

Jordan, Barbara 288

Lifesaving Service 20

Madam C. J. Walker 140
María in School 186
Metro Map 257
Museum Announcement 255
My Father's Song 112

Nye, Naomi Shihab 82, *103*

Old Woman Who Lived with the Wolves, The 218
Ortiz, Simon J. 112, *113*

Pinkney, Andrea Davis 230, *239*
Poem for Langston Hughes, A 180
Poiley, Joel 294
Polanco, Julio Noboa 133, *134*
Press Release 256

Saldaña, Jr., René 6, *15*
Seventh Grade 38
Smartest Human I Ever Met: My Brother's Dog Shep, The 166
So You Want to Start a Club 314
Soto, Gary 38, *47*

Tate, Eleanora E. 20, *31*
That October 120

Upadhyay, Ritu 267

Villaseñor, Victor 166, *170*
Virtue Goes to Town 68
VividPlayer Download Instructions 261

War of the Wall, The 52
Whistle, The 244
why some people be mad at me sometimes 135

Yep, Laurence 68, *75*

Vocabulary Development

Pronunciation guides, in parentheses, are provided for the vocabulary words in this book. The following key will help you use those pronunciation guides.

As practice in using a pronunciation guide, sound out the words used as examples in the list that follows. See if you can hear the way the same vowel might be sounded in different words. For example, say "at" and "ate" aloud. Can you hear the difference in the way "a" sounds?

The symbol ə is called a **schwa.** A schwa is used by many dictionaries to indicate a sort of weak sound like the "a" in "ago." Some people say the schwa sounds like "eh." A vowel sounded like a schwa is never accented.

The vocabulary words in this book are also provided with a part-of-speech label. The parts of speech are *n.* (noun), *v.* (verb), *pro.* (pronoun), *adj.* (adjective), *adv.* (adverb), *prep.* (preposition), *conj.* (conjunction), and *interj.* (interjection). To learn about the parts of speech, consult the *Holt Handbook.*

To learn more about the vocabulary words, consult your dictionary. You will find that many of the words defined here have several other meanings.

---

at, āte, cär; ten, ēve; is, īce; gō, hôrn, look, tool; oil, out; up, fur; ə *for unstressed vowels, as* a *in* ago, u *in* focus; ' *as in* Latin (lat''n); chin; she; zh *as in* azure (azh'ər); thin, the; ŋ *as in* ring (riŋ)
